PENG

THE SECC
KRISHNAM

Krishnamurti was born in south India of Brahmin parents. In 1911, at the age of fifteen, he was brought to England by Mrs Annie Besant. He was educated privately over here and was groomed for the rôle of World Teacher, but in 1929 he disbanded the organization which had proclaimed him and of which he was the head, and declared that he did not want disciples. Since then he has travelled ceaselessly all over the world giving public talks and private interviews. The essence of his teaching is that only through a complete change of heart in the individual can there come about a change in society and so peace to the world. He believes that this radical change can take place in every individual, not gradually but instantaneously. He helps us to see ourselves as we really are, for it is in seeing with absolute clarity that the inward revolution takes place.

The first *Penguin Krishnamurti Reader* was published in 1970.

THE
SECOND PENGUIN
KRISHNAMURTI
READER

Edited by
MARY LUTYENS

PENGUIN BOOKS

Penguin Books Ltd, Harmondsworth, Middlesex, England
Penguin Books, 625 Madison Avenue, New York, New York 10022, U.S.A.
Penguin Books Australia Ltd, Ringwood, Victoria, Australia
Penguin Books Canada Ltd, 2801 John Street, Markham, Ontario, Canada L3R 1B4
Penguin Books (N.Z.) Ltd, 182–190 Wairau Road, Auckland 10, New Zealand

—

The Only Revolution, The Urgency of Change
published by Gollancz 1970, 1971
Published in Penguin Books 1973
Reprinted 1974, 1976, 1977, 1979, 1982

—

—

Set, printed and bound in Great Britain by
Cox & Wyman Ltd, Reading
Set in Linotype Georgian

Contents

PART ONE

The Only Revolution

INDIA

I

MEDITATION is not an escape from the world; it is not an isolating self-enclosing activity, but rather the comprehension of the world and its ways. The world has little to offer apart from food, clothes and shelter, and pleasure with its great sorrows.

Meditation is wandering away from this world; one has to be a total outsider. Then the world has a meaning, and the beauty of the heavens and the earth is constant. Then love is not pleasure. From this all action begins that is not the outcome of tension, contradiction, the search for self-fulfilment or the conceit of power.

The room overlooked a garden, and thirty or forty feet below was the wide, expansive river, sacred to some, but to others a beautiful stretch of water open to the skies and to the glory of the morning. You could always see the other bank with its village and spreading trees, and the newly planted winter wheat. From this room you could see the morning star, and the sun rising gently over the trees; and the river became the golden path for the sun.

At night the room was very dark and the wide window showed the whole southern sky, and into this room one night came – with a great deal of fluttering – a bird. Turning on the light and getting out of bed one saw it under the bed. It was an owl. It was about a foot and a half high with extremely wide big eyes and a fearsome beak. We gazed at each other quite close, a few feet apart. It was frightened by the light and the closeness of a human being. We looked at each other without blinking for quite a while, and it never lost its height and its fierce dignity. You could see the cruel claws, the light feathers and the wings tightly held against the body. One would have liked to touch it, stroke it, but it would not have allowed that. So presently the light was turned out and for some time there was quietness in the room. Soon there was a fluttering of the wings – you could feel the air against your face – and the owl had gone out of the window. It never came again.

It was a very old temple; they said it might be over three thousand years old, but you know how people exaggerate. It certainly was old; it had been a Buddhist temple and about seven centuries ago it became a Hindu temple and in place of the Buddha they had put a Hindu idol. It was very dark inside and it had a strange atmosphere. There were pillared halls, long corridors carved most beautifully, and there was the smell of bats and of incense.

The worshippers were straggling in, recently bathed, with folded hands, and they walked around these corridors, prostrating each time they passed the image, which was clothed in bright silks. A priest in the innermost shrine was chanting and it was nice to hear well pronounced Sanskrit. He wasn't in a hurry, and the words came out easily and gracefully from the depths of the temple. There were children there, old ladies, young men. The professional people had put away their European trousers and coats and put on dhotis, and with folded hands and bare shoulders they were, with great devotion, sitting or standing.

And there was a pool full of water – a sacred pool – with many steps leading down to it and pillars of carved rock around it. You came into the temple from the dusty road full of noise and bright, sharp sunshine, and in here it was very shady, dark and peaceful. There were no candles, no kneeling people about, but only those who made their pilgrimage around the shrine, silently moving their lips in some prayer.

A man came to see us that afternoon. He said he was a

believer in Vedanta. He spoke English very well for he had been educated in one of the universities and had a bright, sharp intellect. He was a lawyer, earning a great deal of money, and his keen eyes looked at you speculatively, weighing, and somewhat anxious. He appeared to have read a great deal, including something of western theology. He was a middle-aged man, rather thin and tall, with the dignity of a lawyer who had won many cases.

He said: 'I have heard you talk and what you are saying is pure Vedanta, brought up to date but of the ancient tradition.' We asked him what he meant by Vedanta. He replied: 'Sir, we postulate that there is only Brahman who creates the world and the illusion of it, and the Atman – which is in every human being – is of that Brahman. Man has to awaken from this everyday consciousness of plurality and the manifest world, much as he would awaken from a dream. Just as this dreamer creates the totality of his dream so the individual consciousness creates the totality of the manifest world and other people. You, sir, don't say all this but surely you mean all this for you have been born and bred in this country and, though you have been abroad most of your life, you are part of this ancient tradition. India has produced you, whether you like it or not; you are the produce of India and you have an Indian mind. Your gestures, your statue-like stillness when you talk, and your very looks are part of this ancient heritage. Your teaching is surely the continuation of what our ancients have taught since time immemorial.'

Let us brush aside whether the speaker is an Indian brought up in this tradition, conditioned in this culture, and whether he is the summation of this ancient teaching. First of all he is not an Indian, that is to say, he does not belong to this nation or to the community of Brahmins, though he was born in it. He denies the very tradition with which you invest him. He denies that his teaching is the continuity of the ancient teachings. He has not read any of the sacred books of India or of the West because they are unnecessary for a man who is aware of what is going on in the world – of the behaviour of human beings with their endless theories, with the accepted propaganda of two thousand or five thousand years which has become the tradition, the truth, the revelation.

To such a man who denies totally and completely the acceptance of the word, the symbol with its conditioning, to him truth is not a second-hand affair. If you had listened to him, sir, he has from the very beginning said that any acceptance of authority is the very denial of truth, and he has insisted that one must be outside all culture, tradition and social morality. If you had listened, then you would not say that he is an Indian or that he is continuing the ancient tradition in modern language. He totally denies the past, its teachers, its interpreters, its theories and its formulas.

Truth is never in the past. The truth of the past is the ashes of memory; memory is of time, and in the dead ashes of yesterday there is no truth. Truth is a living thing, not within the field of time.

So, having brushed all that aside, we can now take up the central issue of Brahman, which you postulate. Surely, sir, the very assertion is a theory invented by an imaginative mind – whether it be Shankara or the modern scholarly theologian. You can experience a theory and say that it is so, but that is like a man who has been brought up and conditioned in the Catholic world having visions of Christ. Obviously such visions are the projection of his own conditioning; and those who have been brought up in the tradition of Krishna have experiences and visions born of their culture. So experience does not prove a thing. To recognize the vision as Krishna or Christ is the outcome of conditioned knowledge; therefore it is not real at all but a fancy, a myth, strengthened through experience and utterly invalid. Why do you want a theory at all, and why do you postulate any belief? This constant assertion of belief is an indication of fear – fear of everyday life, fear of sorrow, fear of death and of the utter meaninglessness of life. Seeing all this you invent a theory and the more cunning and erudite the theory the more weight it has. And after two thousand or ten thousand years of propaganda that theory invariably and foolishly becomes 'the truth'.

But if you do not postulate any dogma, then you are face to face with what actually is. The 'what is', is thought, pleasure, sorrow and the fear of death. When you understand the structure of your daily living – with its competition, greed, ambition and the search for power – then you will see not only the absurdity of theories, saviours and gurus, but you may find an ending to sorrow, an ending to the whole structure which thought has put together.

The penetration into and the understanding of this structure is meditation. Then you will see that the world is not an illusion but a terrible reality which man, in his relationship with his fellow man, has constructed. It is this which has to be understood and not your theories of Vedanta, with the rituals and all the paraphernalia of organized religion.

When man is free, without any motive of fear, of envy or of sorrow, then only is the mind naturally peaceful and still. Then it can see not only the truth in daily life from moment to moment but also go beyond all perception; and therefore there is the ending of the observer and the observed, and duality ceases.

But beyond all this, and not related to this struggle, this vanity and despair, there is – and this is not a theory – a stream that has no beginning and no end; a measureless movement that the mind can never capture.

When you hear this, sir, obviously you are going to make a theory of it, and if you like this new theory you will propagate it. But what you propagate is not the truth. The truth is only when you are free from the ache, anxiety and aggression which now fill your heart and mind. When you see all this and when you come upon that benediction called love, then you will know the truth of what is being said.

II

WHAT is important in meditation is the quality of the mind and the heart. It is not what you achieve, or what you say you attain, but rather the quality of a mind that is innocent and vulnerable. Through negation there is the positive state. Merely to gather, or to live in, experience, denies the purity of meditation. Meditation is not a means to an end. It is both the means and the end. The mind can never be made innocent through experience. It is the negation of experience that brings about that positive state of innocency which cannot be cultivated by thought. Thought is never innocent. Meditation is the ending of thought, not by the meditator, for the meditator is the meditation. If there is no meditation, then you are like a blind man in a world of great beauty, light and colour.

Wander by the seashore and let this meditative quality come upon you. If it does, don't pursue it. What you pursue will be the memory of what it was – and what was is the death of what is. Or when you wander among the hills, let everything tell you the beauty and the pain of life, so that you awaken to your own sorrow and to the ending of it. Meditation is the root, the plant, the flower and the fruit. It is words that divide the fruit, the flower, the plant and the root. In this separation action does not bring about goodness: virtue is the total perception.

It was a long shady road with trees on both sides – a narrow road that wound through the green fields of glistening, ripening wheat. The sun made sharp shadows, and the villages on both sides of the road were dirty, ill-kept and poverty-ridden. The older people looked ill and sad, but the children were shouting and playing in the dust and throwing stones at the birds high up in the trees. It was a very pleasant cool morning and a fresh breeze was blowing over the hills.

The parrots and the mynahs were making a great deal of noise that morning. The parrots were hardly visible among the green leaves of the trees; in the tamarind they had several holes which were their home. Their zig-zag flight was always screechy and raucous. The mynahs were on the ground, fairly tame. They would let you come quite near them before they flew away. And the golden fly-catcher, the green and golden bird, was on the wires across the road. It was a beautiful morning and the sun was not too hot yet. There was a benediction in the air and there was that peace before man wakes up.

On that road a horse-drawn vehicle with two wheels and a platform with four posts and an awning was passing by. On it, stretched across the wheels, wrapped up in a white and red cloth, was a dead body being carried to the river to be burnt on its banks. There was a man sitting beside the driver, probably a relative, and the body was jolting up and down on that not too smooth road. They had come from some distance for the horse was sweating, and the dead body had been shaking all the way and it seemed to be quite rigid.

The man who came to see us later that day said he was a gunnery instructor in the navy. He had come with his wife and two children and he seemed a very serious man. After salutations he said that he would like to find God. He was not too articulate, probably he was rather shy. His hands and face looked capable but there was a certain hardness in his voice and look – for, after all, he was an instructor in the ways of killing. God seemed to be so remote from his everyday activities. It all seemed so weird, for here was a man who said he was in earnest in his search for God and yet his livelihood forced him to teach others the art of killing.

He said he was a religious man and had wandered through many schools of different so-called holy men. He was dissatisfied with them all, and now he had taken a long journey by train and bus to come and see us for he wanted to know how to come upon that strange world which men and saints have sought. His wife and children sat very silent and respectful, and on a branch just outside the window sat a dove, light brown, softly cooing to itself. The man never looked at it, and the children with their mother sat rigid, nervous and unsmiling.

You can't find God; there is no way to it. Man has invented many paths, many religions, many beliefs, saviours and teachers whom he thinks will help him to find the bliss that is not passing. The misery of search is that it leads to some fancy of the mind, to some vision which the mind has projected and measured by things known. The love which he seeks is destroyed by the way of his life. You cannot have a gun in one hand and God in the other. God is only a symbol, a word, that has really lost its meaning, for the churches and places of worship have destroyed it. Of course, if you don't believe in God you are like the believer; both suffer and go through the sorrow of a short and vain life; and the bitterness of every day makes life a meaningless thing. Reality is not at the end of the stream of thought, and the empty heart is filled by the words of thought. We become very clever, inventing new philosophies, and then there is the bitterness of their failure. We have invented theories about how to reach the ultimate, and the devotee goes to the temple and loses himself in the imaginations of his own mind. The monk and the saint do not find that reality for both are part of a tradition, of a culture, that accepts them as being saints and monks.

The dove has flown away, and the beauty of the mountain of cloud is upon the land – and truth is there, where you never look.

III

It was an old Mogul garden with many great trees. There were big monuments, dark inside with marble sepulchres, and the rain and the weather had made the stone dark and the domes still darker. There were hundreds of pigeons on these domes. They and the crows would fight for a place, and lower down on the dome were the parrots, coming from everywhere in groups. There were nicely kept lawns, well trimmed and watered. It was a quiet place and surprisingly there were not too many people. Of an evening the servants of the neighbourhood with their bicycles would gather on a lawn to play cards. It was a game they understood, but an outsider looking on couldn't make head or tail of it. There were parties of children playing on a lawn of a different tomb.

There was one tomb which was especially grand, with great arches, well proportioned, and a wall behind it which was asymmetrical. It was made of bricks and the sun and the rain had made it dark, almost black. There was a notice not to pick flowers but nobody seemed to pay much attention to it for they picked them all the same.

There was an avenue of eucalyptus, and behind it a rose garden with crumbling walls around it. This garden, with magnificent roses, was kept beautifully, and the grass was always green and freshly cut. Few people seemed to come to this garden and you could walk around it in solitude, watching the sun set behind the trees and behind the dome of the tomb. Especially in the evening, with the long dark shadows, it was very peaceful there, far from the noise of the town, from the poverty, and the ugliness of the rich. There were gypsies uprooting the weeds from the lawn. It was altogether a beautiful place – but man was gradually spoiling it.

There was a man sitting cross-legged in one of the remote corners of the lawn, his bicycle beside him. He had closed his eyes and his lips were moving. He was there for more than half an hour in that position, completely lost to the world, to the passers-by and to the screech of the parrots. His body was quite still. In his hands there was a rosary covered by a piece of cloth. His fingers were the only movement that one could see, apart from his lips. He came there daily towards the evening, and it must have been after his day's work. He was rather a poor man, fairly well fed, and he always came to that corner and lost himself. If you asked him he would tell you that he was meditating, repeating some prayer or some mantra – and to him that was good enough. He found in it solace from the everyday monotony of life. He was alone on the lawn. Behind him was a flowering jasmine; a great many flowers were on the ground, and the beauty of the moment lay around him. But he never saw that beauty for he was lost in the beauty of his own making.

Meditation is not the repetition of the word, nor the experiencing of a vision, nor the cultivating of silence. The bead and the word do quieten the chattering mind, but this is a form of self-hypnosis. You might as well take a pill.

Meditation is not wrapping yourself in a pattern of thought, in the enchantment of pleasure. Meditation has no beginning, and therefore it has no end.

If you say: 'I will begin today to control my thoughts, to sit quietly in the meditative posture, to breathe regularly' – then you are caught in the tricks with which one deceives oneself. Meditation is not a matter of being absorbed in some grandiose idea or image: that only quietens one for the moment, as a child absorbed by a toy is for the time being quiet. But as soon as the toy ceases to be of interest, the restlessness and the mischief begin again. Meditation is not the pursuit of an invisible path leading to some imagined bliss. The meditative mind is seeing – watching, listening, without the word, without comment, without opinion – attentive to the movement of life in all its relationships throughout the day. And at night, when the whole organism is at rest, the meditative mind has no dreams for it has been awake all day. It is only the indolent who have dreams; only the half-asleep who need the intimation of their own states. But as the mind watches, listens to the movement of life, the outer and the inner, to such a mind comes a silence that is not put together by thought.

It is not a silence which the observer can experience. If he does experience it and recognize it, it is no longer silence. The silence of the meditative mind is not within the borders of recognition, for this silence has no frontier. There is only silence – in which the space of division ceases.

The hills were being carried by the clouds and the rain was polishing the rocks, big boulders that were scattered over the hills. There was a streak of black in the grey granite, and that morning this dark basalt rock was being washed by the rain and was becoming blacker.

The ponds were filling up and the frogs were making deep-throated noises. A whole group of parrots was coming in from the fields for shelter and the monkeys were scrambling up the trees, and the red earth became darker.

There is a peculiar silence when it rains, and that morning in the valley all the noises seemed to have stopped – the noises of the farm, the tractor and the chopping of wood. There was only the dripping from the roof, and the gutters were gurgling.

It was quite extraordinary to feel the rain on one, to get wet to the skin, and to feel the earth and the trees receive the rain with great delight; for it hadn't rained for some time, and now the little cracks in the earth were closing up. The noises of the many birds were made still by the rain; the clouds were coming in from the east, dark, heavily laden, and were being drawn towards the west; the hills were being carried by them, and the smell of the earth was spreading into every corner. All day it rained.

And in the stillness of the night the owls hooted to each other across the valley.

He was a school-teacher, a Brahmin, with a clean dhoti. He was bare-footed and wore a western shirt. He was clean, sharp-eyed, apparently gentle in manner, and his salutation was a show of this humility. He was not too tall, and spoke English quite well, for he was an English teacher in town. He said he didn't earn much, and like all teachers throughout the world he found it very difficult to make both ends meet. Of course he was married, and had children, but he seemed to brush all that aside as though it did not matter at all. He was a proud man, with that peculiar pride, not of achievement, not the pride of the well-born or of the rich, but that pride of an ancient race, of the representative of an ancient tradition and system of thought and morality which, actually, had nothing whatever to do with what he really was. His pride was in the past which he represented, and his brushing aside of the present complications of life was the gesture of a man who considers it all inevitable-but-so-unnecessary. His diction was of the south, hard and loud. He said he had listened to the talks, here under the trees, for many years. In fact his father had brought him when he was a young man, still at college. Later, when he got his present miserable job, he came every year.

'I have listened to you for many years. Perhaps I understand intellectually what you are saying but it doesn't seem to penetrate very deeply. I like the setting of the trees under which you talk, and I look at the sunset when you point it out – as you so often do in your talks – but I cannot *feel* it, I cannot touch the leaf and feel the joy of the dancing shadows on the ground. I have no feelings at all, in fact. I have read a great deal, naturally, both English literature and the literature of this country. I can recite poems, but the beauty which lies beyond the word has escaped me. I am becoming harder, not only with my wife and children but with everybody. In the school I shout more. I wonder why I have lost the delight in the evening sun – if I ever had it! I wonder why I no longer feel strongly about any of the evils that exist in the world. I seem to see everything intellectually and can reason quite well – at least I think I can – with almost anybody. So why is there this gap between the intellect and the heart? Why have I lost love, and the feeling of genuine pity and concern?'

Look at that bougainvilia out of the window. Do you see it at all? Do you see the light on it, its transparency, the colour, the shape and the quality of it?

'I look at it, but it means absolutely nothing to me. And there are millions like me. So I come back to this question – why is there this gap between the intellect and the feelings?'

Is it because we have been badly educated, cultivating only memory and, from earliest childhood, have never been shown a tree, a flower, a bird, or a stretch of water? Is it because we have made life mechanical? Is it because of this over-population? For every job there are thousands who want it. Or is it because of pride, pride in efficiency, pride of race, the pride of cunning thought? Do you think that's it?

'If you're asking me if I'm proud – yes I am.'

But that is only one of the reasons why the so-called intellect dominates. Is it because words have become so extraordinarily important and not what is above and beyond the word? Or is it because you are thwarted, blocked in various ways, of which you may not be conscious at all? In the modern world the intellect is worshipped and the more clever and cunning you are the more you get on.

'Perhaps it may be all these things, but do they matter much? Of course we can go on endlessly analysing, describing the cause, but will that bridge the gap between the mind and the heart? That's what I want to know. I have read some of the psychological books and our own ancient literature but it doesn't set me on fire, so now I have come to you, though perhaps it may be too late for me.'

Do you really care that the mind and heart should come together? Aren't you really satisfied with your intellectual capacities? Perhaps the question of how to unite the mind and the heart is only academic? Why do you bother about bringing the two together? This concern is still of the intellect and doesn't spring, does it, from a real concern at the decay of your feeling, which is part of you? You have divided life into the intellect and the heart and you intellectually observe the heart withering away and you are verbally concerned about it. Let it wither away! Live only in the intellect. Is that possible?

'I do have feelings.'

But aren't those feelings really sentimentality, emotional self-indulgence? We are not talking about that, surely. We are saying: *Be* dead to love; it doesn't matter. Live entirely in your intellect and in your verbal manipulations, your cunning arguments. And when you do actually live there – what takes place? What you are objecting to is the destructiveness of that intellect which you so worship. The destructiveness brings a multitude of problems. You probably see the effect of the intellectual activities in the world – the wars, the competition, the arrogance of power – and perhaps you are frightened of what is going to happen, frightened of the hopelessness and despair of man. So long as there is this division between the feelings and the intellect, one dominating the other, the one must destroy the other; there is no bridging the two. You may have listened for many years to the talks, and perhaps you have been making great efforts to bring the mind and the heart together, but this effort is of the mind and so dominates the heart. Love doesn't belong to either, because it has no quality of domination in it. It is not a thing put together by thought or by sentiment. It is not a word of the intellect or a sensuous response. You say, ' I must have love, and to have it I must cultivate the heart.' But this cultivation is of the mind and so you keep the two always separate; they cannot be bridged or brought together for any utilitarian purpose. Love is at the beginning, not at the end of an endeavour.

'Then what am I to do?'

Now his eyes were becoming brighter; there was a movement in his body. He looked out of the window, and he was slowly beginning to catch fire.

You can't do anything. Keep out of it! And listen; and see the beauty of that flower.

IV

MEDITATION is the unfolding of the new. The new is beyond and above the repetitious past – and meditation is the ending of this repetition. The death that meditation brings about is the immortality of the new. The new is not within the area of thought, and meditation is the silence of thought.

Meditation is not an achievement, nor is it the capture of a vision, nor the excitement of sensation. It is like the river, not to be tamed, swiftly running and overflowing its banks. It is the music without sound; it cannot be domesticated and made use of. It is the silence in which the observer has ceased from the very beginning.

The sun wasn't up yet; you could see the morning star through the trees. There was a silence that was really extraordinary. Not the silence between two noises or between two notes, but the silence that has no reason whatsoever – the silence that must have been at the beginning of the world. It filled the whole valley and the hills.

The two big owls, calling to each other, never disturbed that silence, and a distant dog barking at the late moon was part of this immensity. The dew was especially heavy, and as the sun came up over the hill it was sparkling with many colours and with the glow that comes with the sun's first rays.

The delicate leaves of the jacaranda were heavy with dew, and birds came to have their morning baths, fluttering their wings so that the dew on those delicate leaves filled their feathers. The crows were particularly persistent; they would hop from one branch to another, pushing their heads through the leaves, fluttering their wings and preening themselves. There were about half-a-dozen of them on that one heavy branch, and there were many other birds, scattered all over the tree, taking their morning bath.

And this silence spread, and seemed to go beyond the hills. There were the usual noises of children shouting, and laughter; and the farm began to wake up.

It was going to be a cool day, and now the hills were taking on the light of the sun. They were very old hills – probably the oldest in the world – with oddly shaped rocks that seemed to be carved out with great care, balanced one on top of the other; but no wind or touch could loosen them from this balance.

It was a valley far removed from towns, and the road through it led to another village. The road was rough and there were no cars or buses to disturb the ancient quietness of this valley. There were bullock carts, but their movement was a part of the hills. There was a dry river bed that only flowed with water after heavy rains, and the colour was a mixture of red, yellow and brown; and it, too, seemed to move with the hills. And the villagers who walked silently by were like the rocks.

The day wore on and towards the end of the evening, as the sun was setting over the western hills, the silence came in from afar, over the hills, through the trees, covering the little bushes and the ancient banyan. And as the stars became brilliant, so the silence grew into great intensity; you could hardly bear it.

The little lamps of the village were put out, and with sleep the intensity of that silence grew deeper, wider and incredibly over-powering. Even the hills became more quiet, for they, too, had stopped their whisperings, their movement, and seemed to lose their immense weight.

She said she was forty-five; she was carefully dressed in a

24

sari, with some bangles on her wrists. The older man with her said he was her uncle. We all sat on the floor overlooking a big garden with a banyan tree, a few mango trees, the bright bougainvilia and the growing palms. She was terribly sad. Her hands were restless and she was trying to prevent herself from bursting into speech and perhaps tears. The uncle said: 'We have come to talk to you about my niece. Her husband died a few years ago, and then her son, and now she can't stop crying and has aged terribly. We don't know what to do. The usual doctors' advice doesn't seem to work, and she seems to be losing contact with her other children. She's getting thinner. We don't know where all this is going to end, and she insisted that we should come to see you.'

'I lost my husband four years ago. He was a doctor and died of cancer. He must have hidden it from me, and only in the last year or so did I know about it. He was in agony although the doctors gave him morphine and other sedatives. Before my eyes he withered away and was gone.'

She stopped, almost choking with tears. There was a dove sitting on the branch, quietly cooing. It was brownish-grey, with a small head and a large body – not too large, for it was a dove. Presently it flew off and the branch was swinging up and down from the pressure of its flight.

'I somehow cannot bear this loneliness, this meaningless existence without him. I loved my children; I had three of them, a boy and two girls. One day last year the boy wrote to me from school that he was not feeling well, and a few days later I got a telephone call from the headmaster, saying that he was dead.'

Here she began to sob uncontrollably. Presently she produced a letter from the boy in which he had said that he wanted to come home for he was not feeling well, and that he hoped she was all right. She explained that he had been concerned about her; he hadn't wanted to go to school but had wanted to remain with her. And she more or less forced him to go, afraid that he would be affected by her grief. Now it

25

was too late. The two girls, she said, were not fully aware of all that had happened for they were quite young. Suddenly she burst out: 'I don't know what to do. This death has shaken the very foundations of my life. Like a house, our marriage was carefully built on what we considered a deep foundation. Now everything is destroyed by this enormous event.'

The uncle must have been a believer, a traditionalist, for he added: 'God has visited this on her. She has been through all the necessary ceremonies but they have not helped her. I believe in reincarnation, but she takes no comfort in it. She doesn't even want to talk about it. To her it is all meaningless and we have not been able to give her any comfort.'

We sat there in silence for some time. Her handkerchief was now quite wet; a clean handkerchief from the drawer helped to wipe away the tears on her cheeks. The red bougainvilia was peeping through the window, and the bright southern light was on every leaf.

Do you want to talk about this seriously – go to the root of it? Or do you want to be comforted by some explanation, by some reasoned argument, and be distracted from your sorrow by some satisfying words?

She replied: 'I'd like to go into it deeply, but I don't know whether I have the capacity or the energy to face what you are going to say. When my husband was alive we used to come to some of your talks; but now I may find it very difficult to go along with you.'

Why are you in sorrow? Don't give an explanation, for that will only be a verbal construction of your feeling, which will not be the actual fact. So, when we ask a question, please don't answer it. Just listen, and find out for yourself. Why is there this sorrow of death – in every house, rich and poor, from the most powerful in the land to the beggar? Why are you in sorrow? Is it for your husband – or is it for yourself? If you are crying for him, can your tears help him? He has gone irrevocably. Do what you will, you will never have him back. No tears, no belief, no ceremonies or gods can ever bring him back. It is a fact which you have to accept; you can't do anything about it. But if you are crying for yourself, because of your loneliness, your empty life, because of the sensual pleasures you had and the companionship, then you are crying, aren't you, out of your own emptiness and out of self-pity? Perhaps for the first time you are aware of your own inward poverty. You have invested in your husband, haven't you, if we may gently point it out, and it has given you comfort, satisfaction and pleasure? All you are feeling now – the sense of loss, the agony of loneliness and anxiety – is a form of self-pity, isn't it? Do look at it. Don't harden your heart against it and say: 'I love my husband, and I wasn't thinking a bit about myself. I wanted to protect him, even though I often tried to dominate him; but it was all for his sake and there was never a thought for myself.' Now that he has gone you are realizing, aren't you, your own actual state? His death has shaken you and shown you the actual state of your mind and heart. You may not be willing to look at it; you may reject it out of fear, but if you observe a little more you will see that you are crying out of your own loneliness, out of your inward poverty – which is, out of self-pity.

'You are rather cruel, aren't you, sir?' she said. 'I have come to you for real comfort, and what are you giving me?'

It is one of the illusions most people have – that there is such a thing as inward comfort; that somebody else can give it to you or that you can find it for yourself. I am afraid there is no such thing. If you are seeking comfort you are bound to live in illusion, and when that illusion is broken you become sad because the comfort is taken away from you. So, to understand sorrow or to go beyond it, one must see actually what is inwardly taking place, and not cover it up. To point out all this is not cruelty, is it? It's not something ugly from which to shy away. When you see all this, very clearly, then you come out of it immediately, without a scratch, unblemished, fresh, untouched by the events of life.

27

Death is inevitable for all of us; one cannot escape from it. We try to find every kind of explanation, cling to every kind of belief in the hope of going beyond it, but do what you will it is always there; tomorrow, or round the corner, or many years away – it is always there. One has to come into touch with this enormous fact of life.

'But . . .' said the uncle, and out came the traditional belief in Atman, the soul, the permanent entity which continues. He was on his own ground now, well-trodden with cunning arguments and quotations. You saw him suddenly sit up straight and the light of battle, the battle of words, came into his eyes. Sympathy, love and understanding were gone. He was on his sacred ground of belief, of tradition, trodden down by the heavy weight of conditioning: 'But the Atman is in every one of us! It is reborn and continues until it realizes that it is Brahman. We must go through sorrow to come to that reality. We live in illusion; the world is an illusion. There is only one reality.'

And he was off! She looked at me, not paying much attention to him, and a gentle smile began to appear on her face; and we both looked at the dove which had come back, and the bright red bougainvilia.

There is nothing permanent either on earth or in ourselves. Thought can give continuity to something it thinks about; it can give permanency to a word, to an idea, to a tradition. Thought thinks itself permanent, but is it permanent? Thought is the response of memory, and is that memory permanent? It can build an image and give to that image a continuity, a permanency, calling it Atman or whatever you like, and it can remember the face of the husband or the wife and hold on to it. All this is the activity of thought which creates fear, and out of this fear there is the drive for permanency – the fear of not having a meal tomorrow, or shelter – the fear of death. This fear is the result of thought, and Brahman is the product of thought, too.

The uncle said: 'Memory and thought are like a candle. You put it out and re-light it again; you forget, and you remember again later on. You die and are re-born again into another life. The flame of the candle is the same – and not the same. So in the flame there is a certain quality of continuity.'

But the flame which has been put out is not the same flame as the new. There is an ending of the old for the new to be. If there is a constant modified continuity, then there is no new thing at all. The thousand yesterdays cannot be made new; even a candle burns itself out. Everything must end for the new to be.

The uncle now cannot rely on quotations or beliefs or on the sayings of others, so he withdraws into himself and becomes quiet, puzzled and rather angry, for he has been exposed to himself, and, like his niece, doesn't want to face the fact.

'I am not concerned about all this,' she said. 'I am utterly miserable. I have lost my husband and my son, and there are these two children left. What am I to do?'

If you are concerned about the two children, you can't be concerned about yourself and your misery. You have to look after them, educate them rightly, bring them up without the usual mediocrity. But if you are consumed by your own self-pity, which you call 'the love for your husband', and if you withdraw into isolation, then you are also destroying the other two children. Consciously or unconsciously we are all utterly selfish, and so long as we get what we want we consider everything is all right. But the moment an event takes place to shatter this, we cry out in despair, hoping to find other comforts which, of course, will again be shattered. So this process goes on, and if you want to be caught in it, knowing full well all the implications of it, then go ahead. But if you see the absurdity of it all, then you will naturally stop crying, stop isolating yourself, and live with the children with a new light and with a smile on your face.

V

SILENCE has many qualities. There is the silence between two noises, the silence between two notes and the widening silence in the interval between two thoughts. There is that peculiar, quiet, pervading silence that comes of an evening in the country; there is the silence through which you hear the bark of a dog in the distance or the whistle of a train as it comes up a steep grade; the silence in a house when everybody has gone to sleep, and its peculiar emphasis when you wake up in the middle of the night and listen to an owl hooting in the valley; and there is that silence before the owl's mate answers. There is the silence of an old deserted house, and the silence of a mountain; the silence between two human beings when they have seen the same thing, felt the same thing, and acted.

That night, particularly in that distant valley with the most ancient hills with their peculiar-shaped boulders, the silence was as real as the wall you touched. And you looked out of the window at the brilliant stars. It was not a self-generated silence; it was not that the earth was quiet and the villagers were asleep, but it came from everywhere – from the distant stars, from those dark hills and from your own mind and heart. This silence seemed to cover everything from the tiniest grain of sand in the river-bed – which only knew running water when it rained – to the tall, spreading banyan tree and a slight breeze that was now beginning. There is the silence of the mind which is never touched by any noise, by any thought or by the passing wind of experience. It is this silence that is innocent, and so endless. When there is this silence of the mind action springs from it, and this action does not cause confusion or misery.

The meditation of a mind that is utterly silent is the benediction that man is ever seeking. In this silence every quality of silence is.

There is that strange silence that exists in a temple or in an empty church deep in the country, without the noise of tourists and worshippers; and the heavy silence that lies on water is part of that which is outside the silence of the mind.

The meditative mind contains all these varieties, changes and movements of silence. This silence of the mind is the true religious mind, and the silence of the gods is the silence of the earth. The meditative mind flows in this silence, and love is the way of this mind. In this silence there is bliss and laughter.

The uncle came back again, this time without the niece who had lost her husband. He was a little more carefully dressed, also more disturbed and concerned, and his face had become darker because of his seriousness and anxiety. The floor on which we were sitting was hard, and the red bougainvilia was there, looking at us through the window. And the dove would probably come a little later. It always came about this time of the morning. It always sat on that branch in the same place, its back to the window and its head pointing south, and the cooing would come softly through the window.

'I would like to talk about immortality and the perfection of life as it evolves towards the ultimate reality. From what you said the other day, you have direct perception of what is true, and we, not knowing, only believe. We really don't know anything about the Atman at all; we are familiar only with the word. The symbol, for us, has become the real, and if you describe the symbol – which you did the other day – we get frightened. But in spite of this fear we cling to it, because we actually know nothing except what we've been taught, what the previous teachers have said, and the weight of tradition is always with us. So, first of all, I'd like to know for myself if there is this Reality which is permanent, this Reality, call it by whatever name you like – Atman or soul – which continues after death. I'm not frightened of death.

I've faced the death of my wife and several of my children, but I am concerned about this Atman as a reality. Is there this permanent entity in me?'

When we speak of permanency we mean, don't we, something that continues in spite of the constant change around it, in spite of the experiences, in spite of all the anxieties, sorrows and brutalities? Something that is imperishable? First of all, how can one find out? Can it be sought out by thought, by words? Can you find the permanent through the impermanent? Can you find that which is changeless through that which is constantly changing – thought? Thought can give permanency to an idea, Atman or soul, and say, 'This is the real', because thought breeds fear of this constant change, and out of this fear it seeks something permanent – a permanent relationship between human beings, a permanency in love. Thought itself *is* impermanent, *is* changing, so anything that it invents as permanent is, like itself, non-permanent. It can cling to a memory throughout life and call that memory permanent, and then want to know whether it will continue after death. Thought has created this thing, given it continuity, nourished it day after day and held on to it. This is the greatest illusion because thought lives in time, and what it has experienced yesterday it remembers through today and tomorrow; time is born out of this. So there is the permanency of time and the permanency which thought has given to an idea of ultimately attaining the truth. All this is the product of thought – the fear, time and achievement, the everlasting becoming.

'But who is the thinker – this thinker who has all these thoughts?'

Is there a thinker at all, or only thought which puts together the thinker? And having established him, then invents the permanent, the soul, the Atman.

'Do you mean to say that I cease to exist when I don't think?'

Has it ever happened to you, naturally, to find yourself in a state where thought is totally absent? In that state are you conscious of yourself as the thinker, the observer, the experiencer? Thought is the response of memory, and the bundle of memories is the thinker. When there is no thought is there the 'me' at all, about whom we make so much fuss and noise? We are not talking of a person in amnesia, or of one who is day-dreaming or controlling thought to silence it, but of a mind that is fully awake, fully alert. If there is no thought and no word, isn't the mind in a different dimension altogether?

'Certainly there is something quite different when the self is not acting, is not asserting itself, but this need not mean that the self does not exist – just because it does not act.'

Of course it exists! The 'me', the ego, the bundle of memories exists. We see it existing only when it responds to a challenge, but it's here, perhaps dormant or in abeyance, waiting for the next chance to respond. A greedy man is occupied most of the time with his greed; he may have moments when it is not active, but it is always there.

'What is that living entity which expresses itself in greed?'

It is still greed. The two are not separate.

'I understand perfectly what you call the ego, the "me", its memory, its greed, its assertiveness, its demands of all kinds, but is there nothing else except this ego? In the absence of this ego do you mean to say there is oblivion?'

When the noise of those crows stops there is something: this something is the chatter of the mind – the problems, worries, conflicts, even this inquiry into what remains after death. This question can be answered only when the mind is no longer greedy or envious. Our concern is not with what there is after the ego ceases but rather with the ending of all the attributes of the ego. That is really the problem – not what reality is, or if there is something permanent, eternal – but whether the mind, which is so conditioned by the culture in which it lives and for which it is responsible – whether such a mind can free itself and discover.

'Then how am I to begin to free myself?'

You can't free yourself. You are the seed of this misery, and when you ask 'how' you are asking for a method which will destroy the 'you', but in the process of destroying the 'you' you are creating another 'you'.

'If I may ask another question, what then is immortality? Mortality is death, mortality is the way of life with its sorrow and pain. Man has searched everlastingly for an immortality, a deathless state.'

Again, sir, you have come back to the question of something that is timeless, which is beyond thought. What is beyond thought is innocence, and thought, do what it will, can never touch it, for thought is always old. It is innocency, like love, that is deathless, but for that to exist the mind must be free of the thousand yesterdays with their memories. And freedom is a state in which there is no hate, no violence, no brutality. Without putting away all these things how can we ask what immortality is, what love is, what truth is?

VI

IF you set out to meditate it will not be meditation. If you set out to be good, goodness will never flower. If you cultivate humility, it ceases to be. Meditation is like the breeze that comes in when you leave the window open; but if you deliberately keep it open, deliberately invite it to come, it will never appear.

Meditation is not the way of thought, for thought is cunning, with infinite possibilities of self-deception, and so it will miss the way of meditation. Like love, it cannot be pursued.

The river that morning was very still. You could see on it the reflections of the clouds, of the new winter wheat and the wood beyond. Even the fisherman's boat didn't seem to disturb it. The quietness of the morning lay on the land. The sun was just coming up over the tops of the trees, and a distant voice was calling, and nearby a chanting of Sanskrit was in the air.

The parrots and the mynahs had not yet begun their search for food; the vultures, bare-necked, heavy, sat on the top of the tree waiting for the carrion to come floating down the river. Often you would see some dead animal floating by and a vulture or two would be on it, and the crows would flutter around it hoping for a bite. A dog would swim out to it, and not gaining a foothold would return to the shore and wander off. A train would pass by, making a steely clatter across the bridge, which was quite long. And beyond it, up the river, lay the city.

It was a morning full of quiet delight. Poverty, disease and pain were not yet walking on the road. There was a tottering bridge across the little stream; and where this little stream – dirty-brown – joined the big river, there it was supposed to be most holy, and there people came on festive days to bathe, men, women and children. It was cold, but they did not seem to mind. And the temple priest across the way made a lot of money; and the ugliness began.

He was a bearded man and wore a turban. He was in some kind of business and from the look of him he seemed to be prosperous, well-fed. He was slow in his walk and in his thinking. His reactions were still slower. He took several minutes to understand a simple statement. He said he had a guru of his own and, as he was passing by, he felt the urge to come up and talk about things that seemed to him important.

'Why is it,' he asked, 'that you are against gurus? It seems so absurd. They know, and I don't know. They can guide me, help me, tell me what to do, and save me a lot of trouble and pain. They are like a light in the darkness, and one must be guided by them otherwise one is lost, confused and in great misery. They told me that I shouldn't come and see you, for they taught me the danger of those who do not accept the traditional knowledge. They said if I listened to others I would be destroying the house they had so carefully built. But the temptation to come and see you was too strong, so here I am!'

He looked rather pleased at having yielded to temptation.

What is the need of a guru? Does he know more than you do? And what does he know? If he says that he knows, he really doesn't know, and, besides, the word is not the actual state. Can anyone teach you that extraordinary state of mind? They may be able to describe it to you, awaken your interest, your desire to possess it, experience it – but they cannot give it to you. You have to walk by yourself, you have to take the journey alone, and on that journey you have to be your own teacher and pupil.

'But all this is very difficult, isn't it?' he said, 'and the steps can be made easier by those who have experienced that reality.'

They become the authority and all you have to do, according to them, is just to follow, to imitate, obey, accept the image, the system which they offer. In this way you lose all initiative, all direct perception. You are merely following what they think is the way to the truth. But, unfortunately, truth has no way to it.

'What do you mean?' he cried, quite shocked.

Human beings are conditioned by propaganda, by the society in which they have been brought up – each religion asserting that its own path is the best. And there are a thousand gurus who maintain that their method, their system, their way of meditation, is the only path that leads to truth. And, if you observe, each disciple tolerates, condescendingly, the disciples of other gurus. Tolerance is the civilized acceptance of a division between people – politically, religiously and socially. Man has invented many paths, giving comfort to each believer, and so the world is broken up.

'Do you mean to say that I must give up my guru? Abandon all he has taught me? I should be lost!'

But mustn't you be lost to discover? We are afraid to be lost, to be uncertain, and so we run after those who promise heaven in the religious, political or social fields. So they really encourage fear, and hold us prisoners in that fear.

'But can I walk by myself?' he asked in an incredulous voice.

There have been so many saviours, masters, gurus, political leaders and philosophers, and not one of them has saved you from your own misery and conflict. So why follow them? Perhaps there may be quite another approach to all our problems.

'But am I serious enough to grapple with all this on my own?'

You are serious only when you begin to understand – not through somebody else – the pleasures that you are pursuing now. You are living at the level of pleasure. Not that there must not be pleasure, but if this pursuit of pleasure is the whole beginning and end of your life, then obviously you can't be serious.

'You make me feel helpless and hopeless.'

You feel hopeless because you want both. You want to be serious and you want also all the pleasures the world can give. These pleasures are so small and petty, anyway, that you desire in addition the pleasure which you call 'God'. When you see all this for yourself, not according to somebody else, then the seeing of it makes you the disciple and master. This is the main point. When you are the teacher, and the taught, and the teaching.

'But,' he asserted, 'you are a guru. You have taught me something this morning, and I accept you as my guru.'

Nothing has been taught, but you have *looked*. The looking has shown you. The looking is your guru, if you like to put it that way. But it is for you either to look or not to look. Nobody can force you. But if you look because you want to be rewarded or fear to be punished, this motive prevents the looking. To see, you must be free from all authority, tradition, fear, and thought with its cunning words. Truth is not in some far distant place; it is in the looking at what is. To see oneself as one is – in that awareness into which choice does not enter – is the beginning and end of all search.

VII

THOUGHT cannot conceive or formulate to itself the nature of space. Whatever it formulates has within it the limitation of its own boundaries. This is not the space which meditation comes upon. Thought has always a horizon. The meditative mind has no horizon. The mind cannot go from the limited to the immense, nor can it transform the limited into the limitless. The one has to cease for the other to be. Meditation is opening the door into spaciousness which cannot be imagined or speculated upon. Thought is the centre round which there is the space of idea, and this space can be expanded by further ideas. But such expansion through stimulation in any form is not the spaciousness in which there is no centre. Meditation is the understanding of this centre and so going beyond it. Silence and spaciousness go together. The immensity of silence is the immensity of the mind in which a centre does not exist. The perception of this space and silence is not of thought. Thought can perceive only its own projection, and the recognition of it is its own frontier.

You crossed the little stream over a rickety bridge of bamboo and mud. The stream joined the big river and disappeared into the waters of the strong current. The little bridge had holes in it and you had to walk rather carefully. You went up the sandy slope and passed the small temple and, a little further on, a well which was as old as the wells of the earth. It was at the corner of a village where there were many goats and hungry men and women wrapped around in dirty clothes, for it was quite cold. They fished in the big river, but somehow they were still very thin, emaciated, already old, some very crippled. In the village were weavers producing the most beautiful brocade and silk saris in dark dingy little rooms with small windows. It was a trade handed down from father to son, and middlemen and shopkeepers made the money.

You didn't go through the village but turned off to the left and followed a path which had become holy, for it was supposed that upon this path the Buddha had walked some 2,500 years ago, and pilgrims came from all over the country to walk on it. This path led through green fields, among mango groves, guava trees and through scattered temples. There was an ancient village, probably older than the Buddha, and many shrines and places where the pilgrims could spend the night. It had all become dilapidated; nobody seemed to care; the goats wandered about the place. There were large trees; one old tamarind, with vultures on top and a flock of parrots. You saw them coming in and disappearing into the green tree; they became the same colour as the leaves; you heard their screech but you could not see them.

On either side of the path stretched fields of winter wheat; and in the distance were villagers and the smoke of the fires over which they cooked. It was very still, the smoke going straight up. A bull, heavy, fierce-looking, but quite harmless, wandered through the fields, eating the grain as it was driven across the field by the farmer. It had rained during the night and the heavy dust was laid low. The sun would be hot during the day but now there were heavy clouds and it was pleasant to walk even in day-time, to smell the clean earth, to see the beauty of the land. It was a very old land, full of enchantment and human sorrow, with its poverty and those useless temples.

'You have talked a great deal about beauty and love, and after listening to you I see I don't know either what beauty is or what love is. I am an ordinary man, but I have read a great deal, both philosophy and literature. The explanations which they offer seem to be different from what you are saying. I could quote to you what the ancients of this country have said about love and beauty, and also how they have expressed it in the West, but I know you don't like quotations for they smack of authority. But, sir, if you are so inclined, we could go into this matter, and then perhaps I shall be able to understand what beauty and love may mean?'

Why is it that in our lives there is so little beauty? Why are museums with their pictures and statues necessary? Why do you have to listen to music? Or read descriptions of scenery? Good taste can be taught, or perhaps one has it naturally, but good taste is not beauty. Is it in the thing that has been put together – the sleek modern aeroplane, the compact tape-recorder, the modern hotel or the Greek temple – the beauty of line, of the very complex machine, or the curve of a beautiful bridge across a deep cavern?

'But do you mean that there is no beauty in things that are beautifully made and function perfectly? No beauty in superlative artistry?'

Of course there is. When you look at the inside of a watch it is really remarkably delicate and there is a certain quality of beauty in it, and in the ancient pillars of marble, or in the words of a poet. But if that is all beauty is, then it is only the superficial response of the senses. When you see a palm tree, single against the setting sun, is it the colour, the stillness of the palm, the quietness of the evening that make you feel the beautiful, or is beauty, like love, something that lies beyond the touch and the sight? Is it a matter of education, conditioning, that says: 'This is beautiful and that is not'? Is it a matter of custom and habit and style that says: 'This is squalor, but that is order and the flowering of the good'? If it is all a matter of conditioning then it is the product of culture and tradition, and therefore not beauty. If beauty is the outcome or the essence of experience, then to the man from the West and from the East, beauty is dependent upon education and tradition. Is love, like beauty, of the East or of the West, of Christianity or Hinduism, or the monopoly of the State or of an ideology? Obviously it is not any of this.

'Then what is it?'

You know, sir, austerity in self-abandonment is beauty. Without austerity there is no love, and without self-abandonment beauty has no reality. We mean by austerity not the harsh discipline of the saint or of the monk or of the commissar with their proud self-denial, or the discipline which gives them power and recognition – that is not austerity. Austerity is not harsh, not a disciplined assertion of self-importance. It is not the denial of comfort, or vows of poverty, or celibacy. Austerity is the summation of intelligence. This austerity can be only when there is self-abandonment, and it cannot be through will, through choice, through deliberate intent. It is the act of beauty that abandons, and it is love that brings the deep inward clarity of austerity. Beauty is this love, in which measurement has come to an end. Then this love, do what it will, is beauty.

'What do you mean, do what it will? If there is self-abandonment then there is nothing left for one to do.'

The doing is not separate from what is. It is the separation that brings conflict and ugliness. When there is not this separation then living itself is the act of love. The deep inward simplicity of austerity makes for a life that has no duality. This is the journey the mind had to take to come upon this beauty without the word. This journey is meditation.

VIII

MEDITATION is hard work. It demands the highest form of discipline – not conformity, not imitation, not obedience, but a discipline which comes through constant awareness, not only of the things about you outwardly, but also inwardly. So meditation is not an activity of isolation but action in everyday life which demands cooperation, sensitivity and intelligence. Without laying the foundation of a righteous life, meditation becomes an escape and therefore has no value whatsoever. A righteous life is not the following of social morality, but the freedom from envy, greed and the search for power – which all breed enmity. The freedom from these does not come through the activity of will but through being aware of them through self-knowing. Without knowing the activities of the self, meditation becomes sensuous excitement and therefore of very little significance.

At that latitude there is hardly any twilight or dawn, and that morning the river, wide and deep, was of molten lead. The sun was not yet over the land but there was a lightening in the east. The birds had not yet begun to sing their daily chorus of the morning and the villagers were not yet calling out to each other. The morning star was quite high in the sky, and as you watched, it grew paler and paler until the sun was just over the trees and the river became silver and gold.

Then the birds began, and the village woke up. Just then, suddenly, there appeared on the window-sill a large monkey, grey, with a black face and bushy hair over the forehead. His hands were black and his long tail hung over the window-sill into the room. He sat there very quiet, almost motionless, looking at us without a movement. We were quite close, a few feet separated us. And suddenly he stretched out his arm, and we held hands for some time. His hand was rough, black and dusty for he had climbed over the roof, over the little parapet above the window and had come down and sat there. He was quite relaxed, and what was surprising was that he was extraordinarily cheerful. There was no fear, no uneasiness; it was as though he was at home. There he was, with the river bright golden now, and beyond it the green bank and the distant trees. We must have held hands for quite a time; then, almost casually, he withdrew his hand but still remained where he was. We were looking at each other, and you could see his black eyes shining, small and full of strange curiosity. He wanted to come into the room but hesitated, then stretched his arms and his legs, reached for the parapet, and was over the roof and gone. In the evening he was there again on a tree, high up, eating something. We waved to him but there was no response.

The man was a sannyasi, a monk, with rather a nice delicate face and sensitive hands. He was clean, and his robes had been recently washed though not ironed. He said he had come from Rishikesh where he had spent many years under a guru who had now withdrawn into the higher mountains and remained alone. He said he had been to many ashrams. He had left home many years ago, perhaps when he was twenty. He couldn't remember very well at what age he had left. He said he had parents and several sisters and brothers but he had lost touch with them completely. He had come all this way because he had heard from several gurus that he should see us, and also he had read little bits here and there. And recently he had talked to a fellow sannyasi, and so he was here. One couldn't guess his age; he was more than middle-aged, but his voice and his eyes were still young.

'It has been my lot to wander over India visiting the various centres with their gurus, some of whom are scholarly, others ignorant though with a quality which indicates that they have something in them; yet others are mere exploiters giving out mantras; these have often been abroad and become popular. There are very few who have been above all this, but among those few was my recent guru. Now he has withdrawn into a remote and isolated part of the Himalayas. A whole group of us go to see him once a year to receive his blessing.'

Is isolation from the world necessary?

'Obviously one must renounce the world, for the world isn't real, and one must have a guru to teach one, for the guru has experienced reality and he will help those who

43

follow him to realize that reality. He knows, and we don't. We are surprised that you say that no guru is necessary, for you are going against tradition. You yourself have become a guru to many, and truth is not to be found alone. One must have help – the rituals, the guidance of those who know. Perhaps ultimately one may have to stand alone, but not now. We are children and we need those who have advanced along the path. It is only by sitting at the feet of one who knows that one learns. But you seem to deny all this, and I have come to find out seriously why.'

Do look at that river – the morning light on it, and those sparkling, green, luscious wheatfields, and the trees beyond. There is great beauty; and the eyes that see it must be full of love to comprehend it. And to hear the rattling of that train over the iron bridge is as important as to hear the voice of the bird. So do look – and listen to those pigeons cooing. And look at that tamarind tree with those two green parrots. For the eyes to see them there must be a communion with them – with the river, with that boat passing by filled with villagers, singing as they row. This is part of the world. If you renounce it you are renouncing beauty and love – the very earth itself. What you are renouncing is the society of men, but not the things which man had made out of the world. You are not renouncing the culture, the tradition, the knowledge – all of that goes with you when you withdraw from the world. You are renouncing beauty and love because you are frightened of those two words and what lies behind those words. Beauty is associated with sensuous reality, with its sexual implications and the love that is involved in it. This renunciation has made the so-called religious people self-centred – at a higher level perhaps than with the man of the world, but it is still self-centredness. When you have no beauty and love there is no possibility of coming upon that immeasurable thing. If you observe, right through the domain of the sannyasis and the saints, this beauty and love are far from them. They may talk about it, but they are harsh disciplinarians, violent in their controls and demands.

So essentially, though they may put on the saffron robe or the black robe, or the scarlet of the cardinal, they are all very worldly. It is a profession like any other profession; certainly it is not what is called spiritual. Some of them should be business men and not put on airs of spirituality.

'But you know, sir, you are being rather harsh, aren't you?'

No, we are merely stating a fact, and the fact is neither harsh, pleasant nor unpleasant; it is so. Most of us object to facing things as they are. But all this is fairly obvious and quite open. Isolation is the way of life, the way of the world. Each human being, through his self-centred activities, is isolating himself, whether he is married or not, whether he talks of cooperation, or of nationality, achievement and success. Only when this isolation becomes extreme is there a neurosis which sometimes produces – if one has talent – art, good literature, and so on. This withdrawal from the world with all its noise, brutality, hate and pleasure is a part of the isolating process, isn't it? Only the sannyasi does it in the name of religion, or God, and the competitive man accepts it as a part of the social structure.

In this isolation you do achieve certain powers, a certain quality of austerity and abstemiousness, which give a sense of power. And power, whether of the Olympic champion, or of the Prime Minister, or of the Head of the churches and temples, is the same. Power in any form is evil – if one may use that word – and the man of power can never open the door to reality. So isolation is not the way.

Cooperation is necessary in order to live at all; and there is no cooperation with the follower or with the guru. The guru destroys the disciple and the disciple destroys the guru. In this relationship of the teacher and the taught how can there be cooperation, the working together, the inquiring together, taking the journey together? This hierarchical division which is part of the social structure, whether it be in the religious field or in the army or the business world, is essentially worldly. And when one renounces the world one is caught in worldliness.

Unworldliness is not the loin-cloth or one meal a day or repeating some meaningless though stimulating mantra or phrase. It is worldliness when you give up the world and are inwardly part of that world of envy, greed, fear, of accepting authority and the division between the one who knows and the one who doesn't know. It is still worldliness when you seek achievement, whether it be fame or the achievement of what one may call the ideal, or God, or what you will. It is the accepted tradition of the culture that is essentially worldly, and withdrawing into a mountain far from man does not absolve this worldliness. Reality, under no circumstances, lies in that direction.

One must be alone, but this aloneness is not isolation. This aloneness implies freedom from the world of greed, hate and violence with all its subtle ways, and from aching loneliness and despair.

To be alone is to be an outsider who does not belong to any religion or nation, to any belief or dogma. It is this aloneness that comes upon an innocency that has never been touched by the mischief of man. It is innocency that can live in the world, with all its turmoil, and yet not be of it. It is not clothed in any particular garb. The flowering of goodness does not lie along any path, for there is no path to truth.

IX

Do not think that meditation is a continuance and an expansion of experience In experience there is always the witness and he is ever tied to the past. Meditation, on the contrary, is that complete inaction which is the ending of all experience. The action of experience has its roots in the past and so it is time-binding; it leads to action which is inaction, and brings disorder. Meditation is the total inaction which comes out of a mind that sees what is, without the entanglement of the past. This action is not a response to any challenge but is the action of the challenge itself, in which there is no duality. Meditation is the emptying of experience and is going on all the time, consciously or unconsciously, so it is not an action limited to a certain period during the day. It is a continuous action from morning till night – the watching without the watcher. Therefore there is no division between the daily life and meditation, the religious life and the secular life. The division comes only when the watcher is tied to time. In this division there is disarray, misery and confusion, which is the state of society.

So meditation is not individualistic, nor is it social; it transcends both and so includes both. This is love: the flowering of love is meditation.

It was cool in the morning but as the day wore on it began to be quite hot and as you went through the town along the narrow street, over-crowded, dusty, dirty, noisy, you realized that every street was like that. You almost saw the exploding of the population. The car had to go very slowly, for the people were walking right in the middle of the street. It was getting hotter now. Gradually, with a great many hootings, you got out of the town and were glad of it. You drove past the factories, and at last you were in the country.

The country was dry. It had rained some time ago and the trees were now waiting for the next rains – and they would wait for a long time. You went past villagers, cattle, bullock-carts and buffaloes which refused to move out of the middle of the road; and you went past an old temple which had an air of neglect but had the quality of an ancient sanctuary. A peacock came out of the wood; its brilliant blue neck sparkled in the sun. It didn't seem to mind the car, for it walked across the road with great dignity and disappeared in the fields.

Then you began to climb steep hills, sometimes with deep ravines on both sides. Now it was getting cooler, the trees were fresher. After winding for some time through the hills, you came to the house. By then it was quite dark. The stars became very clear. You felt you could almost reach out and touch them. The silence of the night was spreading over the land. Here man could be alone, undisturbed, and look at the stars and at himself endlessly.

The man said a tiger had killed a buffalo the day before and would surely come back to it, and would we all, later in the evening, like to see the tiger? We said we would be delighted. He replied. 'Then I will go and prepare a shelter in a tree near the carcase and tie a live goat to the tree. The tiger will first come to the live goat before going back to the old kill.' We replied that we would rather not see the tiger at the expense of the goat. Presently, after some talk he left. That evening our friend said, 'Let us get into the car and go into the forest, and perhaps we may come upon that tiger.' So towards sunset we drove through the forest for five or six miles and of course there was no tiger. Then we returned, with the headlights lighting the road. We had given up all hope of seeing the tiger and drove on without thinking about it. Just as we turned a corner – there it was, in the middle of the road, huge, its eyes bright and fixed. The car stopped, and the animal, large and threatening, came towards us, growling. It was quite close to us now, just in front of the radiator. Then it turned and came alongside the car. We put out our hand to touch it as it went by, but the friend grabbed the arm and pulled it back sharply, for he knew something of tigers. It was of great length, and as the windows were open you could smell it and its smell was not repulsive. There was a dynamic savagery about it, and great power and beauty. Still growling it went off into the woods and we went on our way, back to the house.

He had come with his family – his wife and several children – and seemed not too prosperous though they were fairly well clothed and well fed. The children sat silently for some time until it was suggested that they should go out and play, then they jumped up eagerly and ran out of the door.

The father was some kind of official; it was a job that he had to do, and that was all. He asked: 'What is happiness, and why is it that it can't continue throughout one's life? I have had moments of great happiness and also, of course, great sorrow. I have struggled to live with happiness, but there is always the sorrow. Is it possible to remain with happiness?'

What is happiness? Do you know when you are happy, or only a moment later when it is over? Is happiness pleasure, and can pleasure be constant?

'I should think, sir, at least for me, that pleasure is part of the happiness I have known. I cannot imagine happiness without pleasure. Pleasure is a primary instinct in man, and if you take it away how can there be happiness?'

We are, are we not, inquiring into this question of happiness? And if you assume anything, or have opinion or judgement in this inquiry, you will not be able to go very far. To inquire into complex human problems there must be freedom from the very beginning. If you haven't got it you are like an animal tethered to a post and can move only as far as the rope will allow. That's what always happens. We have concepts, formulas, beliefs or experiences which tether us, and from those we try to examine, look around, and this naturally prevents a very deep inquiry. So, if we may suggest, don't assume or believe, but have eyes that can see very clearly. If happiness is pleasure, then it is also pain. You cannot separate pleasure from pain. Don't they always go together?

So what is pleasure and what is happiness? You know, sir, if, in examining a flower, you tear its petals away one by one, there is no flower left at all. You will have in your hands bits of the flower and the bits don't make the beauty of the flower. So in looking at this question we are not analysing intellectually, thereby making the whole thing arid, meaningless and empty. We are looking at it with eyes that care very much, with eyes that understand, with eyes that touch but do not tear. So please don't tear at it and go away empty handed. Leave the analytical mind alone.

Pleasure is encouraged by thought, isn't it? Thought can give it a continuity, the appearance of duration which we call happiness; as thought can also give a duration to sorrow. Thought says: 'This I like and that I don't like. I would like to keep this and throw away that.' But thought has made up both, and happiness now has become the way of thought. When you say: 'I want to remain in that state of happiness' – you are the thought, you are the memory of the previous experience which you call pleasure and happiness.

So the past, or yesterday, or many yesterdays ago, which is thought, is saying: 'I would like to live in that state of happiness which I have had.' You are making the dead past into an actuality in the present and you are afraid of losing it tomorrow. Thus you have built a chain of continuity. This continuity has its roots in the ashes of yesterday, and therefore it is not a living thing at all. Nothing can blossom in ashes – and thought is ashes. So you have made happiness a thing of thought, and it *is* for you a thing of thought.

But is there something other than pleasure, pain, happiness and sorrow? Is there a bliss, an ecstasy, that is not touched by thought? For thought is very trivial, and there is nothing original about it. In asking this question, thought must abandon itself. When thought abandons itself there is the discipline of the abandonment, which becomes the grace of austerity. Then austerity is not harsh and brutal. Harsh austerity is the product of thought as a revulsion against pleasure and indulgence.

From this deep self-abandonment – which is thought abandoning itself, for it sees clearly its own danger – the whole structure of the mind becomes quiet. It is really a state of pure attention and out of this comes a bliss, an ecstasy, that cannot be put into words. When it is put into words it is not the real.

X

MEDITATION is a movement in stillness. Silence of the mind is the way of action. Action born of thought is inaction, which breeds disorder. This silence is not the product of thought, nor is it the ending of the chattering of the mind.

A still mind is possible only when the brain itself is quiet. The brain cells – which have been conditioned for so long to react, to project, to defend, to assert – become quiet only through the seeing of what actually is. From this silence, action which does not bring about disorder is possible only when the observer, the centre, the experiencer, has come to an end – for then the seeing is the doing. Seeing is possible only out of a silence in which all evaluation and moral values have come to an end.

This temple is older than its gods. They remained, prisoners in the temple, but the temple itself was far more ancient. It had thick walls and pillars in the corridors, carved with horses, gods and angels. They had a certain quality of beauty, and as you passed them you wondered what would happen if they all came alive, including the innermost god.

They said that this temple, especially the innermost sanctuary, went back far beyond the imagination of time. As you wandered through the various corridors, lit by the morning sun and with sharp, clear shadows, you wondered what it was all about – how man has made gods out of his own mind and carved them with his hands and put them into temples and churches and worshipped them.

The temples of the ancient times had a strange beauty and power. They seemed to be born out of the very earth itself. This temple was almost as old as man, and the gods in it were clothed in silks, garlanded, and awakened from their sleep with chants, with incense and with bells. The incense, which had been burned for many centuries past, seemed to pervade the whole of the temple, which was vast and must have covered several acres.

People seemed to have come here from all over the country, the rich and the poor, but only a certain class were allowed inside the sanctuary itself. You entered through a low stone door, stepping over a parapet which was worn down through time. Outside the sanctuary there were guardians in stone, and when you came into it there were priests, naked down to the waist, chanting, solemn and dignified. They were all rather well fed, with big tummies and delicate hands. Their voices were hoarse, for they had been chanting for so many years; and the God, or the Goddess, was almost shapeless. There must have been a face at one time but the features had almost gone. The jewels must have been beyond price.

When the chanting stopped there was a stillness as though the very earth had stopped in its rotation. In here there was no sunshine, and the light came only from the wicks burning in the oil. Those wicks had blackened the ceiling and the place was quite mysteriously dark.

All gods must be worshipped in mystery and in darkness, otherwise they have no existence.

When you came out into the open strong light of the sun and looked at the blue sky and the tall waving palm trees you wondered why it is that man worships himself as the image which he has made with his hands and mind. Fear, and that lovely blue sky, seemed so far apart.

He was a young man, clean, sharp of face, bright-eyed, with a quick smile. We sat on the floor in a little room overlooking a small garden. The garden was full of roses, from white to almost black. A parrot was on a branch, hanging upside down, with its bright eyes and red beak. It was looking at another much smaller bird.

He spoke English fairly well, but was rather hesitant in the use of words, and for the moment he seemed serious. He asked: 'What is a religious life? I have asked various gurus and they have given the standard replies, and I would like, if I may, to ask you the same question. I had a good job, but as I am not married, I gave it up because I am drawn deeply by religion and want to find out what it means to lead a religious life in a world that is so irreligious.'

Instead of asking what a religious life is, wouldn't it be better, if I may suggest it, to ask what living is? Then perhaps we may understand what a truly religious life is. The so-called religious life varies from clime to clime, from sect to sect, from belief to belief; and man suffers through the propaganda of the organized vested interests of religions. If we could set aside all that – not only the beliefs, the dogmas and rituals but also the respectability which is entailed in the culture of religion – then perhaps we could find out what a religious life is, untouched by the thought of man.

But before we do that, let us, as we said, find out what living is. The actuality of living is the daily grind, the routine, with its struggle and conflict; it is the ache of loneliness, the misery and the squalor of poverty and riches, the ambition, the search for fulfilment, the success and the sorrow – these cover the whole field of our life. This is what we call living – gaining and losing a battle, and the endless pursuit of pleasure.

In contrast to this, or in opposition to this, there is what is called religious living or a spiritual life. But the opposite contains the very seed of its own opposite and so, though it may appear different, actually it is not. You may change the outer garment but the inner essence of what was and of what must be is the same. This duality is the product of thought and so it breeds more conflict; and the corridor of this conflict is endless. All this we know – we have been told it by others or we have felt it for ourselves and all this we call living.

The religious life is not on the other side of the river, it is on this side – the side of the whole travail of man. It is this that we have to understand, and the action of understanding is the religious act – not putting on ashes, wearing a loin cloth or a mitre, sitting in the seat of the mighty or being carried on an elephant.

The seeing of the whole condition, the pleasure and the misery of man, is of the first importance – not the speculation as to what a religious life should be. What should be is a myth; it is the morality which thought and fancy have put together, and one must deny this morality – the social, the religious and the industrial. This denial is not of the intellect but is an actual slipping out of the pattern of that morality which is immoral.

So the question really is: Is it possible to step out of this pattern? It is thought which has created this frightening mess and misery, and which has prevented both religion and the religious life. Thought thinks that it can step out of the pattern, but if it does it will still be an act of thought, for thought has no reality and therefore it will create another illusion.

Going beyond this pattern is not an act of thought. This must be clearly understood, otherwise you will be caught again in the prison of thought. After all, the 'you' is a bundle of memory, tradition and the knowledge of a thousand yesterdays. So only with the ending of sorrow, for sorrow is the result of thought, can you step out of the world of war, hate, envy and violence. This act of stepping out is the religious life. This religious life has no belief whatsoever, for it has no tomorrow.

'Aren't you asking, sir, for an impossible thing? Aren't you asking for a miracle? How can I step out of it all without thought? Thought is my very being!'

That's just it! This very being, which is thought, has to come to an end. This very self-centredness with its activities must naturally and easily die. It is in this death alone that there is the beginning of the new religious life.

XI

IF you deliberately take an attitude, a posture, in order to meditate, then it becomes a plaything, a toy of the mind. If you determine to extricate yourself from the confusion and the misery of life, then it becomes an experience of imagination – and this is not meditation. The conscious mind or the unconscious mind must have no part in it; they must not even be aware of the extent and beauty of meditation – if they are, then you might just as well go and buy a romantic novel.

In the total attention of meditation there is no knowing, no recognition, nor the remembrance of something that has happened. Time and thought have entirely come to an end, for they are the centre which limits its own vision.

At the moment of light, thought withers away, and the conscious effort to experience and the remembrance of it, is the word that has been. And the word is never the actual. At that moment – which is not of time – the ultimate is the immediate, but that ultimate has no symbol, is of no person, of no god.

That morning, especially so early, the valley was extraordinarily quiet. The owl had stopped hooting and there was no reply from its mate over in the distant hills. No dog was barking and the village was not yet awake. In the east there was a glow, a promise, and the Southern Cross had not yet faded. There was not even a whisper among the leaves, and the earth itself seemed to have stopped in its rotation. You could feel the silence, touch it, smell it, and it had that quality of penetration. It wasn't the silence outside in those hills, among the trees, that was still; you were of it. You and it were not two separate things. The division between noise and silence had no meaning. And those hills, dark, without a movement, were of it, as you were.

This silence was very active. It was not the negation of noise, and strangely that morning it had come through the window like some perfume, and with it came a sense, a feeling, of the absolute. As you looked out of the window, the distance between all things disappeared, and your eyes opened with the dawn and saw everything anew.

'I am interested in sex, social equality, and God. These are the only things that matter in life, and nothing else. Politics, religions with their priests and promises, with their rituals and confessions, seem so insulting. They really don't answer a thing, they have never really solved any problems, they have helped only to postpone them. They've condemned sex, in different ways, and they have sustained social inequalities, and the god of their mind is a stone which they have clothed with love and its sentiment. Personally I have no use for it at all. I only tell you this so that we can put all that aside and concern ourselves with these three issues – sex, social misery, and that thing called God.

'To me, sex is necessary as food is necessary. Nature has made man and woman and the enjoyment of the night. To me that is as important as the discovery of that truth which may be called God. And it is as important to feel for your neighbour as to have love for the woman of your house. Sex is not a problem. I enjoy it, but there is in me a fear of some unknown thing, and it is this fear and pain that I must understand – not as a problem to be solved but rather as something that I have to go into so that I am really cleansed of it. So I would like, if you have the time, to consider these things with you.'

Can we begin with the last and not with the first, then perhaps the other issues can be more deeply understood; then perhaps they will have a different content than pleasure can give?

Do you want your belief to be strengthened or do you want actually to see reality – not experience it, but actually see it with a mind and heart that are highly attentive and clear? Belief is one thing and seeing is another. Belief leads to darkness, as faith does. It leads you to the church, to the dark temples and to the pleasurable sensations of rituals. Along that way there is no reality, there is only fancy, the imaginative furnishings that fill the church.

If you deny fear, belief is unnecessary, but if you cling to belief and dogma then fear has its way. Belief is not only according to the religious sanctions; it comes into being though you may not belong to any religion. You may have your own individualistic, exclusive belief – but it is not the light of clarity. Thought invests in belief to protect itself against fear which it has brought into being. And the way of thought is not the freedom of attention which sees truth.

The immeasurable cannot be sought by thought, for thought has always a measure. The sublime is not within the structure of thought and reason, nor is it the product of emotion and sentiment. The negation of thought is attention; as the negation of thought is love. If you are seeking the highest, you will not find it; it must come to you, if you are lucky – and luck is the open window of your heart, not of thought.

'This is rather difficult, isn't it? You are asking me to deny the whole structure of myself, the me that I have very carefully nourished and sustained. I had thought the pleasure of what may be called God to be everlasting. It is my security; in it is all my hope and delight; and now you ask me to put all that aside. Is it possible? And do I really want to? Also, aren't you promising me something as a reward if I put it all aside? Of course I see that you are not actually offering me a reward, but can I actually – not only with my lips – put aside completely the thing that I have always lived on?'

If you try to put it aside deliberately it will become a conflict, pain and endless misery. But if you see the truth of it – as you see the truth of that lamp, the flickering light, the wick and the brass stem – then you will have stepped into another dimension. In this dimension love has no social problems; there is no racial, class or intellectual division. It is only the unequal who feel the necessity for equality. It is the superior who needs to keep his division, his class, his ways. And the inferior is ever striving to become the superior; the oppressed to become the oppressor. So merely to legislate – though such legislation is necessary – does not bring about the end of division with its cruelty; nor does it end the division between labour and status. We use work to achieve status, and the whole cycle of inequality begins. The problems of society are not ended by the morality that society has invented. Love has no morality, and love is not reform. When love becomes pleasure, then pain is inevitable. Love is not thought and it is thought that gives pleasure – as sexual pleasure and as the pleasure of achievement. Thought strengthens and gives continuity to the pleasure of the moment. Thought, by thinking about that pleasure, gives it the vitality of the next moment of pleasure. This demand for pleasure is what we call sex, is it not? With it goes a great deal of affection, tenderness, care, companionship, and all the rest of it, but through it all there is the thread of pain and fear. And thought, by its activity, makes this thread unbreakable.

'But you can't remove pleasure from sex! I live by that pleasure; I like it. To me it is far more important than having money, position or prestige. I also see that pleasure brings with it pain, but the pleasure predominates over the pain, so I don't mind.'

When this pleasure which you so delight in comes to an end – with age, through accident, with time – then you are caught; then sorrow is your shadow. But love is not pleasure, nor is it the product of desire, and that is why, sir, one must enter into a different dimension. In that our problems – and all issues – are resolved. Without that, do what you will, there is sorrow and confusion.

XII

A GREAT many birds were flying overhead, some crossing the wide river and others, high up in the sky, going round in wide circles with hardly a movement of the wing. Those that were high up were mostly vultures and in the bright sun they were mere specks, tacking against the breeze. They were clumsy on land with their naked necks and wide, heavy wings. There were a few of them on the tamarind tree, and the crows were teasing them. One crow, especially, was after a vulture, trying to perch on him. The vulture got bored and took to the wing, and the crow which had been harassing him came in from behind and sat on the vulture's back as it flew. It was really quite a curious sight – the vulture with the black crow on top of it. The crow seemed to be thoroughly enjoying himself and the vulture was trying to get rid of him. Eventually the crow flew off across the river and disappeared into the woods.

The parrots came across the river, zig-zagging, screeching, telling the whole world they were coming. They were bright green, with red beaks, and there were several in that tamarind tree. They would come out in the morning, go down the river and sometimes would come back screeching, but more often they remained away all day and only returned in the late afternoon, having stolen the grain from the fields and whatever fruit they could find. You saw them for a few seconds among the tamarind leaves, and then they would disappear. You couldn't really follow them among the tiny green leaves of the tree. They had a hole in the trunk and there they lived, male and female, and they seemed to be so happy, screeching their joy as they flew out. In the evening and early morning the sun made a path – golden in the morning and silver in the evening – across the river. No wonder men worship rivers; it is better than worshipping images with all the rituals and beliefs. The river was alive, deep and full, always in movement; and the little pools beside the bank were always stagnant.

Each human being isolates himself in the little pool, and there decays; he never enters into the full current of the river. Somehow that river, made so filthy by human beings higher up, was clean in the middle, blue-green and deep. It was a splendid river, especially in the early morning before the sun came up; it was so still, motionless, of the colour of molten silver. And, as the sun came up over the trees, it became golden, and then turned again into a silvery path; and the water came alive.

In that room overlooking the river it was cool, almost cold, for it was early winter. A man, sitting opposite with his wife, was young, and she was younger still. We sat on the carpet placed on a rather cold, hard floor. They weren't interested in looking at the river, and when it was pointed out to them – its width, its beauty, and the green bank on the other side – they acknowledged it with a polite gesture. They had come some distance, from the north by bus and train; and were eager to talk about the things they had in mind; the river was something they could look at later when they had time.

He said: 'Man can never be free; he is tied to his family, to his children, to his job. Until he dies he has responsibilities. Unless, of course,' he added, 'he becomes a sannyasi, a monk.'

He saw the necessity of being free, yet he felt it was something he could not achieve in this competitive, brutal world. His wife listened to him with a rather surprised look, pleased to find that her man could be serious and could express himself quite well in English. It gave her a sense of possessive pride. He was totally unaware of this as she was sitting a little behind him.

'Can one be free, ever?' he asked. 'Some political writers and theorists, like the Communists, say that freedom is something bourgeois, unattainable and unreal, while the democratic world talks a great deal about freedom. So do the capitalists, and, of course, every religion preaches it and promises it, though they see to it that man is made a prisoner of their particular beliefs and ideologies – denying their promises by their acts. I've come to find out, not merely intellectually, if man, if I, can really be free in this world. I'm taking a holiday from my job to come here; for two days I am free from my work – from the routine of the office and the usual life of the little town where I live. If I had more money I'd be freer and be able to go where I like and do what I want to do, perhaps paint, or travel. But that is impossible as my salary is limited and I have responsibilities; I am a prisoner to my responsibilities.'

His wife couldn't make out all this but she pricked up her ears at the word 'responsibilities'. She may have been wondering whether he wanted to leave home and wander the face of the earth.

'These responsibilities,' he went on, 'prevent me from being free both outwardly and inwardly. I can understand that man cannot be completely free from the world of the post office, the market, the office and so on, and I'm not seeking freedom there. What I have come to find out is if it is at all possible to be free inwardly?'

The pigeons on the veranda were cooing, fluttering about, and the parrots screeched across the window and the sun shone on their bright green wings.

What is freedom? Is it an idea, or a feeling that thought breeds because it is caught in a series of problems, anxieties, and so on? Is freedom a result, a reward, a thing that lies at the end of a process? Is it freedom when you free yourself from anger? Or is it being able to do what you want to do? Is it freedom when you find responsibility a burden and push it aside? Is it freedom when you resist, or when you yield? Can thought give this freedom, can any action give it?

'I'm afraid you will have to go a little bit slower.'

Is freedom the opposite of slavery? Is it freedom when, being in a prison and knowing you are in prison and being aware of all the restraints of the prison, you imagine freedom? Can imagination ever give freedom or is it a fancy of thought? What we actually know, and what actually is, is bondage – not only to outward things, to the house, to the family, to the job – but also inwardly, to traditions, to habits, to the pleasure of domination and possession, to fear, to achievement and to so many other things. When success brings great pleasure one never talks about freedom from it, or thinks about it. We talk of freedom only when there is pain. We are bound to all these things, both inwardly and outwardly, and this bondage is what is. And the resistance to what is, is what we call freedom. One resists, or escapes from, or tries to suppress what is, hoping thereby to come to some form of freedom. We know inwardly only two things – bondage and resistance; and resistance creates the bondage.

'Sorry, I don't understand at all.'

When you resist anger or hatred, what has actually taken place? You build a wall against hatred, but it is still there; the wall merely hides it from you. Or you determine not to be angry, but this determination is part of the anger, and the very resistance strengthens the anger. You can see it in yourself if you observe this fact. When you resist, control, suppress, or try to transcend – which are all the same thing for they are all facts of the will – you have thickened the wall of resistance, and so you become more and more enslaved, narrow, petty. And it is from this pettiness, this narrowness, that you want to be free, and that very want is the reaction which is going to create another barrier, more pettiness. So we move from one resistance, one barrier, to another – sometimes giving to the wall of resistance a different colouring, a different quality, or some word of nobility. But resistance is bondage, and bondage is pain.

'Does this mean that, outwardly, one should let anybody kick one around as they will, and that, inwardly, one's anger, etc, should be given free rein?'

It seems that you have not listened to what has been said. When it is a matter of pleasure you don't mind the kick of it,

the feeling of delight; but when that kick becomes painful, then you resist. You want to be free from the pain and yet hold on to the pleasure. The holding on to the pleasure is the resistance.

It is natural to respond; if you do not respond physically to the prick of a pin it means you are numbed. Inwardly, too, if you do not respond, something is wrong. But the way in which you respond and the nature of the response is important, not the response itself. When somebody flatters you, you respond; and you respond when somebody insults you. Both are resistances – one of pleasure and the other of pain. The one you keep and the other you either disregard or wish to retaliate against. But both are resistances. Both the keeping and the rejecting are a form of resistance; and freedom is no resistance.

'Is it possible for me to respond without the resistance of either pleasure or pain?'

What do *you* think, sir? What do *you* feel? Are you putting the question to me or to yourself? If an outsider, an outside agency, answers that question for you, then you rely on it, then that reliance becomes the authority, which is a resistance. Then again you want to be free of *that* authority! So how can you ask this question of another?

'You might point it out to me, and if I then see it, authority is not involved, is it?'

But we have pointed out to you what actually *is*. See what actually is, without responding to it with pleasure or with pain. Freedom is seeing. Seeing is freedom. You can see only in freedom.

'This seeing may be an act of freedom, but what effect has it on my bondage which is the what is, which is the thing seen?'

When you say the seeing *may be* an act of freedom, it is a supposition, so your seeing is also a supposition. Then you don't actually see what is.

'I don't know sir. I see my mother-in-law bullying me; does she stop it because I see it?'

See the action of your mother-in-law, and see your responses, without the further responses of pleasure and pain. See it in freedom. Your action may then be to ignore what she says completely or to walk out. But the walking out or the disregarding her is not a resistance. This choiceless awareness is freedom. The action from that freedom cannot be predicted, systematized, or put into the framework of social morality. This choiceless awareness is non-political, it does not belong to any 'ism'; it is not the product of thought.

XIII

'I want to know God,' he said vehemently; he almost shouted it. The vultures were on the usual tree, and the train was rattling across the bridge, and the river flowed on – here it was very wide, very quiet and very deep. Early that morning you could smell the water from a distance; high on the bank overlooking the river you could smell it – the freshness, the cleanliness of it in the morning air. The day had not yet spoilt it. The parrots were screeching across the window, going to the fields, and later they would return to the tamarind. The crows, by the dozen, were crossing the river, high in the air, and they would come down on the trees and among the fields across the river. It was a clear morning of winter, cold but bright, and there was not a cloud in the sky. As you watched the light of the early morning sun on the river, meditation was going on. The very light was part of that meditation when you looked at the bright dancing water in the quiet morning – not with a mind that was translating it into some meaning, but with eyes that saw the light and nothing else.

Light, like sound, is an extraordinary thing. There is the light that painters try to put on a canvas; there is the light that cameras capture; there is the light of a single lamp in a dark night, or the light that is on the face of another, the light that lies behind the eyes. The light that the eyes see is not the light on the water; that light is so different, so vast that it cannot enter into the narrow field of the eye. That light, like sound, moved endlessly – outward and inward – like the tide of the sea. And if you kept very still, you went with it, not in imagination or sensuously; you went with it unknowingly, without the measure of time.

The beauty of that light, like love, is not to be touched, not to be put into a word. But there it was – in the shade, in the open, in the house, on the window across the way, and in the laughter of those children. Without that light what you see is of so little importance, for the light is everything; and the light of meditation was on the water. It would be there in the evening again, during the night, and when the sun rose over the trees, making the river golden. Meditation is that light in the mind which lights the way for action; and without that light there is no love.

He was a big man, clean-shaven, and his head was shaven too. We sat on the floor in that little room overlooking the river. The floor was cold, for it was winter. He had the dignity of a man who possesses little and who is not greatly frightened of what people say.

'I want to know God. I know it's not the fashionable thing nowadays. The students, the coming generation with their revolts, with their political activities, with their reasonable and unreasonable demands, scoff at all religion. And they are quite right too, for look what the priests have done with it! Naturally the younger generation do not want anything of it. To them, what the temples and churches stand for is the exploitation of man. They distrust completely the hierarchical priestly outlook – with the saviours, the ceremonies, and all that nonsense. I agree with them. I have helped some of them to revolt against it all. But I still want to know God. I have been a Communist but I left the party long ago, for the Communists, too, have their gods, their dogmas and theoreticians. I was really a very ardent Communist, for at the beginning they promised something – a great, a real revolution. But now they have all the things the Capitalists have; they have gone the way of the world. I have dabbled in social reform and have been active in politics, but I have left all that behind because I don't see that man will ever be free of his despair and anxiety and fear through science and technology. Perhaps there's only one way. I'm not in any way superstitious and I don't think I have any fear of life. I have been through it all and, as you see, I have still many years before me. I want to know what God is. I have asked some of the wandering monks, and those who everlastingly say, God *is*, you have only to look, and those who become mysterious and offer some method. I am wary of all those traps. So here I am, for I feel I must find out.'

We sat in silence for some time. The parrots were passing the window, screeching, and the light was on their bright green wings and their red beaks.

Do you think you can find out? Do you think that by seeking you will come upon it? Do you think you can experience it? Do you think that the measure of your mind is going to come upon the measureless? How are you going to find out? How will you know? How will you be able to recognize it?

'I really don't know,' he replied. 'But I will know when it is the real.'

You mean you will know it by your mind, by your heart, by your intelligence?

'No. The knowing is not dependent on any of these. I know very well the danger of the senses. I am aware how easily illusions are created.'

To know is to experience, isn't it? To experience is to recognize, and recognition is memory and association. If what you mean by 'knowing' is the result of a past incident, a memory, a thing that has happened before, then it is the knowing of what *has* happened. Can you know what is happening, what is actually taking place? Or, can you only know it a moment afterwards, when it is over? What is actually happening is out of time; knowing is always in time. You look at the happening with the eyes of time, which names it, translates it, and records it. This is what is called knowing, both analytically and through instant recognition. Into this field of knowing you want to bring that which is on the other side of the hill, or behind that tree. And you insist that you must know, that you must experience it and hold it. Can you hold those sweeping waters in your mind or in your hand? What you hold is the word and what your eyes have seen, and this seeing put into words, and the memory of those words. But the memory is not that water – and never will be.

'All right,' he said, 'then how shall I come upon it? I have in my long and studious life found that nothing is going to save man – no institution, no social pattern, nothing, so I've stopped reading. But man must be saved, he must come out of this somehow, and my urgent demand to find God is the cry out of a great anxiety for man. This violence that is spreading is consuming man. I know all the arguments for and against it. Once I had hope, but now I am stripped of all hope. I am really completely at the end of my tether. I am asking this question out of despair or to renew hope. I just can't see any light. So I have come to ask this one question: Can you help me to uncover reality – if there *is* a reality?'

Again we were silent for some time. And the cooing of pigeons came into the room.

'I see what you mean. I've never before been so utterly silent. The question is there, outside of this silence, and when I look out of this silence at the question, it recedes. So you mean that it is only in this silence, in this complete and unpremeditated silence, that there is the measureless?'

Another train was rattling across the bridge.

This invites all the foolishness and the hysteria of mysticism – a vague, inarticulate sentiment which breeds illusion. No, sir, this is not what we mean. It's hard work to put away all illusions – the political, the religious, the illusion of the future. We never discover anything for ourselves. We think we do, and that is one of the greatest illusions, which is thought. It is hard work to see clearly into this mess, into the insanity which man has woven around himself. You need a very, very sane mind to see, and to be free. These two, seeing and freedom, are absolutely necessary. Freedom from the urge to see, freedom from the hope that man always gives to science, to technology and to religious discoveries. This hope breeds illusion. To see this is freedom, and when there is freedom you do not invite. Then the mind itself has become the measureless.

XIV

HE was an old monk, revered by many thousands. He had kept his body well, his head was shaven and he wore the usual saffron-coloured sannyasi robe. He carried a big stick which had seen many seasons, and a pair of sand-shoes, rather worn out. We sat on a bench overlooking the river, high up, with the railway bridge to our right and the river winding down round a big curve to our left. The other side of the bank, that morning, was in heavy mist, and you could just see the tops of the trees. It was as though they were floating on the extended river. There was not a breath of air, and the swallows were flying low near the water's edge. That river was very old and sacred, and people came from very far to die on its banks and to be burnt there. It was worshipped, praised in chants and held most sacred. Every kind of filth was thrown into it; you saw people on the banks meditating, their eyes closed, sitting very straight and still. It was a river that gave abundantly, but man was polluting it. In the rainy season it would rise from twenty to thirty feet, carry away all the filth, and cover the land with silt which gave nourishment to the peasants along its bank. It came down in great curves, and sometimes you would see whole trees going by, uprooted by the strong current. You would also see dead animals, on which were perched vultures and crows, fighting with each other, and occasionally an arm or a leg or even the whole body of some human being.

That morning the river was lovely, there was not a ripple on it. The other bank seemed far away. The sun had been up for several hours and the mist had not yet gone, and the river, like some mysterious being, flowed on. The monk was very familiar with that river; he had spent many years on its banks, surrounded by his disciples. and he took it almost for granted that it would be there always, that as long as man lived it would live also. He had got used to it, and therein lay the pity of it. Now he looked at it with eyes that had seen it many thousands of times. One gets used to beauty and to ugliness, and the freshness of the day is gone.

'Why are you,' he asked, in a rather authoritative voice, 'against morality, against the scriptures which we hold most sacred? Probably you have been spoilt by the West where freedom is licentiousness and where they do not even know, except the few, what real discipline means. Obviously you have not read any of our sacred books. I was here the other morning when you were talking and I was rather aghast at what you were saying about the gods, the priests, the saints and the gurus. How can man live without any of these? If he does, he becomes materialistic, worldly, utterly brutal. You seem to deny all the knowledge that we hold most sacred. Why? I know you are serious. We have followed you from a distance for many years. We have watched you as a brother. We thought you belonged to us. But since you have renounced all these things we have become strangers, and it seems a thousand pities that we are walking on different paths.'

What is sacred? Is the image in the temple, the symbol, the word, sacred? Where does sacredness lie? In that tree, or in that peasant-woman carrying that heavy load? You invest sacredness, don't you, in things you consider holy, worth-while, meaningful? But what value has the image, carved by the hand or by the mind? That woman, that tree, that bird, the living things, seem to have but a passing importance for you. You divide life into that which is sacred and that which is not, that which is immoral and that which is moral. This division begets misery and violence. Either everything is sacred, or nothing is sacred. Either what you say, your words, your thoughts, your chants are serious, or they are there to beguile the mind into some kind of enchantment, which becomes illusion, and therefore not serious at all. There *is* something sacred, but it is not in the word, not in the statue or in the image that thought has built.

He looked rather puzzled and not at all sure where this was leading, so he interrupted: 'We are not actually discussing what is and what is not sacred, but rather, one would like to know why you decry discipline?'

Discipline, as it is generally understood, is conformity to a pattern of silly political, social or religious sanctions. This conformity implies, doesn't it, imitation, suppression, or some form of transcendence of the actual state? In this discipline there is obviously a continuous struggle, a conflict that distorts the quality of the mind. One conforms because of a promised or hoped-for reward. One disciplines oneself in order to get something. In order to achieve something one obeys and submits, and the pattern – whether it be the Communist pattern, the religious pattern or one's own – becomes the authority. In this there is no freedom at all. Discipline means to learn; and learning denies all authority and obedience. To see all this is not an analytical process. To see the implications involved in this whole structure of discipline is itself discipline, which is to learn all about this structure. And the learning is not a matter of gathering information, but of seeing the structure and the nature of it immediately. That is true discipline, because you are learning, and not conforming. To learn there must be freedom.

'Does this imply,' he asked, 'that you do just what you want? That you disregard the authority of the State?'

Of course not, sir. Naturally you have to accept the law of the State or of the policeman, until such law undergoes a change. You have to drive on one side of the road, not all over the road, for there are other cars too, so one has to follow the rule of the road. If one did exactly what one liked – which we surreptitiously do anyway – there would be utter chaos; and that is exactly what there is. The businessman, the politician and almost every human being is pursuing, under cover of respectability, his own secret desires and appetites, and this is producing chaos in the world. We want to cover this up by passing laws, sanctions, and so on. This is not freedom. Throughout the world there are people who have sacred books, modern or ancient. They repeat from them, put them into song, and quote them endlessly, but in their hearts they are violent, greedy, searching for power. Do these so-called sacred books matter at all? They have no actual meaning. What matters is man's utter selfishness, his constant violence, hate and enmity – not the books, the temples, the churches, the mosques.

Under the robe the monk is frightened. He has his own appetites, he is burning with desire, and the robe is merely an escape from this fact.

In transcending these agonies of man we spend our time quarrelling about which books are more sacred than others, and this is so utterly immature.

'Then you must also deny tradition . . . Do you?'

To carry the past over to the present, to translate the movement of the present in terms of the past, destroys the living beauty of the present. This land, and almost every land, is burdened with tradition, entrenched in high places and in the village hut. There is nothing sacred about tradition, however ancient or modern. The brain carries the memory of yesterday, which is tradition, and is frightened to let go, because it cannot face something new. Tradition becomes our security, and when the mind is secure it is in decay. One must take the journey unburdened, sweetly, without any effort, never stopping at any shrine, at any monument, or for any hero, social or religious – alone with beauty and love.

'But we monks are always alone, aren't we?' he asked. 'I have renounced the world and taken a vow of poverty and chastity.'

You are not alone, sir, because the very vow binds you – as it does the man who takes the vow when he gets married. If we may point out, you are not alone because you are a Hindu, just as you would not be alone if you were a Buddhist or a Muslim, or a Christian or a Communist. You are committed, and how can a man be alone when he is committed, when he has given himself over to some form of ideation, which brings its own activity? The word itself, 'alone', means what it says – uninfluenced, innocent, free and whole, not broken up. When you are alone you may live in this world but you will always be an outsider. Only in aloneness can there be complete action and co-operation; for love is always whole.

XV

THAT morning the river was tarnished silver, for it was cloudy and cold. The leaves were covered with dust, and everywhere there was a thin layer of it – in the room, on the veranda and on the chair. It was getting colder; it must have snowed heavily in the Himalayas; one could feel the biting wind from the north, even the birds were aware of it. But the river that morning had a strange movement of its own; it didn't seem to be ruffled by the wind, it seemed almost motionless and had that timeless quality which all waters seem to have. How beautiful it was! No wonder people have made it into a sacred river. You could sit there, on that veranda, and meditatively watch it endlessly. You weren't day-dreaming; your thoughts weren't in any direction – they were simply absent.

And as you watched the light on that river, somehow you seemed to lose yourself, and as you closed your eyes there was a penetration into a void that was full of blessing. This was bliss.

He came again that morning, with a young man. He was the monk who had talked about discipline, sacred books and the authority of tradition. His face was freshly washed, and so were his robes. The young man seemed rather nervous. He had come with the monk, who was probably his guru, and was waiting for him to speak first. He looked at the river but he was thinking of other things. Presently the sannyasi said:

'I have come again but this time to talk about love and sensuality. We, who have taken the vows of chastity, have our sensuous problems. The vow is only a means of resisting our uncontrollable desires. I am an old man now, and these desires no longer burn me. Before I took the vows I was married. My wife died, and I left my home and went through a period of agony, of intolerable biological urges; I fought them night and day. It was a very difficult time, full of loneliness, frustration, fears of madness, and neurotic outbursts. Even now I daren't think about it too much. And this young man has come with me because I think he is going through the same problem. He wants to give up the world and take the vow of poverty and chastity, as I did. I have been talking to him for many weeks, and I thought it might be worthwhile if we could both talk over this problem with you, this problem of sex and love. I hope you don't mind if we talk quite frankly.'

If we are going to concern ourselves with this matter, first, if we may suggest it, don't start to examine from a position or an attitude, or a principle, for this will prevent you from exploration. If you are against sex, or if you insist that it is necessary to life, that it is a part of living, any such assumption will prevent real perception. We should put away any conclusion, and so be free to look, to examine.

There were a few drops of rain now, and the birds had become quiet, for it was going to rain heavily, and the leaves once again would be fresh and green, full of light and colour. There was a smell of rain, and the strange quietness that comes before a storm was on the land.

So we have two problems – love and sex. The one is an abstract idea, the other is an actual daily biological urge – a fact that exists and cannot be denied. Let us first find out what love is, not as an abstract idea but what it actually is. What is it? Is it merely a sensuous delight, cultivated by thought as pleasure, the remembrance of an experience which has given great delight or sexual enjoyment? Is it the beauty of a sunset, or the delicate leaf that you touch or see, or the perfume of the flower that you smell? Is love pleasure, or desire? Or is it none of these? Is love to be divided as the sacred and the profane? Or is it something indivisible, whole, that cannot be broken up by thoughts? Does it exist without the object? Or does it come into being only because of the object? Is it because you see the face of a woman that love arises in you – love then being sensation, desire, pleasure, to which thought gives continuity? Or is love a state in you which responds to beauty as tenderness? Is love something cultivated by thought so that its object becomes important, or is it utterly unrelated to thought and, there-fore, independent, free? Without understanding this word and the meaning behind it we shall be tortured, or become neurotic about sex, or be enslaved by it.

Love is not to be broken up into fragments by thought. When thought breaks it up into fragments, as impersonal, personal, sensuous, spiritual, my country and your country, my god and your god, then it is no longer love, then it is something entirely different – a product of memory, of propaganda, of convenience, of comfort and so on.

Is sex the product of thought? Is sex – the pleasure, the delight, the companionship, the tenderness involved in it – is this a remembrance strengthened by thought? In the sexual act there is self-forgetfulness, self-abandonment, a sense of the non-existence of fear, anxiety, the worries of life. Re-membering this state of tenderness and self-forgetfulness,

74

and demanding its repetition, you chew over it, as it were, until the next occasion. Is this tenderness, or is it merely a recollection of something that is over and which, through repetition, you hope to capture again? Is not the repetition of something, however pleasurable, a destructive process?

The young man suddenly found his tongue: 'Sex is a biological urge, as you yourself have said, and if this is destructive then isn't eating equally destructive, because that also is a biological urge?'

If one eats when one is hungry – that is one thing. If one is hungry and thought says: 'I must have the taste of this or that type of food' – then it is thought, and it is this which is the destructive repetition.

'In sex, how do you know what is the biological urge, like hunger, and what a psychological demand, like greed?' asked the young man.

Why do you divide the biological urge and the psychological demand? And there is yet another question, a different question altogether – why do you separate sex from seeing the beauty of a mountain or the loveliness of a flower? Why do you give such tremendous importance to the one and totally neglect the other?

'If sex is something quite different from love, as you seem to say, then is there any necessity at all to do anything about sex?' asked the young man.

We have never said that love and sex are two separate things. We have said that love is whole, not to be broken up, and thought, by its very nature, is fragmentary. When thought dominates, obviously there is no love. Man generally knows – perhaps only knows – the sex of thought, which is the chewing of the cud of pleasure and its repetition. Therefore we have to ask: Is there any other kind of sex which is not of thought or desire?

The sannyasi had listened to all this with quiet attention. Now he spoke: 'I have resisted it, I have taken a vow against it, because by tradition, by reason, I have seen that one must have energy for the religious dedicated life. But I now see that this resistance has taken a great deal of energy. I have spent more time on resisting, and wasted more energy on it, than I have ever wasted on sex itself. So what you have said – that a conflict of any kind is a waste of energy – I now understand. Conflict and struggle are far more deadening than the seeing of a woman's face, or even perhaps than sex itself.'

Is there love without desire, without pleasure? Is there sex, without desire, without pleasure? Is there love which is whole, without thought entering into it? Is sex something of the past, or is it something each time new? Thought is obviously old, so we are always contrasting the old and the new. We are asking questions from the old, and we want an answer in terms of the old. So when we ask: Is there sex without the whole mechanism of thought operating and working, doesn't it mean that we have not stepped out of the old? We are so conditioned by the old that we do not feel our way into the new. We said love is whole, and always new – new not as opposed to the old, for that again is the old. Any assertion that there is sex without desire is utterly valueless, but if you have followed the whole meaning of thought, then perhaps you will come upon the other. If, however, you demand that you must have your pleasure at any price, then love will not exist.

The young man said: 'That biological urge you spoke about is precisely such a demand, for though it may be different from thought it engenders thought.'

'Perhaps I can answer my young friend,' said the sannyasi, 'for I have been through all this. I have trained myself for years not to look at a woman. I have ruthlessly controlled the biological demand. The biological urge does not engender thought; thought captures it, thought utilizes it, thought makes images, pictures out of this urge – and then the urge is a slave to the thought. It is thought which engenders the urge so much of the time. As I said, I am beginning to see the extraordinary nature of our own deception and dishonesty. There is a great deal of hypocrisy in us. We can never see things as they are but must create illusions about them. What you are telling us, sir, is to look at everything with clear eyes, without the memory of yesterday; you have repeated this so often in your talks. Then life does not become a problem. In my old age I am just beginning to realize this.'

The young man looked not completely satisfied. He wanted life according to *his* terms, according to the formula which he had carefully built.

This is why it is very important to know oneself, not according to any formula or according to any guru. This constant choiceless awareness ends all illusions and all hypocrisy.

Now it was coming down in torrents, and the air was very still, and there was only the sound of the rain on the roof and on the leaves.

CALIFORNIA

I

MEDITATION is not the mere experiencing of something beyond everyday thought and feeling nor is it the pursuit of visions and delights. An immature and squalid little mind can and does have visions of expanding consciousness, and experiences which it recognizes according to its own conditioning. This immaturity may be greatly capable of making itself successful in this world and achieving fame and notoriety. The gurus whom it follows are of the same quality and state. Meditation does not belong to such as these. It is not for the seeker, for the seeker finds what he wants, and the comfort he derives from it is the morality of his own fears.

Do what he will, the man of belief and dogma cannot enter into the realm of meditation. To meditate, freedom is necessary. It is not meditation first and freedom afterwards; freedom – the total denial of social morality and values – is the first movement of meditation. It is not a public affair where many can join in and offer prayers. It stands alone, and is always beyond the borders of social conduct. For truth is not in the things of thought or in what thought has put together and calls truth. The complete negation of this whole structure of thought is the positive of meditation.

The sea was very calm that morning; it was very blue, almost like a lake, and the sky was clear. Seagulls and pelicans were flying around the water's edge – the pelicans almost touching the water, with their heavy wings and slow flight. The sky was very blue and the hills beyond were sunburnt except for a few bushes. A red eagle came out of those hills, flew over the gully and disappeared among the trees.

The light in that part of the world had a quality of penetration and brilliance, without blinding the eye. There was the smell of sumac, orange and eucalyptus. It hadn't rained for many months and the earth was parched, dry, cracked. You saw deer in the hills occasionally, and once, wandering up the hill, there was a bear, dusty and ill-kempt. Along that path rattlers often went by and occasionally you saw a horned toad. On the trail you hardly passed anybody. It was a dusty, rocky and utterly silent trail.

Just in front of you was a quail with its chicks. There must have been more than a dozen of them, motionless, pretending they didn't exist. The higher you climbed the wilder it became for there was no habitation at all there, for there was no water. There were also no birds, and hardly any trees. The sun was very strong; it bit into you.

At that high altitude, suddenly, very close to you was a rattler, shrilly rattling his tail, giving a warning. You jumped. There it was, the rattler with its triangular head, all coiled up with its rattles in the centre and its head pointed towards you. You were a few feet away from it and it couldn't strike you from that distance. You stared at it, and it stared back with its unblinking eyes. You watched it for some time, its fat suppleness, its danger; and there was no fear. Then, as you watched, it uncoiled its head and tail towards you and moved backwards away from you. As you moved towards it, again it coiled, with its tail in the middle, ready to strike. You played this game for some time until the snake got tired and you left it and came down to the sea.

It was a nice house and the windows opened on to the lawn. The house was white inside and well-proportioned. On cold nights there was a fire. It is lovely to watch a fire with its thousand flames and many shadows. There was no noise, except the sound of the restless sea.

There was a small group of two or three in that room, talking about things in general – modern youth, the cinema, and so on. Then one of them said: 'May we ask a question?' And it seemed a pity to disturb the blue sea and the hills.

'We want to ask what time means to you. We know more or less what the scientists say about it, and the science-fiction writers. It seems to me that man has always been caught in this problem of time – the endless yesterdays and tomorrows. From the most remote periods to the present day, time has occupied man's mind. Philosophers have speculated about it, and religions have their own explanations. Can we talk about it?'

Shall we go into this matter rather deeply, or do you merely want to touch upon it superficially and let it go at that? If we want to talk about it seriously we must forget what religions, philosophers and others have said – for really you can't trust any of them. One doesn't distrust them just out of callous indifference or out of arrogance, but one sees that in order to find out, all authorities must be set aside. If one is prepared for that, then perhaps we could go into this matter very simply.

Is there – apart from the clock – time at all? We accept so many things; obedience has been so instilled into us that acceptance seems natural. But is there time at all, apart from the many yesterdays? Is time a continuity as yesterday, today and tomorrow, and is there time without yesterday? What gives to the thousand yesterdays a continuity?

A cause brings its effect, and the effect in turn becomes the cause; there is no division between them, it is one movement. This movement we call time, and with this movement, in our eyes and in our hearts, we see everything. We see with the eyes of time, and translate the present in terms of the past; and this translation meets the tomorrow. This is the chain of time.

Thought, caught in this process, asks the question: 'What is time?' This very inquiry is of the machinery of time. So the inquiry has no meaning, for thought *is* time. The yesterday has produced thought and so thought divides space as yesterday, today and tomorrow. Or it says: 'There is only the present', forgetting that the present itself is the outcome of yesterday.

Our consciousness is made up of this chain of time, and within its borders we are asking 'What is time? And, if there is not time, what happens to yesterday?' Such questions are within the field of time, and there is no answer to a question put by thought about time.

Or is there no tomorrow and no yesterday, but only the now? This question is not put by thought. It is put when the structure and nature of time is seen – but with the eyes of thought.

Is there actually tomorrow? Of course there is if I have to catch a train; but inwardly, is there the tomorrow of pain and pleasure, or of achievement? Or is there only the now, which is not related to yesterday? Time has a stop only when thought has a stop. It is at the moment of stopping that the now is. This now is not an idea, it is an actual fact, but only when the whole mechanism of thought has come to an end. The *feeling* of now is entirely different from the word, which is of time. So do not let us be caught in the words yesterday, today and tomorrow. The realization of the now exists only in freedom, and freedom is not the cultivation of thought.

Then the question arises: 'What is the action of the now?' We only know action which is of time and memory and the interval between yesterday and the present. In this interval or space all the confusion and the conflict begin. What we are really asking is: If there is no interval at all, what is action? The conscious mind might say: 'I did something spontaneously', but actually this is not so; there is no such thing as spontaneity because the mind is conditioned. The actual is the only fact; the actual is the now, and, unable to meet it, thought builds images about it. The interval between the image and what is, is the misery which thought has created.

To see what is without yesterday, is the now. The now is the silence of yesterday.

II

MEDITATION is a never-ending movement. You can never say that you are meditating or set aside a period for meditation. It isn't at your command. Its benediction doesn't come to you because you lead a systemized life or follow a particular routine or morality. It comes only when your heart is really open. Not opened by the key of thought, not made safe by the intellect, but when it is as open as the skies without a cloud; then it comes without your knowing, without your invitation. But you can never guard it, keep it, worship it. If you try, it will never come again: do what you will, it will avoid you. In meditation, you are not important, you have no place in it; the beauty of it is not you, but in itself. And to this you can add nothing. Don't look out of the window hoping to catch it unawares, or sit in a darkened room waiting for it; it comes only when you are not there at all, and its bliss has no continuity.

The mountains looked down on the endless blue sea, stretching out for miles. The hills were almost barren, sunburned, with small bushes, and in their folds there were trees, sunburned and fire-burned, but they were still there, flourishing and very quiet. There was one tree especially, an enormous old oak, that seemed to dominate all the hills around it. And on the top of another hill there was a dead tree, burnt by fire; there it stood naked, grey, without a single leaf. When you looked at those mountains, at their beauty and their lines against the blue sky, this tree alone was seen to hold the sky. It had many branches, all dead, and it would never feel the spring again. Yet it was intensely alive with grace and beauty; you felt you were part of it, alone with nothing to lean on, without time. It seemed it would be there for ever, like that big oak in the valley too. One was living and the other was dead, and both were the only things that mattered among these hills, sunburnt, scorched by the fire, waiting for the winter rains. You saw the whole of life, including your own life, in those two trees – one living, one dead. And love lay in between, sheltered, unseen, undemanding.

Under the house lived a mother with four of her young. The day we arrived they were there on the veranda, the mother racoon with her four babies. They were immediately friendly – with their sharp black eyes and soft paws – demanding to be fed and at the same time nervous. The mother was aloof. The next evening they were there again and they took their food from your hands and you felt their soft paws; they were ready to be tamed, to be petted. And you wondered at their beauty and their movement. In a few days they would be all over you, and you felt the immensity of life in them.

It was a lovely clear day and every little tree and bush stood out clearly against the bright sun. The man had come from the valley, up the hill to the house which overlooked a gully and, beyond it, a whole range of mountains. There were a few pines near the house and tall bamboos.

He was a young man full of hope, and the brutality of civilization had not yet touched him. What he wanted was to sit quiet, to be silent, made silent not only by the hills but also by the quietness of his own urgency.

'What part do I play in this world? What is my relationship to the whole existing order? What is the meaning of this endless conflict? I have a love; we sleep together. And yet that is not the end. All this seems like a distant dream, fading and coming back, throbbing one moment, meaningless the next. I have seen some of my friends taking drugs. They have become stupid, dull-witted. Perhaps I too, even without drugs, will be made dull by the routine of life and the ache of my own loneliness. I don't count among these many millions of people. I shall go the way the others have gone, never coming upon a jewel that is incorruptible, that can never be stolen away, that can never tarnish. So I thought I'd come up here and talk to you, if you have the time. I'm not asking for any answers to my questions. I am perturbed; though I am very young I am already discouraged. I see the old, hopeless generation around me with their bitterness, cruelty, hypocrisy, compromise and prudence. They have nothing to give and, strangely enough, I don't want anything from them. I don't know what I want, but I do know that I must live a life that is very rich, that is full of meaning. I certainly don't want to enter some office and gradually become somebody in that shapeless, meaningless existence. I sometimes cry to myself at the loneliness and the beauty of the distant stars.'

We sat quietly for some time, and the pine and the bamboo were caught in the breeze.

The lark and the eagle in their flight leave no mark; the scientist leaves a mark, as do all specialists. You can follow them step by step and add more steps to what they have found and accumulated; and you know, more or less, where their accumulation is leading. But truth is not like that; it is really a pathless land; it may be at the next curve of the road, or a thousand miles away. You have to keep going and then you will find it beside you. But if you stop and trace out a way for another to follow, or a design for your own way of life, it will never come near you.

'Is this poetic, or actual?'

What do you think? For us everything must be cut and dried so that we can do something practical with it, build something with it, worship it. You can bring a stick into the house, put it on a shelf, put a flower before it every day, and after some days the stick will have a great deal of meaning. The mind can give meaning to anything, but the meaning it gives is meaningless. When one asks what is the purpose of life, it's like worshipping that stick. The terrible thing is that the mind is always inventing new purposes, new meanings, new delights, and always destroying them. It is never quiet. A mind that is rich in its quietness never looks beyond what is. One must be both the eagle and the scientist, knowing well that the two can never meet. This doesn't mean that they are two separate things. Both are necessary. But when the scientist wants to become the eagle, and when the eagle leaves its footprints, there is misery in the world.

You are quite young. Don't ever lose your innocency and the vulnerability that it brings. That is the only treasure that man can have, and must have.

'Is this vulnerability the be-all and end-all of existence? Is it the only priceless jewel that can be discovered?'

You can't be vulnerable without innocency, and though you have a thousand experiences, a thousand smiles and tears, if you don't die to them, how can the mind be innocent? It is only the innocent mind – in spite of its thousand experiences – that can see what truth is. And it is only truth that makes the mind vulnerable – that is, free.

'You say you can't see truth without being innocent, and you can't be innocent without seeing truth. This is a vicious circle, isn't it?'

Innocency can be only with the death of yesterday. But we never die to yesterday. We always have a remnant, a tattered part of yesterday remaining, and it is this that keeps the mind anchored, held by time. So time is the enemy of innocency. One must die every day to everything that the mind has captured and holds on to. Otherwise there is no freedom. In freedom there is vulnerability. It is not the one thing after the other – it is all one movement, both the coming and the going. It is really the fullness of heart that is innocent.

III

MEDITATION is emptying the mind of the known. The known is the past. The emptying is not at the end of accumulation but rather it means not to accumulate at all. What has been is emptied only in the present, not by thought but by action, by the doing of what is. The past is the movement of conclusion to conclusion, and the judgement of what is by the conclusion. All judgement is conclusion, whether it be of the past or the present, and it is this conclusion that prevents the constant emptying of the mind of the known; for the known is always conclusion, determination.

The known is the action of will, and the will in operation is the continuation of the known, so the action of will cannot possibly empty the mind. The empty mind cannot be purchased at the altar of demand; it comes into being when thought is aware of its own activities – not the thinker being aware of his thought.

Meditation is the innocency of the present, and therefore it is always alone. The mind that is completely alone, untouched by thought, ceases to accumulate. So the emptying of the mind is always in the present. For the mind that is alone, the future – which is of the past – ceases. Meditation is a movement, not a conclusion, not an end to be achieved.

The forest was very large, with pine trees, oaks, shrubs and redwood. There was a little stream that went by down the slope, making a constant murmuring. There were butterflies, small ones, blue and yellow, which seemed to find no flowers to rest on, and they drifted down towards the valley.

This forest was very old, and the redwoods were older still. They were enormous trees of great height, and there was that peculiar atmosphere which comes when man is absent with his guns, his chattering and the display of his knowledge. There was no road through the forest. You had to leave the car at some distance and walk along a track covered with pine needles.

There was a jay, warning everybody of human approach. The warning had effect, for all animal movement seemed to stop, and there was that feeling of the intensity of watching. It was difficult for the sun to penetrate here, and there was a stillness which you could almost touch.

Two red squirrels, with long bushy tails, came down the pine tree, chattering, their claws making a scratching sound. They chased each other round and round the trunk, up and down, with a fury of pleasure and delight. There was a tension between them – the chord of play, of sex, and fun. They were really enjoying themselves. The top one would suddenly stop and watch the lower one who was still in movement, then the lower one too would stop, and they would look at each other, with their tails up and their noses twitching, pointed towards each other. Their sharp eyes were taking each other in, and also the movement around them. They had scolded the watcher, sitting under the tree, and now they had forgotten him; but they were aware of each other, and you could almost feel their utter delight in each other's company. Their nest must have been high up, and presently they got tired; one ran up the tree and the other along the ground, disappearing behind another tree.

The jay, blue, sharp and curious, had been watching them and the man sitting under the tree, and he too flew off, loudly calling.

There were clouds coming up and probably in an hour or two there would be a thunderstorm.

She was an analyst with a degree, and was working in a large clinic. She was quite young, in modern dress, the skirt right above the knee; she seemed very intense, and you could see that she was very disturbed. At the table she was unnecessarily talkative, expressing strongly what she thought about things, and it seemed that she never looked out of the big window at the flowers, the breeze among the leaves, and the tall, heavy eucalyptus, gently swaying in the wind. She ate haphazardly, not particularly interested in what she was eating.

In the adjoining small room, she said: 'We analysts help sick people to fit into a sicker society and we sometimes, perhaps very rarely, succeed. But actually any success is nature's own accomplishment. I have analysed many people.

I don't like what I am doing, but I have to earn a living, and there are so many sick people. I don't believe one can help them very much, though of course we are always trying new drugs, chemicals and theories. But apart from the sick, I am myself struggling to be different – different from the ordinary average person.'

Aren't you, in your very struggle to be different, the same as the others? And why all this struggle?

'But if I don't struggle, fight, I'll be just like the ordinary bourgeois housewife. I want to be different, and that's why I don't want to marry. But I am really very lonely, and my loneliness has pushed me into this work.'

So this loneliness is gradually leading you to suicide, isn't it?

She nodded; she was almost in tears.

Isn't the whole movement of the consciousness leading to isolation, to fear, and to this incessant struggle to be different? It is all part of this urge to fulfil, to identify oneself with something, or to identify oneself with what one is. Most of the analysts have their teachers according to whose theories and established schools they operate, merely modifying them and adding a new twist to them.

'I belong to the new school; we approach without the symbol and face reality actually. We have discarded the former masters with their symbols and we see the human being as he is. But all this is something that is also becoming another school, and I am not here to discuss various types of schools, theories and masters, but rather to talk about myself. I don't know what to do.'

Are you not just as sick as the patients whom you are trying to cure? Aren't you part of society – which is perhaps more confused and more sick than yourself? So the issue is more fundamental, isn't it?

You are the result of this enormous weight of society, with its culture and its religions, and it is driving you, both economically and inwardly. Either you have to make your peace with society, which is to accept its maladies and live with

88

them, or totally refute it, and find a new way of living. But you can't find the new way without letting go of the old.

What you really want is security, isn't it? That's the whole search of thought – to be different, to be more clever, more sharp, more ingenious. In this process you are trying to find a deep security, aren't you? But is there such a thing at all? Security denies order. There is no security in relationship, in belief, in action, and because one is seeking it one creates disorder. Security breeds disorder, and when you face the ever-mounting disorder in yourself, you want to end it all.

Within the area of consciousness with its wide and narrow frontiers, thought is ever trying to find a secure spot. So thought is creating disorder; order is not the outcome of thought. When disorder ends there is order. Love is not within the regions of thought. Like beauty, it cannot be touched by the paintbrush. One has to abandon the total disorder of oneself.

She became very silent, withdrawn into herself. It was difficult for her to control the tears that were coming down her cheeks.

IV

SLEEP is as important as keeping awake, perhaps more so. If during the day time the mind is watchful, self-recollected, observing the inward and outward movements of life, then at night meditation comes as a benediction. The mind wakes up, and out of the depth of silence there is the enchantment of meditation, which no imagination or flight of fancy can ever bring about. It happens without the mind ever inviting it: it comes into being out of the tranquillity of consciousness – not within it but outside of it, not in the periphery of thought but beyond the reaches of thought. So there is no memory of it, for remembrance is always of the past, and meditation is not the resurrection of the past. It happens out of the fullness of the heart and not out of intellectual brightness and capacity. It may happen night after night, but each time, if you are so blessed, it is new – not new in being different from old, but new without the background of the old, new in its diversity and changeless change. So sleep becomes a thing of extraordinary importance, not the sleep of exhaustion, not the sleep brought about through drugs and physical satisfaction, but a sleep that is as light and quick as the body is sensitive. And the body is made sensitive through alertness. Sometimes meditation is as light as a breeze that passes by; at other times its depth is beyond all measure. But if the mind holds one or the other as a remembrance to be indulged in, then the ecstasy of meditation comes to an end. It is important never to possess or desire possession of it. The quality of possessiveness must never enter into meditation, for meditation has no root, nor any substance which the mind can hold.

The other day as we went up the deep canyon which lay in shadow with the arid mountains on both sides, it was full of birds, insects, and the quiet activity of small animals. You walked up and up the gentle slope to a great height, and from there you watched all the surrounding hills and mountains with the light of the setting sun upon them. It looked as though they were lit from within, never to be put out. But as you watched, the light faded, and in the west the evening star became brighter and brighter. It was a lovely evening, and somehow you felt that the whole universe was there beside you, and a strange quietness surrounded you.

We have no light within ourselves: we have the artificial light of others; the light of knowledge, the light that talent and capacity give. All this kind of light fades and becomes a pain. The light of thought becomes its own shadow. But the light that never fades, the deep, inward brilliance which is not a thing of the market place, cannot be shown to another. You can't seek it, you can't cultivate it, you can't possibly imagine it or speculate upon it, for it is not within the reach of the mind.

He was a monk of some repute, having lived both in a monastery and alone outside it, seeking, and deeply earnest.

'The things you say about meditation seem true; it is out of reach. This means, doesn't it, that there must be no seeking, no wishing, no gesture of any kind towards it, whether the deliberate gesture of sitting in a special posture, or the gesture of an attitude towards life or towards oneself? So what is one to do? What is the point of any words at all?'

You seek out of emptiness, reach out either to fill that emptiness or to escape from it. This outward movement from inward poverty is conceptual, speculative, dualistic. This is conflict, and it is endless. So don't reach out! But the energy which was reaching out turns from reaching out to reaching inwards, seeking and searching, asking something which it now calls 'within'. The two movements are essentially the same. They must both come to an end.

'Are you asking us simply to be content with this emptiness?'

Certainly not.

'So the emptiness remains, and a settled kind of despair. The despair is even greater if one may not even seek!'

Is it despair if you see the truth that the inward and outward movement have no meaning? Is it contentment with what is? Is it the acceptance of this emptiness? It is none of these. So: you have dispelled the going out, the coming in, the accepting. You have denied all movement of the mind that is faced with this emptiness. Then the mind itself is empty, for the movement is the mind itself. The mind is empty of all movement, therefore there is no entity to initiate any movement. Let it remain empty. Let it *be* empty. The mind has purged itself of the past, the future and the present; it has purged itself of becoming, and becoming is time. So there is no time; there is no measurement. *Then* is it emptiness?

'This state comes and goes often. Even if it is not emptiness, it is certainly not the ecstasy of which you speak.'

Forget what has been said. Forget also that it comes and goes. When it comes and goes it is of time; then there is the observer who says, 'It is here, it has gone.' This observer is the one who measures, compares, evaluates, so it is not the emptiness of which we are talking.

'Are you anaesthetizing me?' And he laughed.

When there is no measurement and no time, is there a frontier or an outline to emptiness? Then can you ever call it emptiness or nothingness? Then everything is in it, and nothing is in it.

V

IT had been raining quite a bit during the night, and now, early in the morning as you were getting up, there was the strong smell of sumac, sage, and damp earth. It was red earth, and red earth seems to give a stronger smell than brown earth. Now the sun was on the hills with that extraordinary colour of burnt-sienna, and every tree and every bush was sparkling, washed clean by last night's rain, and everything was bursting with joy. It hadn't rained for six or eight months, and you can imagine how the earth was rejoicing, and not only the earth but everything on it – the huge trees, the tall eucalyptus, the pepper trees and the live-oaks. The birds seemed to have a different song that morning, and as you watched the hills and the distant blue mountains, you were somehow lost in them. You didn't exist, neither did those around you. There was only this beauty, this immensity, only the spreading, widening earth. That morning, out of those hills that went on for miles and miles, came a tranquillity which met your own quietness. It was like the earth and the heavens meeting, and the ecstasy was a benediction.

The same evening, as you walked up the canyon into the hills, the red earth was damp under your feet, soft, yielding, and full of promise. You went up the steep incline for many miles, and then came down suddenly. As you turned the corner you came upon that complete silence which was already descending on you, and as you entered the deep valley it became more penetrating, more urgent, more insistent. There was no thought, only that silence. As you walked down, it seemed to cover the whole earth, and it was astonishing how every bird and tree became still. There was no breeze among the trees and with the darkness they were withdrawing into their solitude. It is strange how during the day they would welcome you, and now, with their fantastic shapes, they were distant, aloof and withdrawn. Three hunters went by with their powerful bows and arrows, electric torches strapped to their foreheads. They were out to kill the night birds and seemed to be utterly impervious to the beauty and the silence about them. They were intent only on the kill, and it seemed as though everything was watching them, horrified, and full of pity.

That morning a group of young people had come to the house. There were about thirty of them, students from various universities. They had grown up in this climate, and were strong, well fed, tall, and enthusiastic. Only one or two of them sat on chairs, most of us were on the floor, and the girls in their mini-skirts sat uncomfortably. One of the boys spoke, with quivering lips, and with his head down.

'I want to live a different kind of life. I don't want to be caught in sex and drugs and the rat race. I want to live out of this world, and yet I am caught in it. I have sex, and the next day I am utterly depressed. I know I want to live peacefully, with love in my heart, but I am torn by my urges, by the pull of the society in which I live. I want to obey these urges, yet I rebel against them. I want to live at the mountain top yet I am always descending into the valley, for my life is there. I don't know what to do. I'm getting bored with everything. My parents can't help me, nor can the professors with whom I sometimes try to discuss these matters. They are as confused and miserable as I am, more so in fact, because they are much older.'

What is important is not to come to any conclusion, or any decision for or against sex, not to get caught in conceptual ideologies. Let us look at the whole picture of our existence. The monk has taken a vow of celibacy because he thinks that to gain his heaven he has to shun contact with a woman; but for the rest of his life he is struggling against his own physical demands: he is in conflict with heaven and with earth, and spends the rest of his days in darkness, seeking light. Each one of us is caught in this ideological battle, just like the monk, burning with desire and trying to suppress it for the promise of heaven. We have a physical body and it has its demands. They are encouraged and influenced by the society in which we live, by the advertisements, by the half-naked girls, by the insistence on fun, amusement, entertainment, and by the morality of society, the morality of the social order, which is disorder and immorality. We are physically stimulated – more and tastier food, drink, television. The whole of modern existence focuses your attention on sex. You are stimulated in every way – by books, by talk, and by an utterly permissive society. All this surrounds you; it's no good merely shutting your eyes to it. You have to see this whole way of life with its absurd beliefs and divisions, and the utter meaninglessness of a life spent in an office or a factory. And at the end of it all there is death. You have to see all this confusion very clearly.

Now look out of that window and see those marvellous mountains, freshly washed by last night's rain, and that extraordinary light of California which exists nowhere else. See the beauty of the light on those hills. You can smell the clean air and the newness of the earth. The more alive you are to it, the more sensitive you are to all this immense, incredible light and beauty, the more you are with it – the more your perception is heightened. That is also sensuous, just like seeing a girl. You can't respond with your senses to this mountain and then cut them off when you see the girl; in this way you divide life, and in this division there is sorrow and conflict. When you divide the mountain-top from the valley, you are in conflict. This doesn't mean that you avoid conflict or escape from it, or get so lost in sex or some other appetite that you cut yourself off from conflict. The understanding of conflict doesn't mean that you vegetate or become like a cow.

To understand all this is not to be caught in it, not to depend on it. It means never to deny anything, never to come to any conclusion or to reach any ideological, verbal state, or principle, according to which you try to live. The very perception of this whole map which is being unfolded is already intelligence. It is this intelligence that will act and not a conclusion, a decision or an ideological principle.

Our bodies have been made dull, just as our minds and hearts have been dulled, by our education, by our conformity to the pattern which society has set and which denies the sensitivity of the heart. It sends us to war, destroying all our beauty, tenderness and joy. The observation of all this not verbally or intellectually but actually, makes our body and mind highly sensitive. The body will then demand the right kind of food; then the mind will not be caught in words, in symbols, in platitudes of thought. Then we shall know how to live both in the valley and on the mountain-top; then there will be no division or contradiction between the two.

EUROPE

I

MEDITATION is a movement in attention. Attention is not an achievement, for it is not personal. The personal element comes in only when there is the observer as the centre, from which he concentrates or dominates; thus all achievement is fragmentary and limited. Attention has no border, no frontier to cross; attention is clarity, clear of all thought. Thought can never make for clarity for thought has its roots in the dead past; so thinking is an action in the dark. Awareness of this is to be attentive. Awareness is not a method that leads to attention; such attention is within the field of thought and so can be controlled or modified; being aware of this inattention is attention. Meditation is not an intellectual process – which is still within the area of thought. Meditation is the freedom from thought, and a movement in the ecstasy of truth.

It was snowing that morning. A bitter wind was blowing; and the movement upon the trees was a cry for spring. In that light, the trunks of the large beech and the elm had that peculiar quality of grey-green that one finds in old woods where the earth is soft and covered with autumn leaves. Walking among them you had the feeling of the wood – not of the separate individual trees with their particular shapes and forms – but rather of the entire quality of all the trees.

Suddenly the sun came out, and there was a vast blue sky towards the east, and a dark, heavily-laden sky against the west. In that moment of bright sunlight, spring began. In the quiet stillness of the spring day you felt the beauty of the earth and the sense of unity of the earth and all things upon it. There was no separation between you and the tree and the varying, astonishing colours of the sparkling light on the holly. You, the observer, had ceased, and so the division, as space and time, had come to an end.

He said he was a religious man – not belonging to any particular organization or belief – but he felt religious. Of course he had been through the drill of talking with all the religious leaders, and had come away from them all rather despairingly, but without becoming a cynic. Yet he had not found the bliss he sought. He had been a professor at a university, and had given it up to lead a life of meditation and inquiry.

'You know,' he said, 'I am always aware of the fragmentation of life. I, myself, am a fragment of that life – broken, different, endlessly struggling to become the whole, an integral part of this universe. I have tried to find my own identity, for modern society is destroying all identity. I wonder if there is a way out of all this division into something that cannot be divided, separated?'

We have divided life as the family and the community, the family and the nation, the family and the office, politics and the religious life, peace and war, order and disorder – an endless division of the opposites. Along this corridor we walk, trying to bring about a harmony between mind and heart, trying to keep a balance between love and envy. We know all this too well, and we try to make out of it some kind of harmony.

What makes this division? Obviously there *is* division, contrast – black and white, man and woman, and so on – but what is the source, the essence, of this fragmentation? Unless we find it, fragmentation is inevitable. What do you think is the root cause of this duality?

'I can give many causes for this seemingly endless division, and many ways in which one has tried to build a bridge between opposites. Intellectually I can expose the reasons for this division, but it leads nowhere. I have played this game often, with myself and with others. I have tried, through meditation, through the exercise of will, to feel the unity of things, to be one with everything – but it is a barren attempt.'

Of course the mere discovery of the cause of the separation does not necessarily dissolve it. One knows the cause of fear, but one is still afraid. The intellectual exploration loses its immediacy of action when the sharpness of thought is all that matters. The fragmentation of the I and the not-I is surely the basic cause of this division, though the I tries to identify itself with the not-I, which may be the wife, the family, the community, or the formula of God which thought has made. The I is ever striving to find an identity, but what it identifies itself with is still a concept, a memory, a structure of thought.

Is there a duality at all? Objectively there is, such as light and shade, but psychologically is there? We accept the psychological duality as we accept the objective duality; it is part of our conditioning. We never question this conditioning. But is there, psychologically, a division? There is only what is, not what should be. The what should be is a division which thought has put together in the avoiding or the overcoming of the reality of what is. Hence the struggle between the actual and the abstraction. The abstraction is the fanciful, the romantic, the ideal. What is actual is what is, and everything else is non-real. It is the non-real that brings about the fragmentation, not the actual. Pain is actual; non-pain is the pleasure of thought which brings about the division between the pain and the state of non-pain. Thought is always separative; it is the division of time, the space between the observer and the thing observed. There is only what is, and to see what is, without thought as the observer, is the ending of fragmentation.

Thought is not love; but thought, as pleasure, encloses love and brings pain within that enclosure. In the negation of what is not, what is remains. In the negation of what is not love, love emerges in which the I and the non-I cease.

II

INNOCENCY and spaciousness are the flowering of meditation. There is no innocency without space. Innocency is not immaturity. You may be mature physically, but the vast space that comes with love is not possible if the mind is not free from the many marks of experience. It is these scars of experience that prevent innocency. Freeing the mind from the constant pressure of experience is meditation.

Just as the sun is setting there comes a strange quietness and a feeling that everything about you has come to an end, though the bus, the taxi and the noise go on. This sense of aloofness seems to penetrate the whole universe. You must have felt this too. Often it comes most unexpectedly; strange stillness and peace seem to pour down from the heavens and cover the earth. It is a benediction, and the beauty of the evening is made boundless by it. The shiny road after the rain, the waiting cars, the empty park, seem to be part of it; and the laughter of the couple who pass by does not in any way disturb the peace of the evening.

The naked trees, black against the sky, with their delicate branches, were waiting for the spring, and it was just round the corner, hastening to meet them. There was already new grass, and the fruit trees were in bloom. The country was slowly becoming alive again, and from this hill-top you could see the city with many, many domes, and one more haughty and higher than the others. You could see the flat tops of the pine trees, and the evening light was upon the clouds. The whole horizon seemed to be filled with these clouds, range after range, piling up against the hills in the most fantastic shapes, castles such as man had never built. There were deep chasms and towering peaks. All these clouds were alight with a dark red glow and a few of them seemed to be afire, not by the sun, but within themselves.

These clouds didn't make the space; they were in the space, which seemed to stretch infinitely, from eternity to eternity.

A blackbird was singing in a bush close by, and that was the everlasting blessing.

There were three or four who had brought their wives and we all sat on the floor. From this position the windows were too high for one to see the garden or the wall opposite. They were all professionals. One said he was a scientist, another a mathematician, another, an engineer; they were specialists, not overflowing beyond their boundaries – as the river does after heavy rain. It is the overflowing that enriches the soil.

The engineer asked: 'You have often talked about space and we are all interested to know what you mean by it. The bridge covers the space between two banks or between two hills. Space is made by a dam which is filled by water. There is space between us and the expanding universe. There is space between you and me. Is this what you mean?'

The others seconded the question; they must have talked over before they came. One said: 'I could put it differently, in more scientific terms, but it comes to more or less the same thing.'

There is space that divides and encloses, and space that is unlimited. The space between man and man, in which grows mischief, is the limited space of division; there is division between you as you are and the image you have about yourself; there is division between you and your wife; there is division between what you are and the ideal of what you should be; there is division between hill and hill. And there is the beauty of space that is without the boundary of time and line.

Is there space between thought and thought? Between remembrances? Between actions? Or is there no space at all between thought and thought? Between reason and reason? Between health and ill-health – cause becoming the effect, and the effect becoming the cause?

If there were a break between thought and thought, then thought would be always new, but because there is no break, no space, all thought is old. You may not be conscious of the continuity of a thought; you may pick it up a week later after dropping it, but it has been working within the old boundaries.

So the whole of consciousness, both the conscious and the unconscious – which is an unfortunate word to have to use – is within the limited, narrow space of tradition, culture, custom and remembrance. Technology may take you to the moon, you may build a curving bridge over a chasm or bring some order within the limited space of society, but this again will breed disorder.

Space exists not only beyond the four walls of this room; there is also the space which the room makes. There is the enclosing space, the sphere, which the observer creates around himself, through which he sees the observed – which also creates a sphere around itself.

When the observer looks at the stars of an evening, his space is limited. He may be able, through a telescope, to see many thousands of light years away, but he is the maker of space and therefore it is finite. The measurement between the observer and the observed is space, and time to cover that space.

There is not only physical space but the psychological dimension in which thought covers itself – as yesterday, today and tomorrow. So long as there is an observer, space is the narrow yard of the prison in which there is no freedom at all.

'But we'd like to ask if you are trying to convey space without the observer? That seems to be utterly impossible, or it might be a fancy of your own.'

Freedom, sir, is not within the prison, however comfortable and decorated it may be. If one has a dialogue with freedom it cannot possibly exist within the boundaries of memory, knowledge and experience. Freedom demands that you break the prison walls, though you may enjoy the limited disorder, the limited slavery, the toil within this boundary.

Freedom is not relative; either there is freedom or there is not. If there is not, then one must accept the narrow, limited life with its conflicts, sorrows and aches – merely bringing about a little change here and there.

Freedom is infinite space. When there is a lack of space there is violence – as with the predator, and the bird who claims his space, his territory, for which he will fight. This violence may be relative under the law and the policeman just as the limited space the predators and the birds demand, for which they will fight, is limited violence. Because of the limited space between man and man aggression must exist.

'Are you trying to tell us, sir, that man will always be in conflict within himself and with the world so long as he lives within the sphere of his own making?'

Yes, sir. So we come to the central issue of freedom. Within the narrow culture of society there is no freedom, and because there is no freedom there is disorder. Living within this disorder man seeks freedom in ideologies, in theories, in what he calls God. This escape is not freedom. It is the yard of the prison again which separates man from man. Can thought, which has brought this conditioning upon itself, come to an end, break down this structure, and go beyond and above it? Obviously it cannot, and that is the first factor to see. The intellect cannot possibly build a bridge between itself and freedom. Thought, which is the response of memory, experience and knowledge, is always old, as is the intellect, and the old cannot build a bridge to the new. Thought is essentially the observer with his prejudices, fears and anxieties, and this thinking-image – because of his isolation – obviously makes a sphere around himself. Thus there is a distance between the observer and the observed. The observer tries to establish a relationship preserving this distance – and so there is conflict and violence.

In all this there is no fancy. Imagination in any form destroys truth. Freedom is beyond thought; freedom means infinite space not created by the observer. Coming upon this freedom is meditation.

There is no space without silence, and silence is not put together by time as thought. Time will never give freedom; order is possible only when the heart is not covered over with words.

III

A MEDITATIVE mind is silent. It is not the silence which thought can conceive of; it is not the silence of a still evening; it is the silence when thought – with all its images, its words and perceptions – has entirely ceased. This meditative mind is the religious mind – the religion that is not touched by the church, the temples or by chants.

The religious mind is the explosion of love. It is this love that knows no separation. To it, far is near. It is not the one or the many, but rather that state of love in which all division ceases. Like beauty, it is not of the measure of words. From this silence alone the meditative mind acts.

It had rained the day before and in the evening the sky had been full of clouds. In the distance, the hills were covered with clouds of delight, full of light, and as you watched them they were taking different shapes.

The setting sun, with its golden light, was touching only one or two mountains of cloud, but those clouds seemed as solid as the dark cypress. As you looked at them you naturally became silent. The vast space and the solitary tree on the hill, the distant dome, and the talking going on around one – were all part of this silence. You knew that the next morning it would be lovely, for the sunset was red. And it was lovely; there wasn't a cloud in the sky and it was very blue. The yellow flowers and the white flowering tree against the dark hedge of cypress, and the smell of spring, filled the land. The dew was on the grass, and slowly spring was coming out of darkness.

He said he had just lost his son who had had a very good job and who would soon have become one of the directors of a large company. He was still under the shock of it, but he had great control over himself. He wasn't the type that cried – tears would not come to him easily. He had been schooled all his life by hard work in a matter-of-fact technology. He was not an imaginative man, and the complex, subtle, psychological problems of life had hardly touched him.

The recent death of his son was an unacknowledged blow. He said: 'It is a sad event.'

This sadness was a terrible thing for his wife and children. 'How can I explain to them the ending of sorrow, of which you have talked? I myself have studied and perhaps can understand it, but what of the others who are involved in it?'

Sorrow is in every house, round every corner. Every human being has this engulfing grief, caused by so many incidents and accidents. Sorrow seems like an endless wave that comes upon man, almost drowning him; and the pity of sorrow breeds bitterness and cynicism.

Is the sorrow for your son, or for yourself, or for the break in the continuity of yourself through your son? Is there the sorrow of self-pity? Or is there sorrow because he was so promising in the worldly sense?

If it is self-pity, then this self-concern, this isolating factor in life – though there is the outward semblance of relation-ship – must inevitably cause misery. This isolating process, this activity of self-concern in everyday life, this ambition, this pursuit of one's own self-importance, this separative way of living, whether one is aware of it or not, must bring about the loneliness from which we try to escape in so many different ways. Self-pity is the ache of loneliness, and this pain is called sorrow.

Then there is also the sorrow of ignorance – not the ignorance of the lack of books or of technical knowledge or the lack of experience, but the ignorance we have accepted as time, as evolution, the evolution from what is to what should be – the ignorance which makes us accept authority with all its violence, the ignorance of conformity with its dangers and pains, the ignorance of not knowing the whole structure of oneself. This is the sorrow that man has spread wherever he has been.

So we must be clear about what it is that we call sorrow – sorrow being grief, the loss of what was the supposed good, the sorrow of insecurity and the constant demand for security. Which is it that you are caught in? Unless this is clear there is no ending to sorrow.

This clarity is not a verbal explanation nor is it the result of a clever intellectual analysis. You must be aware of what your sorrow is as clearly as you become aware, sensually, when you touch that flower.

Without understanding this whole way of sorrow, how can you end it? You can escape from it by going to the temple or the church or taking to drink – but all escapes, whether to God or to sex, are the same, for they do not solve sorrow.

So you have to lay down the map of sorrow and trace every path and road. If you allow time to cover this map, then time will strengthen the brutality of sorrow. You have to see this whole map at a glance – seeing the whole and then the detail, not the detail first and then the whole. In ending sorrow, time must come to an end.

Sorrow cannot end by thought. When time stops, thought as the way of sorrow ceases. It is thought and time that divide and separate, and love is not thought or time.

See the map of sorrow not with the eyes of memory. Listen to the whole murmur of it; be of it, for you are both the observer and the observed. Then only can sorrow end. There is no other way.

IV

MEDITATION is never prayer. Prayer, supplication, is born of self-pity. You pray when you are in difficulty, when there is sorrow; but when there is happiness, joy, there is no supplication. This self-pity, so deeply embedded in man, is the root of separation. That which is separate, or thinks itself separate, ever seeking identification with something which is not separate, brings only more division and pain. Out of this confusion one cries to heaven, or to one's husband, or to some deity of the mind. This cry may find an answer, but the answer is the echo of self-pity, in its separation.

The repetition of words, of prayers, is self-hypnotic, self-enclosing and destructive. The isolation of thought is always within the field of the known, and the answer to prayer is the response of the known.

Meditation is far from this. In that field, thought cannot enter; there is no separation, and so no identity. Meditation is in the open; secrecy has no place in it. Everything is exposed, clear; then the beauty of love is.

It was an early spring morning with a few flakey clouds moving gently across the blue sky from the west. A cock began to crow, and it was strange to hear it in a crowded town. It began early, and for nearly two hours it kept announcing the arrival of the day. The trees were still empty, but there were thin, delicate leaves against the clear morning sky.

If you were very quiet, without any thought flashing across the mind, you could just hear the deep bell of some cathedral. It must have been far away, and in the short silences between the cock's crowing you could hear the waves of this sound coming towards you and going beyond you – you almost rode on them, going far away, disappearing into the immensities. The crowing of the cock and the deep

sound of the distant bell had a strange effect. The noises of
the town had not yet begun. There was nothing to interrupt
the clear sound. You didn't hear it with your ears, you heard
it with your heart, not with thought that knows 'the bell'
and 'the cock', and it was pure sound. It came out of silence
and your heart picked it up and went with it from everlasting to everlasting. It was not an organized sound, like music,
it was not the sound of silence between two notes; it was not
the sound you hear when you have stopped talking. All such
sounds are heard by the mind or by the ear. When you hear
with your heart, the world is filled with it and your eyes see
clearly.

She was quite a young lady, well turned out, her hair cut
short, highly efficient and capable. From what she said she
had no illusions about herself. She had children and a certain quality of seriousness. Perhaps she was somewhat romantic and very young, but for her the Orient had lost its
aura of mysticism – which was just as well. She talked
simply, without any hesitation.

'I think I committed suicide a long time ago, when a certain event took place in my life; with that event my life
ended. Of course I have carried on outwardly, with the children and all the rest of it, but I have stopped living.'

Don't you think that most people, knowingly or unknowingly, are always committing suicide? The extreme
form of it is jumping out of the window. But it begins, probably, when there is the first resistance and frustration. We
build a wall around ourselves behind which we lead our own
separate lives – though we may have husbands, wives and
children. This separative life is the life of suicide, and that is
the accepted morality of religion and society. The acts of
separation are of a continuous chain and lead to war and to
self-destruction. Separation is suicide, whether of the individual or of the community or of the nation. Each one wants
to live a life of self-identity, of self-centred activity, of the
self-enclosing sorrow of conformity. It is suicide when belief

and dogma hold you by the hand. Before the event, you invested your life and the whole movement of it in the one against the many, and when the one dies, or the god is destroyed, your life goes with it and you have nothing to live for. If you are terribly clever you invent a meaning to life – which the experts have always done – but having committed yourself to that meaning you are already committing suicide. All commitment is self-destruction, whether it be in the name of God or in the name of Socialism, or anything else.

You, madam – and this is not said in cruelty – ceased to exist because you could not get what you wanted; or it was taken away from you; or you wanted to go through a particular, special door which was tightly shut. As sorrow and pleasure are self-enclosing, so acceptance and insistence bring their own darkness of separation. We do not live, we are always committing suicide. Living begins when the act of suicide ends.

'I understand what you mean. I see what I have done. But now what am I to do? How am I to come back from the long years of death?'

You can't come back; if you came back you would follow the old pattern, and sorrow would pursue you as a cloud is driven by the wind. The only thing you can do is to see that to lead one's own life, separately, in secret, demanding the continuity of pleasure – is to invite the separation of death. In separation there is no love. Love has no identity. Pleasure, and the seeking of it, build the enclosing wall of separation. There is no death when all commitment ceases. Self-knowledge is the open door.

V

MEDITATION is the ending of the word. Silence is not induced by a word, the word being thought. The action out of silence is entirely different from the action born of the word;

meditation is the freeing of the mind from all symbols, images and remembrances.

That morning the tall poplars with their fresh, new leaves were playing in the breeze. It was a spring morning and the hills were covered with flowering almonds, cherries and apples. The whole earth was tremendously alive. The cypresses were stately and aloof, but the flowering trees were touching, branch to branch, and rows of poplars were casting swaying shadows. Beside the road there was running water which would eventually become the old river.

There was scent in the air, and every hill was different from the others. On some of them stood houses surrounded by olives and rows of cypresses leading to the house. The road wound through all these soft hills.

It was a sparkling morning, full of intense beauty, and the powerful car was somehow not out of place. There seemed to be extraordinary order, but, of course, inside each house there was disorder – man plotting against man, children crying or laughing; the whole chain of misery was stretching unseen from house to house. Spring, autumn and winter never broke this chain.

But that morning there was a rebirth. Those tender leaves never knew the winter nor the coming autumn; they were vulnerable and therefore innocent.

From the window one could see the old dome of the striped marble cathedral and the many-coloured campanile; and within were the dark symbols of sorrow and hope. It was really a lovely morning, but strangely there were few birds, for here people kill them for sport, and their song was very still.

He was an artist, a painter. He said he had a talent for it as another might have a talent for the building of bridges. He had long hair, delicate hands and was enclosed within the dream of his own gifts. He would come out of it – talk, explain – and then go back into his own den. He said his pictures were selling and he had had several one-man exhibitions. He was rather proud of this, and his voice told of it.

There is the army, within its own walls of self-interest; and the businessman enclosed within steel and glass; and the housewife pottering about the house waiting for her husband and her children. There is the museum keeper, and the orchestra conductor, each living within a fragment of life, each fragment becoming extraordinarily important, unrelated, in contradiction to other fragments, having its own honours, its own social dignity, its own prophets. The religious fragment is unrelated to the factory, and the factory to the artist; the general is unrelated to the soldiers, as the priest is to the layman. Society is made up of these fragments, and the do-gooder and the reformer are trying to patch up the broken pieces. But through these separative, broken, specialized parts, the human being carries on with his anxieties, guilt and apprehensions. In that we are all related, not in our specialized fields.

In the common greed, hate and aggression, human beings are related and this violence builds the culture, the society, in which we live. It is the mind and the heart that divide – God and hate, love and violence – and in this duality the whole culture of man expands and contracts.

The unity of man does not lie in any of the structures which the human mind has invented. Cooperation is not the nature of the intellect. Between love and hate there can be no unity, and yet it is what the mind is trying to find and establish. Unity lies totally outside this field, and thought cannot reach it.

Thought has constructed this culture of aggression, competition and war, and yet this very thought is groping after order and peace. But thought will never find order and peace, do what it will. Thought must be silent for love to be.

VI

THE mind freeing itself from the known is meditation. Prayer goes from the known to the known; it may produce results, but it is still within the field of the known – and the known is the conflict, the misery and confusion. Meditation is the total denial of everything that the mind has accumulated. The known is the observer, and the observer sees only through the known. The image is of the past, and the meditation is the ending of the past.

It was a fairly large room overlooking a garden with many cypresses for a hedge, and beyond it was a monastery, red-roofed. Early in the morning, before the sun rose, there was a light there and you could see the monks moving about. It was a very cold morning. The wind was blowing from the north and the big eucalyptus – towering over every other tree and over the houses – was swaying in the wind most unwillingly. It liked the breezes that came from the sea because they were not too violent; and it took delight in the soft movement of its own beauty. It was there in the morning early and it was there when the sun was setting, catching the evening light, and somehow it conveyed the certainty of nature. It gave assurance to all the trees and bushes and little plants. It must have been a very old tree. But man never looked at it. He would cut it down if necessary to build a house and never feel the loss of it; for in this country trees are not respected and nature has very little place except, perhaps, as a decoration. The magnificent villas with their gardens had trees showing off the graceful curves of the houses. But this eucalyptus was not decorative to any house. It stood by itself, splendidly quiet and full of silent movement; and the monastery with its garden, and the room with its enclosed green space, were within its shadow. It was there, year after year, living in its own dignity.

There were several people in the room. They had come to carry on a conversation which had been started a few days before. They were mostly young people, some with long hair, others with beards, tight trousers, skirts very high, painted lips and piled-up hair.

The conversation began very lightly; they were not quite sure of themselves or where this conversation was going to lead. 'Of course we cannot follow the established order,' said one of them, 'but we are caught in it. What is our relationship with the older generation and their activity?'

Mere revolt is not the answer, is it? Revolt is a reaction, a response which will bring about its own conditioning. Every generation is conditioned by the past generation, and merely to rebel against conditioning does not free the mind which has been conditioned. Any form of obedience is also a resistance which brings about violence. Violence among the students, or the riots in the cities, or war, whether far removed from yourself or within yourself, will in no way bring clarity.

'But how are we to act within the society to which we belong?'

If you act as a reformer then you are patching up society, which is always degenerating, and so sustaining a system which has produced wars, divisions and separativeness. The reformer, really, is a danger to the fundamental change of man. You have to be an outsider to all communities, to all religions and to the morality of society, otherwise you will be caught in the same old pattern, perhaps somewhat modified.

You are an outsider only when you cease to be envious and vicious, cease to worship success or its power motive. To be psychologically an outsider is possible only when you understand yourself who are part of the environment, part of the social structure which you yourself have built – you being the many yous of many thousands of years, the many, many generations that have produced the present. In understanding yourself as a human being you will find your relationship with the older passing generations.

'But how can one be free of the heavy conditioning as a Catholic? It is so deeply ingrained in us, deeply buried in the unconscious.'

Whether one is a Catholic, or a Muslim, or Hindu, or a Communist, the propaganda of a hundred, two hundred, or five thousand years is part of this verbal structure of images which goes to make up your consciousness. We are conditioned by what we eat, by the economic pressures, by the culture and society in which we live. We *are* that culture, we *are* that society. Merely to revolt against it is to revolt against ourselves. If you rebel against yourself, not knowing what you are, your rebellion is utterly wasted. But to be aware, without condemnation, of what you are – such awareness brings about action which is entirely different from the action of a reformer or a revolutionary.

'But, sir, our unconscious is the collective racial heritage and according to the analysts this must be understood.'

I don't see why you give such importance to the unconscious. It is as trivial and shoddy as the conscious mind, and giving it importance only strengthens it. If you see its true worth it drops away as a leaf in the autumn. We think certain things are important to keep and that others can be thrown away. War does produce certain peripheral improvements, but war itself is the greatest disaster for man. Intellect will in no way solve our human problems. Thought has tried in many, many ways to overcome and go beyond our agonies and anxieties. Thought has built the church, the saviour, the guru; thought has invented nationalities; thought has divided the people in the nation into different communities, classes, at war with each other. Thought has separated man from man, and having brought anarchy and great sorrow, it then proceeds to invent a structure to bring people together. Whatever thought does must inevitably breed danger and anxiety. To call oneself an Italian or an Indian or an American is surely insanity, and it is the work of thought.

'But love is the answer to all this, isn't it?'

Again you're off! Are you free from envy, ambition, or are you merely using that word 'love' to which thought has given a meaning? If thought has given a meaning to it, then it is not love. The word love is not love – no matter what you mean by that word. Thought is the past, the memory, the experience, the knowledge from which the response to every challenge comes. So this response is always inadequate, and hence there is conflict. For thought is always old; thought can never be new. Modern art is the response of thought, the intellect, and though it pretends to be new it is really as old, though not as beautiful, as the hills. It is the whole structure built by thought – as love, as God, as culture, as the ideology of the polit-buro – which has to be totally denied for the new to be. The new cannot fit into the old pattern. You are really afraid to deny the old pattern completely.

'Yes, sir, we are afraid, for if we deny it what is there left? With what do we replace it?'

This question is the outcome of thought which sees the danger and so is afraid and wants to be assured that it will find something to replace the old. So again you are caught in the net of thought. But if factually, not verbally or intellectually, you denied this whole house of thought, then you might perhaps find the new – the new way of living, seeing, acting. Negation is the most positive action. To negate the false, not knowing what is true, to negate the apparent truth in the false, and to negate the false as the false, is the instant action of a mind that is free from thought. To see this flower with the image that thought has built about it is entirely different from seeing it without that image. The relationship between the observer and the flower is the image which the observer has about the observed, and in this there is a great distance between them.

When there is no image the time interval ceases.

VII

MEDITATION is always new. It has not the touch of the past for it has no continuity. The word new doesn't convey the quality of a freshness that has not been before. It is like the light of a candle which has been put out and relit. The new light is not the old, though the candle is the same. Meditation has a continuity only when thought colours it, shapes it and gives it a purpose. The purpose and meaning of meditation given by thought becomes a time-binding bondage. But the meditation that is not touched by thought has its own movement, which is not of time. Time implies the old and the new as a movement from the roots of yesterday to the flowing of tomorrow. But meditation is a different flowering altogether. It is not the outcome of the experience of yesterday, and therefore it has no roots at all in time. It has a continuity which is not that of time. The word continuity in meditation is misleading, for that which was, yesterday, is not taking place today. The meditation of today is a new awakening, a new flowering of the beauty of goodness.

The car went slowly through all the traffic of the big town with its buses, lorries and cars, and all the noise along the narrow streets. There were endless flats, filled with families, and endless shops, and the town was spreading on all sides, devouring the countryside. At last we came out into the country, the green fields and the wheat and the great patches of flowering mustard, intense in their yellowness. The contrast between the intense green and the yellow was as striking as the contrast between the noise of the town and the quietness of the countryside. We were on the auto route to the north which went up and down the land. And there were woods, streams, and the lovely blue sky.

It was a spring morning, and there were great patches of

bluebells in the wood, and beside the wood was the yellow mustard, stretching almost to the horizon; and then the green wheatfield that stretched as far as the eye could see. The road passed villages and towns, and a side road led to a lovely wood with new fresh spring leaves and the smell of damp earth; and there was that peculiar feeling of spring, and the newness of life. You were very close to nature then as you watched your part of the earth – the trees, the new delicate leaf, and the stream that went by. It was not a romantic feeling or an imaginative sensation, but actually you were all this – the blue sky and the expanding earth.

The road led to an old house with an avenue of tall beeches with their young, fresh leaves, and you looked up through them at the blue sky. It was a lovely morning, and the copper-beech was still quite young, though very tall.

He was a big, heavy man with very large hands, and he filled that enormous chair. He had a kindly face and he was ready to laugh. It is strange how little we laugh. Our hearts are too oppressed, made dull, by the weary business of living, by the routine and the monotony of everyday life. We are made to laugh by a joke or a witty saying, but there is no laughter in ourselves; the bitterness which is man's ripening fruit seems so common. We never see the running water and laugh with it; it is sad to see the light in our eyes grow duller and duller each day; the pressures of agony and despair seem to colour our whole life with their promise of hope and pleasure, which thought cultivates.

He was interested in that peculiar philosophy of the origin and acceptance of silence – which probably he had never come upon. You can't buy silence as you would buy good cheese. You can't cultivate it as you would a lovely plant. It doesn't come about by any activity of the mind or of the heart. The silence that music produces as you listen to it is the product of that music, induced by it. Silence isn't an experience; you know it only when it is over.

Sit, sometime, on the bank of a river and look into the

water. Don't be hypnotized by the movement of the water, by the light, the clarity and the depth of the stream. Look at it without any movement of thought. The silence is all round you, in you, in the river, and in those trees that are utterly still. You can't take it back home, hold it in your mind or your hand and think you have achieved some extraordinary state. If you have, then it is not silence; then it is merely a memory, an imagining, a romantic escape from the daily noise of life.

Because of silence everything exists. The music you heard this morning came to you out of silence, and you heard it because you were silent, and it went beyond you in silence.

Only we don't listen to the silence because our ears are full of the chatter of the mind. When you love, and there is no silence, thought makes of it a plaything of society whose culture is envy and whose gods are put together by the mind and the hand. Silence is where you are, in yourself and beside yourself.

VIII

MEDITATION is the summation of all energy. It is not to be gathered little by little, denying this and denying that, capturing this and holding on to that; but rather, it is the total denial, without any choice, of all wasteful energy. Choice is the outcome of confusion; and the essence of wasted energy is confusion and conflict. To see clearly what is at any time needs the attention of all energy; and in this there is no contradiction or duality. This total energy does not come about through abstinence, through the vows of chastity and poverty, for all determination and action of will is a waste of energy because thought is involved in it, and thought is wasted energy: perception never is. The *seeing* is not a determined effort. There is no 'I will see', but only seeing. Observation puts aside the observer, and in this there is no waste of energy. The thinker who attempts to observe, spoils energy. Love is not wasted energy, but when thought makes it into pleasure, then pain dissipates energy. The summation of energy, of meditation, is ever expanding, and action in daily life becomes part of it.

The poplar this morning was being stirred by the breeze that came from the west. Every leaf was telling something to the breeze; every leaf was dancing, restless in its joy of the spring morning. It was very early. The blackbird on the roof was singing. It is there every morning and evening, sometimes sitting quietly looking all around and at other times calling and waiting for a reply. It would be there for several minutes and then fly off. Now its yellow beak was bright in the early light. As it flew away the clouds were coming over the roof, the horizon was filled with them, one on top of another, as though someone had very carefully arranged them in neat order. They were moving, and it seemed as if the whole earth was being carried by them – the chimneys, the television antennae and the very tall building across the way. They presently passed, and there was the blue, spring sky, clear, with the light freshness that only spring can bring. It was extraordinarily blue and, at that time of the morning, the street outside was almost silent. You could hear the noise of heels on the pavement and in the distance a lorry went by. The day would soon begin. As you looked out of the window at the poplar you saw the universe, the beauty of it.

He asked: 'What is intelligence? You talk a great deal about it and I would like to know your opinion of it.'

Opinion, and the exploration of opinion, is not truth. You can discuss indefinitely the varieties of opinion, the rightness and the wrongness of them, but however good and reasonable, opinion is not the truth. Opinion is always biased, coloured by the culture, the education, the knowledge which one has. Why should the mind be burdened with opinions at all, with what you think about this or that person, or book, or idea? Why shouldn't the mind be empty? Only when it is empty can it see clearly.

'But we are all full of opinions. My opinion of the present political leader has been formed by what he has said and done, and without that opinion I would not be able to vote for him. Opinions are necessary for action, aren't they?'

Opinions can be cultivated, sharpened and hardened, and most actions are based on this principle of like and dislike. The hardening of experience and knowledge expresses itself in action, but such action divides and separates man from man; it is opinion and belief that prevent the observation of what actually is. The seeing of *what is* is part of that intelligence which you are asking about. There is no intelligence if there is no sensitivity of the body and of the mind – the sensitivity of feeling and the clarity of observation. Emotionalism and sentimentality prevent the sensitivity of feeling. Being sensitive in one area and dull in another leads to contradiction and conflict – which deny intelligence. The integration of the many broken parts into a whole does not bring about intelligence. Sensitivity is attention, which is intelligence. Intelligence has nothing to do with knowledge or information. Knowledge is always the past; it can be called upon to act in the present but it limits the present. Intelligence is always in the present, and of no time.

IX

MEDITATION is the freeing of the mind from all dishonesty. Thought breeds dishonesty. Thought, in its attempts to be honest, is comparative and therefore dishonest. All comparison is a process of evasion and hence breeds dishonesty. Honesty is not the opposite of dishonesty. Honesty is not a principle. It is not conformity to a pattern, but rather it is the total perception of what is. And meditation is the movement of this honesty in silence.

The day began rather cloudy and dull, and the naked trees were silent in the wood. Through the wood you could see crocuses, daffodils and bright yellow forsythia. You looked at it all from a distance and it was a patch of yellow against a green lawn. As you came close to it you were blinded by the brightness of that yellow – which was God. It was not that you identified yourself with the colour, or that you became the expanse that filled the universe with yellow – but that there was no you to look at it. Only it existed, and nothing else – not the voices around you, not the blackbird singing its melody of the morning, not the voices of the passers-by, not the noisy car that scraped by you on the road. *It* existed, nothing else. And beauty and love were in that existence.

You walked back into the wood. A few rain drops fell, and the wood was deserted. Spring had just come, but here in the north the trees had no leaves. They were dreary from the winter, from the waiting for sunshine and mild weather. A horseman went by and the horse was sweating. The horse, with its grace, its movement, was more than the man; the man, with his breeches, highly polished boots and riding-cap, looked insignificant. The horse had breeding, it held its head high. The man, although he rode the horse, was a stranger to the world of nature, but the horse seemed part of nature, which man was slowly destroying.

The trees were large – oaks, elms and beeches. They stood very silent. The ground was soft with winter's leaves, and here the earth seemed very old. There were few birds. The blackbird was calling, and the sky was clearing.

When you went back in the evening the sky was very clear and the light on these huge trees was strange and full of silent movement.

Light is an extraordinary thing; the more you watch it the deeper and vaster it becomes; and in its movement the trees were caught. It was startling; no canvas could have caught the beauty of that light. It was more than the light of the setting sun; it was more than your eyes saw. It was as though love was on the land. You saw again that yellow patch of forsythia, and the earth rejoiced.

She came with her two daughters but left them to play outside. She was a young woman, rather nice-looking and quite well dressed; she seemed rather impatient and capable. She said her husband worked in some kind of office, and life went by. She had a peculiar sadness which was covered up with a swift smile. She asked: 'What is relationship? I have been married to my husband for some years now. I suppose we love each other – but there is something terribly lacking in it.'

You really want to go into this deeply?

'Yes, I have come a long way to talk to you about it.'

Your husband works in his office, and you work in your house, both of you with your ambitions, frustrations, agonies and fears. He wants to be a big executive and is afraid that he may not make it – that others may get there before him. He is enclosed in his ambition, his frustration, his search for fulfilment, and you in yours. He comes home tired, irritable, with fear in his heart, and brings home that tension. You also are tired after your long day, with the children, and all the rest of it. You and he take a drink to ease your nerves, and fall into uneasy conversation. After some talk – food, and then the inevitable bed. This is what is called relationship – each one living in his own self-centred activity and meeting in bed; this is called love. Of course, there is a little tenderness, a little consideration, a pat or two on the head for the children. Then there will follow old age and death. This is what is called living. And you accept this way of life.

'What else can one do? We are brought up in it, educated for it. We want security, some of the good things of life. I don't see what else one can do.'

Is it the desire for security that binds us? Or is it custom, the acceptance of the pattern of society – the idea of husband, wife and family? Surely in all this there is very little happiness?

'There is some happiness, but there is too much to do, too many things to see to. There is so much to read if one is to be well-informed. There isn't much time to think. Obviously one is not really happy, but one just carries on.'

All this is called living in relationship – but obviously there is no relationship at all. You may be physically together for a little while but each one is living in his own world of isolation, breeding his own miseries, and there is no actual coming together, not just physically, but at a much deeper and wider level. It is the fault of society, isn't it, of the culture in which we have been brought up and in which we so easily get caught? It is a rotten society, a corrupt and immoral society which human beings have created. It is this that must be changed, and it cannot be changed unless the human being who has built it changes himself.

'I may perhaps understand what you say, and maybe change, but what of him? It gives him great pleasure to strive, to achieve, to become somebody. He is not going to change, and so we are back again where we were – I, feebly attempting to break through my enclosure, and he more and more strengthening his narrow cell of life. What is the point of it all?'

There is no point in this kind of existence at all. We have made this life, the everyday brutality and ugliness of it, with occasional flashes of delight; so we must die to it all. You know, madam, actually there is no tomorrow. Tomorrow is the invention of thought in order to achieve its shoddy ambitions and fulfilment. Thought builds the many tomorrows, but actually there is no tomorrow. To die tomorrow is to live completely today. When you do, the whole of existence changes. For love is not tomorrow, love is not a thing of thought, love has no past or future. When you live completely today there is a great intensity in it, and in its beauty – which is untouched by ambition, by jealousy or by time –

there is relationship not only with man but with nature, with the flowers, the earth and the heavens. In that there is the intensity of innocence; living, then, has a wholly different meaning.

X

You can never set about to meditate: it must happen without your seeking it out. If you seek it, or ask how to meditate, then the method will not only condition you further but also strengthen your own present conditioning. Meditation, really, is the denial of the whole structure of thought. Thought is structural, reasonable or unreasonable, objective or unhealthy, and when it tries to meditate from reason or from a contradictory and neurotic state it will inevitably project that which it is, and will take its own structure as a serious reality. It is like a believer meditating upon his own belief; he strengthens and sanctifies that which he, out of fear, has created. The word is the picture or the image whose idolatry becomes the end.

Sound makes its own cage, and then the noise of thought is of the cage, and it is this word and its sound which divides the observer and the observed. The word is not only a unit of language, not only a sound, but also a symbol, a recollection of any event which unleases the movement of memory, of thought. Meditation is the complete absence of this word. The root of fear is the machinery of the word.

It was early spring and in the Bois it was strangely gentle. There were few new leaves, and the sky was not yet that intense blue that comes with the delight of spring. The chestnuts were not yet out, but the early smell of spring was in the air. In that part of the Bois there was hardly anybody, and you could hear the cars going by in the distance. We were walking in the early morning and there was that gentle sharpness of the early spring. He had been discussing, questioning, and asking what he should do.

'It seems so endless, this constant analysis, introspective examination, this vigilance. I have tried so many things; the clean-shaven gurus and the bearded gurus, and several systems of meditation – you know the whole bag of tricks – and it leaves one rather dry-mouthed and hollow.'

Why don't you begin from the other end, the end you don't know about – from the other shore which you cannot possibly see from this shore? Begin with the unknown rather than with the known, for this constant examination, analysis, only strengthens and further conditions the known. If the mind lives from the other end, then these problems will not exist.

'But how am I to begin from the other end? I don't know it, I can't see it.'

When you ask: 'How am I to begin from the other end?' you are still asking the question from this end. So don't ask it, but start from the other shore, of which you know nothing, from another dimension which cunning thought cannot capture.

He remained silent for some time, and a cock pheasant flew by. It looked brilliant in the sun, and it disappeared under some bushes. When it reappeared a little later there were four or five hen pheasants almost the colour of the dead leaves, and this big pheasant stood mightily amongst them.

He was so occupied that he never saw the pheasant, and when we pointed it out to him he said: 'How beautiful!' – which were mere words, because his mind was occupied with the problem of how to begin from something he didn't know. An early lizard, long and green, was on a rock, sunning itself.

'I can't see how I am going to begin from that end. I don't really understand this vague assertion, this statement which, at least to me, is quite meaningless. I can go only to what I know.'

But what do you know? You know only something which is already finished, which is over. You know only the yesterday, and we are saying: Begin from that which you don't know, and live from there. If you say: 'How am I to live from there?' then you are inviting the pattern of yesterday. But if you live with the unknown you are living in freedom, acting from freedom, and, after all, that is love. If you say, 'I know what love is,' then you don't know what it is. Surely it is not a memory, a remembrance of pleasure. Since it isn't, then live with that which you don't know.

'I really don't know what you are talking about. You are making the problem worse.'

I'm asking a very simple thing. I'm saying that the more you dig, the more there is. The very digging is the conditioning, and each shovelful makes steps which lead nowhere. You want new steps made for you, or you want to make your own steps which will lead to a totally different dimension. But if you don't know what that dimension is – actually, not speculatively – then whatever steps you make or tread can lead only to that which is already known. So drop all this and start from the other end. Be silent, and you will find out.

'But I don't know how to be silent!'

There you are, back again in the 'how', and there is no end to the how. All knowing is on the wrong side. If you know, you are already in your grave. The being is not the knowing.

XI

IN the light of silence, all problems are dissolved. This light is not born of the ancient movement of thought. It is not born, either, out of self-revealing knowledge. It is not lit by time nor by any action of will. It comes about in meditation. Meditation is not a private affair; it is not a personal search for pleasure; pleasure is always separative and dividing. In meditation the dividing line between you and me disappears; in it the light of silence destroys the knowledge of the me. The me can be studied indefinitely, for it varies from day to day, but its reach is always limited, however extensive it is thought to be. Silence is freedom, and freedom comes with the finality of complete order.

It was a wood by the sea. The constant wind had misshapen the pine trees, keeping them short, and the branches were bare of needles. It was spring, but spring would never come to these pine trees. It was there, but far away from them, far away from the constant wind and the salt air. It was there, flowering, and every blade of grass and every leaf was shouting, every chestnut tree was in bloom, its candles lit by the sun. The ducks with their chicks were there, the tulips and the narcissi. But here it was bare, without shadow, and every tree was in agony, twisted, stunted, bare. It was too near the sea. This place had its own quality of beauty but it looked at those far-away woods with silent anguish, for that day the cold wind was very strong; there were high waves and the strong winds drove the spring further inland. It was foggy over the sea, and the racing clouds covered the land, carrying with them the canals, the woods and the flat earth. Even the low tulips, so close to the earth, were shaken and their brilliant colour was a wave of bright light over the field. The birds were in the woods, but not among the pines. There were one or two blackbirds, with their bright yellow beaks, and a pigeon or two. It was a marvellous thing to see the light on the water.

He was a big man, heavily built, with large hands. He must have been a very rich man. He collected modern pictures and was rather proud of his collection which the critics had said was very good. As he told you this you could see the light of pride in his eyes. He had a dog, big, active and full of play; it was more alive than its master. It wanted to be out in the grass among the dunes, racing against the wind, but it sat obediently where its master had told it to sit, and soon it went to sleep from boredom.

Possessions possess us more than we possess them. The castle, the house, the pictures, the books, the knowledge, they become far more vital, far more important, than the human being.

He said he had read a great deal, and you could see from the books in the library that he had all the latest authors. He spoke about spiritual mysticism and the craze for drugs that was seeping over the land. He was a rich, successful man, and behind him was emptiness and the shallowness that can never be filled by books, by pictures, or by the knowledge of the trade.

The sadness of life is this – the emptiness that we try to fill with every conceivable trick of the mind. But that emptiness remains. Its sadness is the vain effort to possess. From this attempt comes domination and the assertion of the me, with its empty words and rich memories of things that are gone and never will come back. It is this emptiness and loneliness that isolating thought breeds and keeps nourished by the knowledge it has created.

It is this sadness of vain effort that is destroying man. His thought is not so good as the computer, and he has only the instrument of thought with which to meet the problems of life, so he is destroyed by them. It is this sadness of wasted life which probably he will be aware of only at the moment of his death – and then it will be too late.

So the possessions, the character, the achievements, the domesticated wife, become terribly important, and this sadness drives away love. Either you have one or the other; you cannot have both. One breeds cynicism and bitterness which are the only fruit of man; the other lies beyond all woods and hills.

XII

IMAGINATION and thought have no place in meditation. They lead to bondage; and meditation brings freedom. The good and the pleasurable are two different things; the one brings freedom and the other leads to the bondage of time. Meditation is the freedom from time. Time is the observer, and experiencer, the thinker, and time is thought; meditation is the going beyond and above the activities of time.

Imagination is always in the field of time, and however concealed and secretive it may be, it will act. This action of thought will inevitably lead to conflict and to the bondage of time. To meditate is to be innocent of time.

You could see the lake from many miles away. You got to it through winding roads that wandered through fields of grain and the pine forests. It was a very tidy country. The roads were very clean and the farms with their cattle, horses, chickens and pigs were well-ordered. You went through the rolling hills down to the lake, and on every side were mountains covered with snow. It was very clear, and the snow was sparkling in the early morning.

There had been no wars in this country for many centuries, and one felt the great security, the undisturbed routine of everyday life, bringing with it the dullness and indifference of the established society of a good government.

It was a smooth well-kept road, wide enough for cars to pass each other easily; and now, as you came over the hill, you were among orchards. A little farther on there was a great patch of tobacco. As you came near it you could smell the strong smell of ripening tobacco flowers.

That morning, coming down from an altitude, it was beginning to get warm and the air was rather heavy. The peace of the land entered your heart, and you became part of the earth.

It was an early spring day. There was a cool breeze from the north, and the sun was already beginning to make sharp shadows. The tall, heavy eucalyptus was gently swaying against the house, and a single blackbird was singing; you could see it from where you sat. It must have felt rather lonely, for there were very few birds that morning. The sparrows were lined up on the wall overlooking the garden. The garden was rather ill-kept; the lawn needed mowing. The children would come out and play in the afternoon and you could hear their shouts and laughter. They would chase each other among the trees, playing hide-and-seek, and high laughter would fill the air.

There were about eight people around the table at lunch. One was a film director, another a pianist, and there was also a young student from some university. They were talking about politics and the riots in America, and the war that seemed to be going on and on. There was an easy flow of conversation about nothing. The director said, suddenly: 'We of the older generation have no place in the coming modern world. A well-known author spoke the other day at the university – and the students tore him to pieces and he was left flat. What he was saying had no relation to what the students wanted, or thought about, or demanded. He was asserting his views, his importance, his way of life, and the students would have none of it. As I know him, I know what he felt. He was really lost, but would not admit it. He wanted to be accepted by the younger generation and they would not have his respectable, traditional way of life – though in his books he wrote about a formalized change ... I, personally,' went on the director, 'see that I have no relation or contact with anyone of the younger generation. I feel that we are hypocrites.'

This was said by a man who had many well-known avant-garde films to his name. He was not bitter about it. He was just stating a fact, with a smile and a shrug of his shoulders. What was specially nice about him was his frankness, with that touch of humility which often goes with it.

The pianist was quite young. He had given up his promising career because he thought the whole world of impresarios, concerts, and the publicity and money involved in it, was a glorified racket. He himself wanted to live a different kind of life, a religious life.

He said: 'It is the same all the world over. I have just come from India. There the gap between the old and the new is perhaps even wider. There the tradition and the vitality of the old are tremendously strong, and probably the younger generation will be sucked into it. But at least there will be a few, I hope, who will resist and start a different movement.

'And I have noticed, for I have travelled quite a bit, that the younger people (and I am old compared with the young) are breaking away more and more from the establishment. Perhaps they get lost in the world of drugs and oriental mysticism, but they have a promise, a new vitality. They reject the church, the fat priest, the sophisticated hierarchy of the religious world. They don't want to have anything to do with politics or wars. Perhaps out of them will come a germ of the new.'

The university student had been silent all this time, eating his spaghetti and looking out of the window; but he was taking in the conversation, as were the others. He was rather shy, and though he disliked study he went to the university and listened to the professors – who couldn't teach him properly. He read a great deal; he liked English literature as well as that of his own country, and had talked about it at other meals and at other times.

He said: 'Though I am only twenty I am already old compared with the fifteen-year-olds. Their brains work faster, they are keener, they see things more clearly, they get to the point before I do. They seem to know much more, and I feel old compared with them. But I entirely agree with what you said. You feel you are hypocrites, say one thing and do another. This you can understand in the politicians and in the priests, but what puzzles me is – why should others join this world of hypocrisy? Your morality stinks; you *want* wars.

'As for us, we don't hate the Negro, or the brown man, or any other colour. We feel at home with all of them. I know this because I have moved about with them.

'But you, the older generation, have created this world of racial distinctions and war – and we don't want any of it. So we revolt. But again, this revolt is made fashionable and exploited by the different politicians, and so we lose our original revulsion against all this. Perhaps we, too, will become respectable, moral citizens. But now we hate your morality and have no morality at all.'

There was a minute or two of silence; and the eucalyptus was still, almost listening to the words going on around the table. The blackbird had gone, and so had the sparrows.

We said: Bravo, you are perfectly right. To deny all morality is to be moral, for the accepted morality is the morality of respectability, and I'm afraid we all crave to be respected – which is to be recognized as good citizens in a rotten society. Respectability is very profitable and ensures you a good job and a steady income. The accepted morality of greed, envy and hate is the way of the establishment.

When you totally deny all this, not with your lips but with your heart, then you are really moral. For this morality springs out of love and not out of any motive of profit, of achievement, of place in the hierarchy. There cannot be this love if you belong to a society in which you want to find fame, recognition, a position. Since there is no love in this, its morality is immorality. When you deny all this from the very bottom of your heart, then there is a virtue that is encompassed by love.

XIII

To meditate is to transcend time. Time is the distance that thought travels in its achievements. The travelling is always along the old path covered over with a new coating, new sights, but always the same road, leading nowhere – except to pain and sorrow.

It is only when the mind transcends time that truth ceases to be an abstraction. Then bliss is not an idea derived from pleasure but an actuality that is not verbal.

The emptying of the mind of time is the silence of truth, and the seeing of this is the doing; so there is no division between the seeing and the doing. In the interval between seeing and doing is born conflict, misery and confusion. That which has no time is the everlasting.

On every table there were daffodils, young, fresh, just out of the garden, with the bloom of spring on them still. On a side table there were lilies, creamy-white with sharp yellow centres. To see this creamy-white and the brilliant yellow of those many daffodils was to see the blue sky, ever expanding, limitless, silent.

Almost all the tables were taken by people talking very loudly and laughing. At a table nearby a woman was surreptitiously feeding her dog with the meat she could not eat. They all seemed to have huge helpings, and it was not a pleasant sight to see people eating; perhaps it may be barbarous to eat publicly. A man across the room had filled himself with wine and meat and was just lighting a big cigar, and a look of beatitude came over his fat face. His equally fat wife lit a cigarette. Both of them appeared to be lost to the world.

And there they were, the yellow daffodils, and nobody seemed to care. They were there for decorative purposes that had no meaning at all; and as you watched them their yellow brilliance filled the noisy room. Colour has this strange effect upon the eye. It wasn't so much that the eye absorbed the colour, as that the colour seemed to fill your being. You *were* that colour; you didn't become that colour – you were of it, without identification or name; the anonymity which is innocence. Where there is no anonymity there is violence, in all its different forms.

But you forgot the world, the smoke-filled room, the cruelty of man, and the red, ugly meat; those shapely daffodils seemed to take you beyond all time.

Love is like that. In it there is no time, space or identity. It is the identity that breeds pleasure and pain; it is the identity that brings hate and war and builds a wall around people, around each one, each family and community. Man reaches over the wall to the other man – but he too is enclosed; morality is a word that bridges the two, and so it becomes ugly and vain.

Love isn't like that; it is like that wood across the way, always renewing itself because it is always dying. There is no permanency in it, which thought seeks; it is a movement which thought can never understand, touch or feel. The feeling of thought and the feeling of love are two different things; the one leads to bondage and the other to the flowering of goodness. The flowering is not within the area of any society, of any culture or of any religion, whereas the bondage belongs to all societies, religious beliefs and faith in otherness. Love is anonymous, therefore not violent. Pleasure is violent, for desire and will are moving factors in it. Love cannot be begotten by thought, or by good works. The denial of the total process of thought becomes the beauty of action, which is love. Without this there is no bliss of truth.

And over there, on that table, were the daffodils.

XIV

MEDITATION is the awakening of bliss; it is both of the senses and transcending them. It has no continuity, for it is not of time. The happiness and the joy of relationship, the sight of a cloud carrying the earth, and the light of spring on the leaves, are the delight of the eye and of the mind. This delight can be cultivated by thought and given a duration in the space of memory, but it is not the bliss of meditation in which is included the intensity of the senses. The senses must be acute and in no way distorted by thought, by the discipline of conformity and social morality. The freedom of the senses is not the indulgence of them: the indulgence is the pleasure of thought. Thought is like the smoke of a fire and bliss is the fire without the cloud of smoke that brings tears to the eyes. Pleasure is one thing, and bliss another. Pleasure is the bondage of thought, and bliss is beyond and above thought. The foundation of meditation is the understanding of thought and of pleasure, with their morality and the discipline which gives comfort. The bliss of meditation is not of time or duration; it is beyond both and therefore not measurable. Its ecstasy is not in the eye of the beholder, nor is it an experience of the thinker.

Thought cannot touch it with its words and symbols and the confusion it breeds; it is not a word that can take root in thought and be shaped by it. This bliss comes out of complete silence.

It was a lovely morning with fleeting clouds and a clear blue sky. It had rained, and the air was clean. Every leaf was new and the dreary winter was over; each leaf knew, in the sparkling sunshine, that it had no relation to last year's spring. The sun shone through the new leaves, shedding a soft green light on the wet path that led through the woods to the main road that went on to the big city.

There were children playing about, but they never looked at that lovely spring day. They had no need to look, for they were the spring. Their laughter and their play were part of the tree, the leaf and the flower. You felt this, you didn't imagine it. It was as though the leaves and the flowers were taking part in the laughter, in the shouting, and in the balloon that went by. Every blade of grass, and the yellow dandelion, and the tender leaf that was so vulnerable, all were part of the children, and the children were part of the whole earth. The dividing line between man and nature disappeared; but the man on the race-course in his car, and the woman returning from market, were unaware of this. Probably they never even looked at the sky, at the trembling leaf, the white lilac. They were carrying their problems in their hearts, and the heart never looked at the children or at the brightening spring day. The pity of it was that they bred these children and the children would soon become the man on the race-course and the woman returning from the market; and the world would be dark again. Therein lay the unending sorrow. The love on that leaf would be blown away with the coming autumn.

He was a young man with a wife and children. He seemed highly educated, intellectual, and good at the use of words. He was rather lean and sat comfortably in the arm-chair – legs crossed, hands folded on his lap and his glasses sparkling with the light of the sun from the window. He said he had always been seeking – not only philosophical truths but the truth that was beyond the word and the system.

I suppose you are seeking because you are discontented?

'No, I am not exactly discontented. Like every other human being I am dissatisfied, but that's not the reason for the search. It isn't the search of the microscope, or of the telescope, or the search of the priest for his God. I can't say what I'm seeking; I can't put my finger on it. It seems to me I was born with this, and though I am happily married, the search still goes on. It isn't an escape. I really don't know what I want to find. I have talked it over with some clever philosophers and with religious missionaries from the East, and they have all told me to continue in my search and never stop seeking. After all these years it is still a constant disturbance.'

Should one seek at all? Seeking is always for something over there on the other bank, in the distance covered by time and long strides. The seeking and the finding are in the future – over there, just beyond the hill. This is the essential meaning of seeking. There is the present and the thing to be found in the future. The present is not fully active and alive and so, of course, that which is beyond the hill is more alluring and demanding. The scientist, if he has his eyes glued to the microscope, will never see the spider on the wall, although the web of his life is not in the microscope but in the life of the present.

'Are you saying, sir, that it is vain to seek; that there is no hope in the future; that all time is in the present?'

All life is in the present, not in the shadow of yesterday or in the brightness of tomorrow's hope. To live in the present one has to be free of the past, and of tomorrow. Nothing is found in the tomorrow, for tomorrow is the present, and yesterday is only a remembrance. So the distance between that which is to be found and that which *is*, is made ever wider by the search – however pleasant and comforting that search may be.

Constantly to seek the purpose of life is one of the odd escapes of man. If he finds what he seeks it will not be worth that pebble on the path. To live in the present the mind must not be divided by the remembrance of yesterday or the bright hope of tomorrow: it must have no tomorrow and no yesterday. This is not a poetic statement but an actual fact. Poesy and imagination have no place in the active present. Not that you deny beauty, but love is that beauty in the present which is not to be found in the seeking.

'I think I'm beginning to see the futility of the years I have spent in the search, in the questions I have asked of myself and of others, and the futility of the answers.'

The ending is the beginning, and the beginning is the first step, and the first step is the only step.

XV

Hᴇ was rather a blunt man, full of interest and drive. He had read extensively, and spoke several languages. He had been to the East and knew a little about Indian philosophy, had read the so-called sacred books and had followed some guru or other. And here he was now, in this little room overlooking a verdant valley smiling in the morning sun. The snow peaks were sparkling and there were huge clouds just coming over the mountains. It was going to be a very nice day, and at that altitude the air was clear and the light penetrating. It was the beginning of summer and there was still in the air the cold of spring. It was a quiet valley, especially at this time of the year, full of silence, and the sound of cowbells, and the smell of pine and new mown grass. There were a lot of children shouting and playing, and that morning, early, there was delight in the air and the beauty of the land lay upon one's senses. The eye saw the blue sky and the green earth, and there was rejoicing.

'Behaviour is righteousness – at least, that's what you have said. I have listened to you for some years, in different parts of the world, and I have grasped the teaching. I am not trying to put that teaching into action in life for then it becomes another pattern, another form of imitation, the acceptance of a new formula. I see the danger of this. I have absorbed a great deal of what you have said and it has almost become part of me. This may prevent a freedom of action – upon which you so insist. One's life is never free and spontaneous. I have to live my daily life but I'm always watchful to see that I'm not merely following some new pattern which I have made for myself. So I seem to lead a double life; there is the ordinary activity, family, work, and so on, and on the other hand there is the teaching that you have been giving, in which I am deeply interested. If I follow the teaching then I'm the same as any Catholic who conforms to a dogma. So, from what does one act in daily life if one lives the teaching without simply conforming to it?'

It is necessary to put aside the teaching and the teacher and also the follower who is trying to live a different kind of life. There is only learning: in the learning is the doing. The learning is not separate from the action. If they are separate, then learning is an idea or a set of ideals according to which action takes place, whereas learning is the doing in which there is no conflict. When this is understood, what is the question? The learning is not an abstraction, an idea, but an actual learning about something. You cannot learn without doing; you cannot learn about yourself except in action. It is not that you first learn about yourself and then act from that knowledge for then that action becomes imitative, conforming to your accumulated knowledge.

'But, sir, every moment I am challenged, by this or by that, and I respond as I always have done – which often means there is conflict. I'd like to understand the pertinence of what you say about learning in these everyday situations.'

Challenges must always be new, otherwise they are not challenges, but the response, which is old, is inadequate, and therefore there is conflict. You are asking what there is to learn about this. There is the learning about responses, how they come into being, their background and conditioning, so there is a learning about the whole structure and nature of the response. This learning is not an accumulation from which you are going to respond to the challenge. Learning is a movement not anchored in knowledge. If it is anchored it is not a movement. The machine, the computer, *is* anchored. That is the basic difference between man and the machine. Learning is watching, seeing. If you see from accumulated knowledge then the seeing is limited and there is no new thing in the seeing.

'You say one learns about the whole structure of response. This does seem to mean that there is a certain accumulated volume of what is learnt. On the other hand you say that the learning you speak of is so fluid that it accumulates nothing at all.'

Our education is the gathering of a volume of knowledge, and the computer does this faster and more accurately. What need is there for such an education? The machines are going to take over most of the activities of man. When you say, as people do, that learning is the gathering of a volume of knowledge then you are denying, aren't you, the movement of life, which is relationship and behaviour? If relationship and behaviour are based on previous experience and knowledge, then is there true relationship? Is memory, with all its associations, the true basis of relationship? Memory is images and words, and when you base your relationship on symbols, images and words, can it ever bring about true relationship?

As we said, life is a movement in relationship, and if that relationship is tethered to the past, to memory, its movement is limited and becomes agonizing.

'I understand very well what you say, and I ask again, from what do you act? Are you not contradicting yourself when you say that one learns in observing the whole structure of one's responses, and at the same time say that learning precludes accumulation?'

The seeing of the structure is alive, it is moving; but when that seeing adds to the structure then the structure becomes far more important than the seeing, which is the living. In this there is no contradiction. What we are saying is that the seeing is far more important than the nature of the structure. When you give importance to learning about the structure and not to learning as the seeing, then there *is* a contradiction; then seeing is one thing and learning about the structure is another.

You ask, sir, what is the source from which one acts? If there is a source of action then it is memory, knowledge, which is the past. We said the seeing *is* the acting; the two things are not separate. And the seeing is always new and so the acting is always new. Therefore the seeing of the everyday response brings out the new, which is what you call spontaneity. At the very moment of anger there is no recognition of it as anger. The recognition takes place a few seconds later as 'being angry'. Is this seeing of that anger a choiceless awareness of that anger, or is it again choice based on the old? If it is based on the old, then all the responses to that anger – repression, control, indulgence and so on – are the traditional activity. But when the seeing is choiceless, there is only the new.

From all this arises another interesting problem: our dependence on challenges to keep us awake, to pull us out of our routine, tradition, established order, either through bloodshed, revolt, or some other upheaval.

'Is it possible for the mind not to depend on challenges at all?'

It is possible when the mind is undergoing constant change and has no resting place, safe anchorage, vested interest or commitment. An awakened mind, a mind which is alight – what need has it of challenges of any kind?

XVI

MEDITATION is the action of silence. We act out of opinion, conclusion and knowledge, or out of speculative intentions. This inevitably results in contradiction in action between what is and what should be, or what has been. This action out of the past, called knowledge, is mechanical, capable of adjustment and modification but having its roots in the past. And so the shadow of the past always covers the present. Such action in relationship is the outcome of the image, the symbol, the conclusion; relationship then is a thing of the past, and so it is memory and not a living thing. Out of this chatter, disarray and contradiction, activities proceed, breaking up into patterns of culture, communities, social institutions and religious dogmas. From this endless noise, the revolution of a new social order is made to appear as though it really were something new, but as it is from the known to the known it is not a change at all. Change is possible only when denying the known; action then is not according to a pattern but out of an intelligence that is constantly renewing itself.

Intelligence is not discernment and judgement or critical evaluation. Intelligence is the seeing of what is. The what is is constantly changing, and when the seeing is anchored in the past, the intelligence of seeing ceases. Then the dead weight of memory dictates the action and not the intelligence of perception. Meditation is the seeing of all this at a glance. And to see, there must be silence, and from this silence there is action which is entirely different from the activities of thought.

It had been raining all day, and every leaf and every petal was dripping with water. The stream had swollen and the clear water had gone; now it was muddy and fast-running. Only the sparrows were active, and the crows – and the big black-and-white magpies. The mountains were hidden by the clouds, and the low-lying hills were barely visible. It hadn't rained for some days and the smell of fresh rain on dry earth was a delight. If you had been in tropical countries where it doesn't rain for months and every day there is a bright, hot sun which parches the earth, then, when the first rains come, you would smell the fresh rain falling on the old, bare earth, as a delight that enters into the very depths of your heart. But here in Europe there was a different kind of smell, more gentle, not so strong, not so penetrating. It was like a gentle breeze that soon passes away.

The next day there was a clear blue sky early in the morning; all the clouds were gone, and there was sparkling snow on those mountain peaks, fresh grass in the meadows and a thousand new flowers of the spring. It was a morning full of unutterable beauty; and love was on every blade of grass.

He was a well-known film director and, surprisingly, not at all vain. On the contrary he was very friendly, with a ready smile. He had made many successful pictures, and others were copying them. Like all the more sensitive directors he was concerned with the unconscious, with fantastic dreams, conflicts to be expressed in pictures. He had studied the gods of the analysts and had taken drugs himself for experimental purposes.

The human mind is heavily conditioned by the culture it lives in – by its traditions, by its economic condition, and especially by its religious propaganda. The mind strenuously objects to being a slave to a dictator or to the tyranny of the State, yet willingly submits to the tyranny of the Church or of the Mosque, or of the latest, most fashionable psychiatric dogmas. It cleverly invents – seeing so much helpless misery – a new Holy Ghost or a new Atman which soon becomes the image to be worshipped.

The mind, which has created such havoc in the world, is basically frightened of itself. It is aware of the materialistic outlook of science, its achievements, its increasing domination over the mind, and so it begins to put together a new philosophy; the philosophies of yesterday give place to new theories, but the basic problems of man remain unsolved.

Amidst all this turmoil of war, dissension and utter selfishness, there is the main issue of death. Religions, the very ancient or the recent, have conditioned man to certain dogmas, hopes and beliefs which give a ready-made answer to this issue; but death is not answerable by thought, by the intellect; it is a fact, and you cannot get round it.

You have to die to find what death is, and that, apparently, man cannot do, for he is frightened of dying to everything he knows, to his most intimate, deep-rooted hopes and visions.

There is really no tomorrow, but many tomorrows are between the now of life and the future of death. In this dividing gap man lives, with fear and anxiety, but always keeps an eye on that which is inevitable. He doesn't want even to talk about it, and decorates the grave with all the things he knows.

To die to everything one knows – not to particular forms of knowledge but to all knowing – is death. To invite the future – death – to cover the whole of today is the total dying; then there is no gap between life and death. Then death is living and living is death.

This, apparently, no man is willing to do. Yet man is always seeking the new; always holding in one hand the old and groping with the other into the unknown for the new. So there is the inevitable conflict of duality – the me and the not-me, the observer and the observed, the fact and the what should be.

This turmoil completely ceases when there is the ending of the known. This ending is death. Death is not an idea, a symbol, but a dreadful reality and you cannot possibly escape from it by clinging to the things of today, which are of yesterday, nor by worshipping the symbol of hope.

One has to die to death; only then is innocence born, only then does the timeless new come into being. Love is always new, and the remembrance of love is the death of love.

XVII

IT was a wide, luxuriant meadow with green hills round it. That morning it was brilliant, sparkling with dew, and the birds were singing to the heavens and to the earth. In this meadow with so many flowers, there was a single tree, majestic and alone. It was tall and shapely, and that morning it had a special meaning. It made a long, deep shadow, and between the tree and the shadow there was an extraordinary silence. They were communicating with each other – the reality and the unreality, the symbol and the fact. It was really a splendid tree with its late spring leaves all aflutter in the breeze, healthy, not worm-eaten yet; there was great majesty in it. It wasn't clothed in the robes of majesty but it was in itself splendid and imposing. With the evening it would withdraw into itself, silent and unconcerned, though there might be a gale blowing; and as the sun rose it would wake up too and give out its luxuriant blessing over the meadow, over the hills, over the earth.

The blue jays were calling and the squirrels were very active that morning. The beauty of the tree in its solitude gripped your heart. It wasn't the beauty of what you saw; its beauty lay in itself. Though your eyes had seen more lovely things, it was not the accustomed eye that saw this tree, alone, immense and full of wonder. It must have been very old but you never thought of it as being old. As you went and sat in its shadow, your back against the trunk, you felt the earth, the power in that tree, and its great aloofness. You could almost talk to it and it told you many things. But there was always that sense of its being far away although you touched it and felt its harsh bark which had many ants going up it. This morning its shadow was very sharp and clear and seemed to stretch beyond the hills to other hills. It was really a place of meditation if you know how to meditate. It was very quiet, and your mind, if it was sharp, clear, also became quiet, uninfluenced by the surroundings, a part of that brilliant morning, with the dew still on the grass and on the reeds. There would always be that beauty there, in the meadow with that tree.

He was a middle-aged man, well kept, trim and dressed with good taste. He said he had travelled a great deal though not on any particular business. His father had left him a little money and he had seen a bit of the world, not only what lay upon it but also all those rare things in the very rich museums. He said he liked music and played occasionally. He also seemed well-read. In the course of his conversation, he said: 'There's so much violence, anger, and hatred of man against man. We seem to have lost love, to have no beauty in our hearts; probably we have never had it. Love has been made into such a cheap commodity, and artificial beauty has become more important than the beauty of the hills, the trees and the flowers. The beauty of children soon fades. I have been wondering about love and beauty. Do let us talk about it if you can spare a little time.'

We were sitting on a bench by a stream. Behind us was a railway line and hills dotted with chalets and farmhouses.

Love and beauty cannot be separated. Without love there is no beauty; they are interlocked, inseparable. We have exercised our minds, our intellect, our cleverness, to such an extent, to such destructiveness, that they predominate, violating what may be called love. Of course, the word is not the real thing at all, any more than that shadow of the tree is the tree. We shan't be able to find out what that love is if we don't step down from our cleverness, our heights of intellectual sophistication, if we don't feel the brilliant water and are not aware of that new grass. Is it possible to find this love in museums, in the ornate beauty of church rituals, in the cinema, or in the face of a woman? Isn't it important for us to find out for ourselves how we have alienated ourselves from the very common things of life? Not that we should neurotically worship nature, but if we lose touch with nature doesn't it also mean that we are losing touch with man, with ourselves? We seek beauty and love outside ourselves, in people, in possessions. They become far more important than love itself. Possessions mean pleasure, and because we hold on to pleasure, love is banished. Beauty is in ourselves, not necessarily in the things about us. When the things about us become more important and we invest beauty in them, then the beauty in ourselves lessens. So more and more, as the world becomes more violent, materialistic, the museums and all those other possessions become the things with which we try to clothe our own nakedness and fill our emptiness.

'Why do you say that when we find beauty in people and in things around us, and when we experience pleasure, it lessens the beauty and the love within us?'

All dependence breeds in us possessiveness, and we become the thing which we possess. I possess this house – I *am* this house. That man on horse-back going by *is* the pride of his possession, though the beauty and dignity of the horse are more significant than the man. So the dependence on the beauty of a line, or on the loveliness of a face, surely must diminish the observer himself; which doesn't mean that we must put away the beauty of a line or the loveliness of a face; it means that when the things outside us become of great meaning, we are inwardly poverty-ridden.

'You are saying that if I respond to that lovely face I am inwardly poor. Yet, if I do not respond to that face or to the line of a building I am isolated and insensitive.'

When there is isolation there must, precisely, be dependence, and dependence breeds pleasure, therefore fear. If you don't respond at all, either there is paralysis, indifference, or a sense of despair which has come about through the hopelessness of continual gratification. So we are everlastingly caught in this trap of despair and hope, fear and pleasure, love and hate. When there is inward poverty there is the urge to fill it. This is the bottomless pit of the opposites, the opposites which fill our lives and create the battle of life. All these opposites are identical for they are branches of the same root. Love is not the product of dependence, and love has no opposite.

'Doesn't ugliness exist in the world? And isn't it the opposite of beauty?'

Of course there is ugliness in the world, as hate, violence, and so on. Why do you compare it to beauty, to non-violence? We compare it because we have a scale of values and we put what we call beauty at the top and ugliness at the bottom. Can you not look at violence non-comparatively? And if you do, what happens? You find you are dealing only with facts, not with opinions or with what should be, not with measurements. We can deal with what is and act immediately; what should be becomes an ideology and so is fanciful, and therefore useless. Beauty is not comparable, nor is love, and when you say: 'I love this one more than that one', then it ceases to be love.

'To return to what I was saying, being sensitive one responds readily and without complications to the lovely face, to the beautiful vase. This unthinking response slides imperceptibly into dependence and pleasure and all the complications you are describing. Dependence therefore seems to me inevitable.'

Is there anything inevitable – except, perhaps, death?

'If it is not inevitable, it means that I can order my conduct, which is therefore mechanical.'

The seeing of the inevitable process is to be *not* mechanical. It is the mind that refuses to see what is that becomes mechanical.

'If I see the inevitable, I still wonder where and how to draw the line?'

You don't draw the line, but the seeing brings its own action. When you say, 'Where am I to draw the line?' it is the interference of thought which is frightened of being caught and wants to be free. Seeing is not this process of thought; seeing is always new, and fresh, and active. Thinking is always old, never fresh. Seeing and thinking are of two different orders, and these two can never come together. So, love and beauty have no opposites and are not the outcome of inward poverty. Therefore love is at the beginning and not at the end.

XVIII

THE sound of the church bells came through the woods across the water and over the deep meadow. The sound was different according to whether it came through the woods or over the open meadows or across the fast-running, noisy stream. Sound, like light, has a quality that silence brings; the deeper the silence the more the beauty of the sound is heard. That evening, with the sun riding just above the western hills, the sound of those church bells was quite extraordinary. It was as though you heard the bells for the first time. They were not as old as in the ancient cathedrals but they carried the feeling of that evening. There wasn't a cloud in the sky. It was the longest day of the year, and the sun was setting as far north as it ever would.

We hardly ever listen to the sound of a dog's bark, or to the cry of a child or the laughter of a man as he passes by. We separate ourselves from everything, and then from this isolation look and listen to all things. It is this separation which is so destructive, for in that lies all conflict and confusion. If you listened to the sound of those bells with complete silence you would be riding on it – or, rather, the sound would carry you across the valley and over the hill. The beauty of it is felt only when you and the sound are not separate, when you are part of it. Meditation is the ending of the separation, not by any action of will or desire, or by seeking the pleasure of things not already tasted.

Meditation is not a separate thing from life; it is the very essence of life, the very essence of daily living. To listen to those bells, to hear the laughter of that peasant as he walks by with his wife, to listen to the sound of the bell on the bicycle of the little girl as she passes by: it is the whole of life, and not just a fragment of it, that meditation opens.

'What, to you, is God? In the modern world, among the students, the workers and the politicians, God is dead. For the priests, it is a convenient word to enable them to hang on to their jobs, their vested interests, both physical and spiritual, and for the average man – I don't think it bothers him very much, except occasionally when there is some kind of calamity or when he wants to appear respectable among his respectable neighbours. Otherwise it has very little meaning. So I've made the rather long journey here to find out from you what you believe, or, if you don't like that word, to find out if God exists in your life. I've been to India and visited various teachers in their places there, with their disciples, and they all believe, or more or less maintain, that there *is* God, and point out the way to him. I would like, if I may, to talk over with you this rather important question which has haunted man for many thousands of years.'

Belief is one thing, reality another. One leads to bondage and the other is possible only in freedom. The two have no relationship. Belief cannot be abandoned or set aside in order to get that freedom. Freedom is not a reward, it is not the carrot in front of the donkey. It is important from the beginning to understand this – the contradiction between belief and reality.

Belief can never lead to reality. Belief is the result of conditioning, or the outcome of fear, or the result of an outer or inner authority which gives comfort. Reality is none of these. It is something wholly different, and there is no passage from this to that. The theologian starts from a fixed position. He believes in God, in a Saviour, or in Krishna or in Christ, and then spins theories according to his conditioning and the cleverness of his mind. He is, like the Communist theoretician, tied to a concept, a formula, and what he spins is the outcome of his own deliberations.

The unwary are caught in this, as the unwary fly is caught in the web of the spider. Belief is born out of fear or tradition. Two thousand or ten thousand years of propaganda is the religious structure of words, with the rituals, dogmas and beliefs. The word, then, becomes extremely important, and the repetition of that word mesmerizes the credulous. The credulous are always willing to believe, accept, obey, whether what is offered is good or bad, mischievous or beneficial. The believing mind is not an inquiring mind, and so it remains within the limits of the formula or the principle. It is like an animal who, tied to a post, can wander only within the limits of the rope.

'But without belief we have nothing! I believe in goodness; I believe in holy matrimony; I believe in the hereafter and in evolutionary growth towards perfection. To me these beliefs are immensely important for they keep me in line, in morality; if you take away belief I am lost.'

Being good, and becoming good, are two different things. The flowering of goodness is not becoming good. Becoming good is the denial of goodness. Becoming better is a denial of what is; the better corrupts the what is. Being good is now, in the present; becoming good is in the future, which is the invention of the mind that is caught in belief, in a formula of comparison and time. When there is measurement, the good ceases.

What is important is not *what* you believe, what your formulas, principles, dogmas and opinions are, but why you have them at all, why your mind is burdened with them. Are they essential? If you put that question to yourself seriously you will find that they are the result of fear, or of the habit of accepting. It is this basic fear which prevents you being involved in what actually *is*. It is this fear that makes for commitment. Being involved is natural; you are involved in life, in your activities; you are *in* life, in the whole movement of it. But to be committed is a deliberate action of a mind that functions and thinks in fragments; one is committed only to a fragment. You cannot deliberately commit yourself to what you consider the whole because this consideration is part of a process of thought, and thought is always separative, it always functions in fragments.

'Yes, you cannot be committed without naming that to which you are committed, and naming is limiting.'

Is that statement of yours merely a series of words or an actuality which you have now realized? If it is merely a series of words then it is a belief and therefore has no value at all. If it is an actual truth that you have now discovered, then you are free and in negation. The negation of the false is not a statement. All propaganda is false, and man has lived on propaganda ranging from soap to God.

'You are forcing me into a corner by your perception, and isn't this also a form of propaganda – to propagate what *you* see?'

Surely not. You are forcing *yourself* into a corner where you have to face things as they are, unpersuaded, uninfluenced. You are beginning to realize for yourself what is actually in front of you, therefore you are free of another, free of all authority – of the word, of the person, of the idea. To *see*, belief is not necessary. On the contrary, to see, the absence of belief is necessary. You can see only when there is a negative state, not the positive state of a belief. Seeing is a negative state in which the 'what is' is alone evident. Belief is a formula of inaction which breeds hypocrisy, and it is this hypocrisy against which all the younger generation are fighting and revolting. But the younger generation get caught in that hypocrisy later on in life. Belief is a danger which must be totally avoided if one is to see the truth of what is. The politician, the priest, the respectable, will always function according to a formula, forcing others to live according to that formula, and the thoughtless, the foolish, are always blinded by their words, their promises, their hopes. The authority of the formula becomes far more important than the love of what is. Therefore authority is evil, whether it be the authority of belief, or of tradition, or of the custom which is called morality.

'Can I be free of this fear?'

Surely you're putting a wrong question, aren't you? You *are* the fear; you and the fear are not two separate things. The separation is fear which breeds the formula that 'I will conquer it, suppress it, escape from it'. This is the tradition which gives a false hope of overcoming fear. When you see that you *are* the fear, that you and fear are not two separate things, fear disappears. Then formulas and beliefs are not necessary at all. Then you live only with what is, and see the truth of it.

'But you've not answered the question about God, have you?'

Go to any place of worship – is God there? In the stone, in the word, in the ritual, in the stimulated feeling of seeing something beautifully done? Religions have divided God as yours and mine, the Gods of the East and the Gods of the West, and each God has killed the other God. Where is God to be found? Under a leaf, in the skies, in your heart, or, is it merely a word, a symbol, representing something that cannot be put into words? Obviously you must put aside the symbol, the place of worship, the web of words that man has woven around himself. Only after having done this, not before, can you begin to inquire if there is or is not a reality which is immeasurable.

'But when you have discarded all this you are completely lost, empty, alone – and in this state how can you inquire?'

You are in this state because you are pitying yourself, and self-pity is an abomination. You are in this state because you have not seen, actually, that the false *is* the false. When you see it, it gives you tremendous energy and freedom to see the truth as the truth, not as an illusion or a fancy of the mind. It is this freedom that is necessary from which to see if there is or is not something which cannot be put into words. But it is not an experience, a personal achievement. All experiences, in this sense, bring about a separative, contradictory existence. It is this separative existence as the thinker, the observer, that demands further and wider experiences, and what he demands he will have – but it is not the truth.

Truth is not yours or mine. What is yours can be organized, enshrined, exploited. That is what is happening in the world. But truth cannot be organized. Like beauty and love, truth is not in the realm of possessions.

XIX

IF you walk through the little town with its one street of many shops – the baker, the camera shop, the bookshop and the open restaurant – under the bridge, past the couturier, over another bridge, past the sawmill, then enter the wood and continue along by the stream, looking at all the things you have passed, with your eyes and all your senses fully awake, but without a single thought in your mind – then you will know what it means to be without separation. You follow that stream for a mile or two – again without a single flutter of thought – looking at the rushing water, listening to its noise, seeing the colour of it, the grey-green mountain stream, looking at the trees and the blue sky through the branches, and at the green leaves – again without a single thought, without a single word – then you will know what it means to have no space between you and the blade of grass.

If you pass on through the meadows with their thousand flowers of every colour imaginable, from bright red to yellow and purple, and their bright green grass washed clean by last night's rain, rich and verdant – again without a single move-ment of the machinery of thought – then you will know what love is. To look at the blue sky, the high full-blown clouds, the green hills with their clear lines against the sky, the rich grass and the fading flower – to look without a word of yesterday; then, when the mind is completely quiet, silent, undisturbed by any thought, when the observer is completely absent – then there is unity. Not that you are united with the flower, or with the cloud, or with those sweeping hills; rather there is a feeling of complete non-being in which the division between you and another ceases. The woman carry-ing those provisions which she bought in the market, the big black Alsatian dog, the two children playing with the ball – if you can look at all these without a word, without a measure, without any association, then the quarrel between you and another ceases. This state, without the word, without thought, is the expanse of mind that has no boundaries, no frontiers within which the I and the not-I can exist. Don't think this is imagination, or some flight of fancy, or some desired mystical experience; it is not. It is as actual as the bee on that flower or the little girl on her bicycle or the man going up the ladder to paint the house – the whole conflict of the mind in its separation has come to an end. You look without the look of the observer, you look without the value of the word and the measurement of yesterday. The look of love is different from the look of thought. The one leads in a direction where thought cannot follow, and the other leads to separation, conflict and sorrow. From this sorrow you cannot go to the other. The distance between the two is made by thought, and thought cannot by any stride reach the other.

As you walk back by the little farmhouses, the meadows and the railway line, you will see that yesterday has come to an end: life begins where thought ends.

'Why is it I cannot be honest?' she asked. 'Naturally, I am dishonest. Not that I want to be, but it slips out of me. I say things I don't really mean. I'm not talking about polite conversation about nothing – then one knows that one is talking just for the sake of talking. But even when I'm serious I find myself saying things, doing things, that are absurdly dishonest. I've noticed it with my husband too. He says one thing and does something entirely different. He promises, but you know so well that while he is saying it he doesn't quite mean it; and when you point it out to him he gets irritated, sometimes very angry. We both know we are dishonest in so many things. The other day he made a promise to somebody whom he rather respected, and that man went away believing my husband. But my husband didn't keep his word and he found excuses to prove that he was right and the other man wrong. You know the game we play with

ourselves and with others – it is part of our social structure
and relationship. Sometimes it reaches the point where it
becomes very ugly and deeply disturbing – and I have come
to that state. I am greatly disturbed, not only about my husband but about myself and all those people who say one
thing and do something else and think something else again.
The politician makes promises and one knows exactly what
his promises mean. He promises heaven on earth and you
know very well he's going to create hell on earth – and he
will blame it all on factors beyond his control. Why is it that
one is so basically dishonest?'

What does honesty mean? Can there be honesty – that is,
clear insight, seeing things as they are – if there is a principle, an ideal, an ennobled formula? Can one be direct if
there is confusion? Can there be beauty if there is the standard of what is beautiful or upright? When there is this
division between what is and what should be, can there be
honesty – or only an edifying and respectable dishonesty?
We are brought up between the two – between what actually
is and what may be. In the interval between these two – the
interval of time and space – is all our education, our morality, our struggle. We keep a distracted look upon the one
and upon the other, a look of fear and a look of hope. And
can there be honesty, sincerity, in this state, which society
calls education? When we say we are dishonest, essentially
we mean there is a comparison between what we have said
and what is. One has said something which one doesn't
mean, perhaps to give passing assurance or because one is
nervous, shy or ashamed to say something which actually *is*.
So nervous apprehension and fear make us dishonest. When
we are pursuing success we must be somewhat dishonest,
play up to another, be cunning, deceitful, to achieve our end.
Or one has gained authority or a position which one wants to
defend. So all resistance, all defence, is a form of dishonesty.
To be honest means to have no illusions about oneself and
no seed of illusion – which is desire and pleasure.

'You mean to say that desire breeds illusion! I desire a nice house – there isn't any illusion in that. I desire my husband to have a better position – I can't see illusion in that either!'

In desire there is always the better, the bigger, the more. In desire there is the measurement, the comparison – and the root of illusion is comparison. The good is not the better, and all our life is spent pursuing the better – whether it be the better bathroom, or the better position, or the better god. Discontent with what is makes the change in what is – which is merely the improved continuity of what is. Improvement is not change, and it is this constant improvement – both in ourselves and in the social morality – which breeds dishonesty.

'I don't know if I follow you, and I don't know if I want to follow you,' she said with a smile. 'I understand verbally what you say, but where are you leading? I find it rather frightening. If I lived, actually, what you are saying, probably my husband would lose his job, for in the business world there is a great deal of dishonesty. Our children, too, are brought up to compete, to fight to survive. And when I realize, from what you are saying, that we are training them to be dishonest – not obviously, of course, but in subtle and devious ways – then I get frightened for them. How can they face the world, which is so dishonest and brutal, unless they themselves have some of this dishonesty and brutality? Oh, I know I'm saying dreadful things, but there it is! I'm beginning to see how utterly dishonest I am!'

To live without a principle, without an ideal, is to live facing that which is every minute. The actual facing of what is – which is to be completely in contact with it, not through the word or through past associations and memories, but directly in touch with it – is to be honest. To know you have lied and make no excuse for it but to see the actual fact of it, *is* honesty; and in this honesty there is great beauty. The beauty does not hurt anybody. To say one is a liar is an acknowledgement of the fact; it is to acknowledge a mistake as a mistake. But to find reasons, excuses and justifications for it is dishonesty, and in this there is self-pity. Self-pity is the darkness of dishonesty. It does not mean that one must become ruthless with oneself, but rather, one is attentive. To be attentive means to care, to look.

'I certainly did not expect all this when I came. I felt rather ashamed of my dishonesty and didn't know what to do about it. The incapacity to do anything about it made me feel guilty, and fighting guilt or resisting it brings in other problems. Now I must carefully think over everything you have said.'

If I may make a suggestion, don't think it over. See it now as it is. From that seeing something new will happen. But if you think it over you are back again in the same old trap.

XX

IN the animal, the instincts to follow and to obey are natural and necessary for survival, but in man they become a danger. To follow and obey, in the individual, becomes imitation, conformity to a pattern of society which he himself has built. Without freedom, intelligence cannot function. To understand the nature of obedience and acceptance in action brings freedom. Freedom is not the instinct to do what one wants. In a vast complex society that isn't possible; hence the conflict between the individual and society, between the many and the one.

It had been very hot for days; the heat was stifling and at this altitude the sun's rays penetrated every pore of your body and made you rather dizzy. The snow was melting rapidly and the stream became more and more brown. The big waterfall cascaded in torrents. It came from a large glacier, perhaps more than a kilometre long. This stream would never be dry.

That evening the weather broke. The clouds were piling

up against the mountains and there were crashes of thunder, and lightning, and it began to rain; you could smell the rain.

There were three or four of them in that little room overlooking the river. They had come from different parts of the world and they seemed to have a common question. The question was not so important as their own state. Their own state of mind conveyed much more than the question. The question was like a door which opened into a house of many rooms. They were not a very healthy lot, and unhappy in their own way. They were educated – whatever that may mean; they spoke several languages, and appeared ill-kempt.

'Why should one not take drugs? You apparently seem to be against it. Your own prominent friends have taken them, have written books about them, encouraged others to take them, and they have experienced with great intensity the beauty of a simple flower. We, too, have taken them and we would like to know why you seem to be opposed to these chemical experiences. After all, our whole physical organism is a bio-chemical process, and adding to it an extra chemical may give us an experience which may be an approximation to the real. You yourself have not taken drugs, have you? So how can you, without experimenting, condemn them?'

No, we have not taken drugs. Must one get drunk to know what sobriety is? Must one make oneself ill to find out what health is? As there are several things involved in taking drugs, let us go into the whole question with care. What is the necessity of taking drugs at all – drugs that promise a psychedelic expansion of the mind, great visions and intensity? Apparently one takes them because one's own perceptions are dull. Clarity is dimmed and one's life is rather shallow, mediocre and meaningless; one takes them to go beyond this mediocrity.

The intellectuals have made of the drugs a new way of life. One sees throughout the world the discord, the neurotic compulsions, the conflicts, the aching misery of life. One is aware of the aggressiveness of man, his brutality, his utter selfishness, which no religion, no law, no social morality has been able to tame.

There is so much anarchy in man – and such scientific capacities. This imbalance brings about havoc in the world. The unbridgable gap between advanced technology and the cruelty of man is producing great chaos and misery. This is obvious. So the intellectual, who has played with various theories – Vedanta, Zen, Communist ideals, and so on – having found no way out of man's predicament, is now turning to the golden drug that will bring about dynamic sanity and harmony. The discovery of this golden drug – the complete answer to everything – is expected of the scientist and probably he will produce it. And the authors and the intellectuals will advocate it to stop all wars, as yesterday they advocated Communism or Fascism.

But the mind, with its extraordinary capacities for scientific discoveries and their implementation, is still petty, narrow and bigoted, and will surely continue, will it not, in its pettiness? You may have a tremendous and explosive experience through one of these drugs, but will the deep-rooted aggression, bestiality and sorrow of man disappear? If these drugs can solve the intricate and complex problems of relationship, then there is nothing more to be said, for then relationship, the demand for truth, the ending of sorrow, are all a very superficial affair to be resolved by taking a pinch of the new golden drug.

Surely this is a false approach, isn't it? It is said that these drugs give an experience approximating to reality, therefore they give hope and encouragement. But the shadow is not the real; the symbol is never the fact. As is observed throughout the world, the symbol is worshipped and not the truth. So isn't it a phoney assertion to say that the result of these drugs is near the truth?

No dynamic golden pill is ever going to solve our human problems. They can be solved only by bringing about a radical revolution in the mind and the heart of man. This demands hard, constant work, seeing and listening, and thus being highly sensitive.

The highest form of sensitivity is the highest intelligence, and no drug ever invented by man will give this intelligence. Without this intelligence there is no love; and love is relationship. Without this love there is no dynamic balance in man. This love cannot be given – by the priests or their gods, by the philosophers, or by the golden drug.

PART TWO

The Urgency of Change

AWARENESS

Questioner: I should like to know what you mean by aware-
ness because you have often said that awareness is really
what your teaching is about. I've tried to understand it by
listening to your talks and reading your books, but I don't
seem to get very far. I know it is not a practice, and I under-
stand why you so emphatically repudiate any kind of prac-
tice, drill, system, discipline or routine. I see the importance
of that, for otherwise it becomes mechanical, and at the end
of it the mind has become dull and stupid. I should like, if I
may, to explore with you to the very end this question of
what it means to be aware. You seem to give some extra,
deeper meaning to this word, and yet it seems to me that we
are aware of what's going on all the time. When I'm angry I
know it, when I'm sad I know it and when I'm happy I know
it.

KRISHNAMURTI: I wonder if we really are aware of anger,
sadness, happiness? Or are we aware of these things only
when they are all over? Let us begin as though we know
nothing about it at all and start from scratch. Let us not
make any assertions, dogmatic or subtle, but let us explore
this question which, if one really went into it very deeply,
would reveal an extraordinary state that the mind had probably never touched, a dimension not touched by superficial
awareness. Let us start from the superficial and work
through.

We see with our eyes, we perceive with our senses the
things about us – the colour of the flower, the humming bird
over the flower, the light of this Californian sun, the thousand sounds of different qualities and subtleties, the depth
and the height, the shadow of the tree and the tree itself. We
feel in the same way our own bodies, which are the instru-

ments of these different kinds of superficial, sensory perceptions. If these perceptions remained at the superficial level there would be no confusion at all. That flower, that pansy, that rose, are there, and that's all there is to it. There is no preference, no comparison, no like and dislike, only the thing before us without any psychological involvement. Is all this superficial sensory perception or awareness quite clear? It can be expanded to the stars, to the depth of the seas, and to the ultimate frontiers of scientific observation, using all the instruments of modern technology.

Questioner: Yes, I think I understand that.

KRISHNAMURTI: So you see that the rose and all the universe and the people in it, your own wife if you have one, the stars, the seas, the mountains, the microbes, the atoms, the neutrons, this room, the door, really are there. Now, the next step; what you think about these things, or what you feel about them, is your psychological response to them. And this we call thought or emotion. So the superficial awareness is a very simple matter: the door is there. But the description of the door is not the door, and when you get emotionally involved in the description you don't see the door. This description might be a word or a scientific treatise or a strong emotional response; none of these is the door itself. This is very important to understand right from the beginning. If we don't understand this we shall get more and more confused. The description is never the described. Though we are describing something even now, and we have to, the thing we are describing is not our description of it. So please bear this in mind right through our talk. Never confuse the word with the thing it describes. The word is never the real, and we are easily carried away when we come to the next stage of awareness where it becomes personal and we get emotional through the word.

So there is the superficial awareness of the tree, the bird, the door, and there is the response to that, which is thought, feeling, emotion. Now when we become aware of this response, we might call it a second depth of awareness. There is the awareness of the rose, and the awareness of the response to the rose. Often we are unaware of this response to the rose. In reality it is the same awareness which sees the rose and which sees the response. It is one movement and it is wrong to speak of the outer and inner awareness. When there is a visual awareness of the tree without any psychological involvement there is no division in relationship. But when there is a psychological response to the tree, this response is a conditioned response, it is the response of past memory, past experiences, and this response is a division in relationship. This response is the birth of what we shall call the 'me' in relationship and the 'non-me'. This is how you place yourself in relationship to the world. This is how you create the individual and the community. The world is seen not as it is, but in its various relationships to the 'me' of memory. This division is the life and the flourishing of everything we call our psychological being, and from this arises all contradiction and division. Are you very clear that you perceive this? When there is the awareness of the tree there is no evaluation. But when there is a response to the tree, when the tree is judged with like and dislike, then a division takes place in this awareness as the 'me' and the 'non-me', the 'me' who is different from the thing observed. This 'me' is the response, in relationship, of past memory, past experiences. Now can there be an awareness, an observation of the tree, without any judgement, and can there be an observation of the response, the reactions, without any judgement? In this way we eradicate the principle of division, the principle of 'me' and 'non-me', both in looking at the tree and in looking at ourselves.

Questioner: I'm trying to follow you. Let's see if I have got it right. There is an awareness of the tree, that I understand. There is a psychological response to the tree, that I understand also. The psychological response is made up of past memories and past experiences, it is like and dislike, it is the division into the tree and the 'me'. Yes, I think I understand all that.

KRISHNAMURTI: Is this as clear as the tree itself, or is it simply the clarity of description? Remember, as we have already said, the described is not the description. What have you got, the thing or its description?

Questioner: I think it is the thing.

KRISHNAMURTI: Therefore there is no 'me' who is the description in the seeing of this fact. In the seeing of any fact there is no 'me'. There is either the 'me' of the seeing; there can't be both. 'Me' is non-seeing. The 'me' cannot see, cannot be aware.

Questioner: May I stop here? I think I've got the feeling of it, but I must let it sink in. May I come again tomorrow?

*

Questioner: I think I have really understood, non-verbally, what you said yesterday. There is the awareness of the tree, there is the conditioned response to the tree, and this conditioned response is conflict, it is the action of memory and past experiences, it is like and dislike, it is prejudice. I also understand that this response of prejudice is the birth of what we call the 'me' or the censor. I see clearly that the 'me', the 'I', exists in all relationships. Now is there an 'I' outside of relationships?

KRISHNAMURTI: We have seen how heavily conditioned our responses are. When you ask if there is a 'me' outside of relationship, it becomes a speculative question as long as there is no freedom from these conditioned responses. Do you see that? So our first question is not whether there is a 'me' or not outside of conditioned responses, but rather, can the mind, in which is included all our feelings, be free of this conditioning, which is the past? The past is the 'me'. There is no 'me' in the present. As long as the mind is operating in the past there is the 'me'. and the mind *is* this past, the mind *is* this 'me'.

You can't say there is the mind and there is the past, whether it is the past of a few days ago or of ten thousand years ago. So we are asking: can the mind free itself from yesterday? Now there are several things involved, aren't there? First of all there is a superficial awareness. Then there is the awareness of the conditioned response. Then there is the realization that the mind is the past, the mind *is* this conditioned response. Then there is the question whether this mind can free itself of the past. And all this is one unitary action of awareness, because in this there are no conclusions. When we say the mind is the past, this realization is not a verbal conclusion but an actual perception of fact. The French have a word for such a perception of a fact, they call it 'constatation'. When we ask whether the mind can be free of the past is this question being asked by the censor, the 'me', who is that very past?

Questioner: Can the mind be free of the past?

KRISHNAMURTI: Who is putting that question? Is it the entity who is the result of a great many conflicts, memories and experiences – is it he who is asking – or does this question arise of itself, out of the perception of the fact? If it is the observer who is putting the question, then he is trying to escape from the fact of himself, because, he says, I have lived so long in pain, in trouble, in sorrow, I should like to go beyond this constant struggle. If he asks the question from that motive his answer will be a taking refuge in some escape. One either turns away from a fact or one faces it. And the word and the symbol are a turning away from it. In fact, just to ask this question at all is already an act of escape, is it not? Let us be aware whether this question is or is not an act of escape. If it is, it is noise. If there is no observer, then there is silence, a complete negation of the whole past.

Questioner: Here I am lost. How can I wipe away the past in few seconds?

KRISHNAMURTI: Let us bear in mind that we are discussing awareness. We are talking over together this question of awareness.

There is the tree, and the conditioned response to the tree, which is the 'me' in relationship, the 'me' who is the very centre of conflict. Now is it this 'me' who is asking the question? – this 'me' who, as we have said, is the very structure of the past? If the question is not asked from the structure of the past, if the question is not asked by the 'me', then there *is* no structure of the past. When the structure is asking the question it is operating in relationship to the fact of itself, it is frightened of itself and it acts to escape from itself. When this structure does not ask the question, it is not acting in relationship to itself. To recapitulate: there is the tree, there is the word, the response to the tree, which is the censor, or the 'me', which comes from the past; and then there is the question: can I escape from all this turmoil and agony? If the 'me' is asking this question it is perpetuating itself.

Now, being aware of that, it doesn't ask the question! Being aware and seeing all the implications of it, the question cannot be asked. It does not ask the question at all because it sees the trap. Now do you see that all this awareness is superficial? It is the same as the awareness which sees the tree.

Questioner: Is there any other kind of awareness? Is there any other dimension to awareness?

KRISHNAMURTI: Again let's be careful, let's be very clear that we are not asking this question with any motive. If there is a motive we are back in the trap of conditioned response. When the observer is wholly silent, not made silent, there is surely a different quality of awareness coming into being?

Questioner: What action could there possibly be in any cir-cumstances without the observer – what question or what action?

KRISHNAMURTI: Again, are you asking this question from this side of the river, or is it from the other bank? If you are on the other bank, you will not ask this question; if you are on that bank, your action will be from that bank. So there is an awareness of this bank, with all its structure, its nature and all its traps, and to try to escape from the trap is to fall into another trap. And what deadly monotony there is in all that! Awareness has shown us the nature of the trap, and therefore there is the negation of all traps; so the mind is now empty. It is empty of the 'me' and of the trap. This mind has a different quality, a different dimension of aware-ness. This awareness is not aware that it is aware.

Questioner: My God, this is too difficult. You are saying things that seem true, that sound true, but I'm not there yet. Can you put it differently? Can you push me out of my trap?

KRISHNAMURTI: Nobody can push you out of your trap – no guru, no drug, no mantra, nobody, including myself – nobody, especially myself. All that you have to do is to be aware from the beginning to the end, not become inattentive in the middle of it. This new quality of awareness is atten-tion, and in this attention there is no frontier made by the 'me'. This attention is the highest form of virtue, therefore it is love. It is supreme intelligence, and there cannot be atten-tion if you are not sensitive to the structure and the nature of these man-made traps.

IS THERE A GOD?

Questioner: I really would like to know if there is a god. If there isn't, life has no meaning. Not knowing god, man has invented him in a thousand beliefs and images. The division and the fear bred by all these beliefs have divided him from his fellow men. To escape the pain and the mischief of this division he creates yet more beliefs, and the mounting misery and confusion have engulfed him. Not knowing, we believe. Can I know God? I've asked this question of many saints both in India and here and they've all emphasized belief. 'Believe and then you will know; without belief you can never know.' What do you think?

KRISHNAMURTI: Is belief necessary to find out? To learn is far more important than to know. Learning about belief is the end of belief. When the mind is free of belief then it can look. It is belief, or disbelief, that binds; for disbelief and belief are the same: they are the opposite sides of the same coin. So we can completely put aside positive or negative belief; the believer and the non-believer are the same. When this actually takes place then the question, 'Is there a god?' has quite a different meaning. The word god with all its tradition, its memory, its intellectual and sentimental connotations – all this is not god. The word is not the real. So can the mind be free of the word?

Questioner: I don't know what that means.

KRISHNAMURTI: The word is the tradition, the hope, the desire to find the absolute, the striving after the ultimate, the movement which gives vitality to existence. So the word itself becomes the ultimate, yet we can see that the word is not the thing. The mind is the word, and the word is thought.

Questioner: And you're asking me to strip myself of the word? How can I do that? The word is the past; it is memory. The wife is the word, and the house is the word. In the beginning was the word. Also the word is the means of communication, identification. Your name is not you, and yet without your name I can't ask about you. And you're asking me if the mind can be free of the word – that is, can the mind be free of its own activity?

KRISHNAMURTI: In the case of the tree the object is before our eyes, and the word refers to the tree by universal agreement. Now with the word god there is nothing to which it refers, so each man can create his own image of that for which there is no reference. The theologian does it in one way, the intellectual in another, and the believer and the non-believer in their own different ways. Hope generates this belief, and then seeking. This hope is the outcome of despair – the despair of all we see around us in the world. From despair hope is born; they also are two sides of the same coin. When there is no hope there is hell, and this fear of hell gives us the vitality of hope. Then illusion begins. So the word has led us to illusion and not to god at all. God is the illusion which we worship; and the non-believer creates the illusion of another god which he worships – the State, or some utopia, or some book which he thinks contains all truth. So we are asking you whether you can be free of the word with its illusion.

Questioner: I must meditate on this.

KRISHNAMURTI: If there is no illusion, what is left?

Questioner: Only what is.

KRISHNAMURTI: That 'what is' is the most holy.

Questioner: If the 'what is' is the most holy then war is most holy, and hatred, disorder, pain, avarice and plunder. Then we must not speak of any change at all. If 'what is' is sacred, then every murderer and plunderer and exploiter can say, 'Don't touch me, what I'm doing is sacred.'

KRISHNAMURTI: The very simplicity of that statement, '"what is" is the most sacred', leads to great misunderstanding, because we don't see the truth of it. If you see that what *is* is sacred, you do not murder, you do not make war, you do not hope, you do not exploit. Having done these things you cannot claim immunity from a truth which you have violated. The white man who says to the black rioter, 'What is is sacred, do not interfere, do not burn', has not seen, for if he had, the Negro would be sacred to him, and there would be no need to burn. So if each one of us sees this truth there must be change. This seeing of the truth is change.

Questioner: I came here to find out if there is god, and you have completely confused me.

KRISHNAMURTI: You came to ask if there is god. We said: the word leads to illusion which we worship, and for this illusion we destroy each other willingly. When there is no illusion the 'what is' is most sacred. Now let's look at what actually is. At a given moment the 'what is' may be fear, or utter despair, or a fleeting joy. These things are constantly changing. And also there is the observer who says, 'These things all change around me, but I remain permanent.' Is that a fact, is that what really is? Is he not also changing, adding to and taking away from himself, modifying, adjusting himself, becoming or not becoming? So both the observer and the observed are constantly changing. *What is* is change. That is a fact. That *is* what is.

Questioner: Then is love changeable? If everything is a movement of change, isn't love also part of that movement? And if love is changeable, then I can love one woman today and sleep with another tomorrow.

172

KRISHNAMURTI: Is that love? Or are you saying that love is different from its expression? Or are you giving to expression greater importance than to love, and therefore making a contradiction and a conflict. Can love ever be caught in the wheel of change? If so then it can also be hate; then love is hate. It is only when there is no illusion that 'what is' is most sacred. When there is no illusion 'what is' is god or any other name that can be used. So god, or whatever name you give it, is when *you* are not. When you are, it is not. When you are not, love is. When you are, love is not.

FEAR

Questioner: I used to take drugs but now I am free of them. Why am I so frightened of everything? I wake up in the mornings paralyzed with fear. I can hardly move out of bed. I'm frightened of going outside, and I'm frightened of being inside. Suddenly as I drive along this fear comes upon me, and I spend a whole day sweating, nervous, apprehensive, and at the end of the day I'm completely exhausted. Sometimes, though very rarely, in the company of a few intimate friends or at the house of my parents, I lose this fear; I feel quiet, happy, completely relaxed. As I came along in my car today, I was frightened of coming to see you, but as I came up the drive and walked to the door I suddenly lost this fear, and now as I sit here in this nice quiet room I feel so happy that I wonder what I was ever frightened about. Now I have no fear. I can smile and truthfully say: I'm very glad to see you! But I can't stay here for ever, and I know that when I leave here the cloud of fear will engulf me again. That is what I'm faced with. I've been to ever so many psychiatrists and analysts, here and abroad, but they merely delve into my memories of childhood – and I'm fed up with it because the fear hasn't gone at all.

KRISHNAMURTI: Let's forget childhood memories and all that nonsense, and come to the present. Here you are, and you say you are not frightened now; you're happy for the moment and can hardly imagine the fear you were in. Why have you no fear now? Is it the quiet, clear, well-proportioned room, furnished with good taste, and this sense of welcoming warmth which you feel? Is that why you are not frightened now?

Questioner: That's part of it. Also perhaps it is you. I heard

174

you talk in Switzerland, and I've heard you here, and I feel a kind of deep friendship for you. But I don't want to depend on nice houses, welcoming atmospheres and good friends in order not to be afraid. When I go to my parents I have this same feeling of warmth. But it is deadly at home; all families are deadly with their little enclosed activities, their quarrels, and the vulgarity of all that loud talk about nothing, and their hypocrisy. I'm fed up with it all. And yet, when I go to them and there is this certain warmth, I do feel, for a while, free of this fear. The psychiatrists can't tell me what my fear is about. They call it a 'floating fear'. It's a black, bottomless, ghastly pit. I've spent a great deal of money and time on being analysed and it really hasn't helped at all. So what am I to do?

KRISHNAMURTI: Is it that being sensitive you need a certain shelter, a certain security, and not being able to find it, you are frightened of the ugly world? Are you sensitive?

Questioner: Yes, I think so. Perhaps not in the way you mean, but I am sensitive. I don't like the noise, the bustle, the vulgarity of this modern existence and the way they throw sex at you everywhere you go today, and the whole business of fighting your way to some beastly little position. I am really frightened of all this – not that I can't fight and get a position for myself, but it makes me sick with fear.

KRISHNAMURTI: Most people who are sensitive need a quiet shelter and a warm friendly atmosphere. Either they create it for themselves or depend on others who can give it to them – the family, the wife, the husband, the friend. Have you got such a friend?

Questioner: No. I'm frightened of having such a friend. I'm frightened of being dependent on him.

KRISHNAMURTI: So there is this issue; being sensitive, demanding a certain shelter, and depending on others to give you that shelter. There is sensitivity, and dependence; the two often go together. And to depend on another is to fear losing him. So you depend more and more, and then the fear increases in proportion to your dependence. It is a vicious circle. Have you inquired why you depend? We depend on the postman, on physical comfort and so on; that's quite simple. We depend on people and things for our physical well-being and survival; it is quite natural and normal. We have to depend on what we may call the organizational side of society. But we also depend psychologically, and this dependence, though comforting, breeds fear. Why do we depend psychologically?

Questioner: You're talking to me about dependence now, but I came here to discuss fear.

KRISHNAMURTI: Let's examine them both because they are inter-related as we shall see. Do you mind if we discuss them both? We were talking about dependence. What is dependence? Why does one psychologically depend on another? Isn't dependence the denial of freedom? Take away the house, the husband, the children, the possessions – what is a man if all these are removed? In himself he is insufficient, empty, lost. So out of this emptiness, of which he is afraid, he depends on property, on people and beliefs. You may be so sure of all the things you depend on that you can't imagine ever losing them – the love of your family, and the comfort. Yet fear continues. So we must be clear that any form of psychological dependence must inevitably breed fear, though the things you depend on may seem almost indestructible. Fear arises out of this inner insufficiency, poverty and emptiness. So now, do you see, we have three issues – sensitivity, dependence and fear? The three are inter-related. Take sensitivity: the more sensitive you are (unless you understand how to remain sensitive without dependence, how to be vulnerable without agony), the more you depend. Then take dependence: the more you depend, the more there is disgust and the demand to be free. This demand for freedom encourages fear, for this demand is a reaction, not freedom from dependence.

Questioner: Are you dependent on anything?

KRISHNAMURTI: Of course I'm dependent physically on food, clothes and shelter, but psychologically, inwardly, I'm not dependent on anything – not on gods, not on social morality, not on belief, not on people. But it is irrelevant whether or not *I* am dependent. So, to continue: fear is the awareness of our inner emptiness, loneliness and poverty, and of not being able to do anything about it. We are concerned only with this fear which breeds dependence, and which is again increased by dependence. If we understand fear we also understand dependence. So to understand fear there must be sensitivity to discover, to understand how it comes into being. If one is at all sensitive one becomes conscious of one's own extraordinary emptiness – a bottomless pit which cannot be filled by the vulgar entertainment of drugs nor by the entertainment of the churches, nor the amusements of society: nothing can ever fill it. Knowing this the fear increases. This drives you to depend, and this dependence makes you more and more insensitive. And knowing this is so, you are frightened of it. So our question now is: how is one to go beyond this emptiness, this loneliness – not how is one to be self-sufficient, not how is one to camouflage this emptiness permanently?

Questioner: Why do you say it is not a quesion of becoming self-sufficient?

KRISHNAMURTI: Because if you are self-sufficient you are no longer sensitive; you become smug and callous, indifferent and enclosed. To be without dependence, to go beyond dependence, doesn't mean to become self-sufficient. Can the mind face and live with this emptiness, and not escape in any direction?

Questioner: It would drive me mad to think I had to live with it for ever.

KRISHNAMURTI: Any movement away from this emptiness is an escape. And this flight away from something, away from 'what is', is fear. Fear is flight away from something. What *is* is not the fear; it is the *flight* which is the fear, and *this* will drive you mad, not the emptiness itself. So what is this emptiness, this loneliness? How does it come about? Surely it comes through comparison and measurement, doesn't it? I compare myself with the saint, the master, the great musician, the man who knows, the man who has arrived. In this comparison I find myself wanting and insufficient: I have no talent I am inferior, I have not 're-alized'; I am not, and that man is. So out of measurement and comparison comes the enormous cavity of emptiness and nothingness. And the flight from this cavity is fear. And the fear stops us from understanding this bottomless pit. It is a neurosis which feeds upon itself. And again, this measurement, this comparison, is the very essence of dependence. So we are back again at dependence, a vicious circle.

Questioner: We have come a long way in this discussion and things are clearer. There is dependence; is it possible not to depend? Yes, I think it is possible. Then we have the fear; is it possible not to run away from emptiness at all, which means, not to escape through fear? Yes, I think it is possible. That means we are left with the emptiness. Is it possible then to face this emptiness since we have stopped running away from it through fear? Yes, I think it is possible. Is it possible finally, not to measure, not to compare? For if we have come this far, and I think we have, only this emptiness remains, and one sees that this emptiness is the outcome of comparison. And one sees that dependence and fear are the outcome of this emptiness. So there is comparison, empti-ness, fear, dependence. Can I really live a life without com-parison, without measurement?

KRISHNAMURTI: Of course you have to measure to put a carpet on the floor!

Questioner: Yes. I mean can I live without psychological comparison?

KRISHNAMURTI: Do you know what it means to live without psychological comparison when all your life you have been conditioned to compare – at school, at games, at the university and in the office? Everything is comparison. To live without comparison! Do you know what it means? It means no dependence, no self-sufficiency, no seeking, no asking; therefore it means to love. Love has no comparison, and so love has no fear. Love is not aware of itself as love, for the word is not the thing.

HOW TO LIVE IN THIS WORLD

Questioner: Please, sir, could you tell me how I am to live in this world? I don't want to be part of it yet I have to live in it, I have to have a house and earn my own living. And my neighbours are of this world; my children play with theirs, and so one becomes a part of this ugly mess, whether one wants to or not. I want to find out how to live in this world without escaping from it, without going into a monastery or around the world in a sailing boat. I want to educate my children differently, but first I want to know how to live surrounded by so much violence, greed, hypocrisy, competition and brutality.

KRISHNAMURTI: Don't let's make a problem of it. When anything becomes a problem we are caught in the solution of it, and then the problem becomes a cage, a barrier to further exploration and understanding. So don't let us reduce all life to a vast and complex problem. If the question is put in order to overcome the society in which we live, or to find a substitute for that society, or to try to escape from it though living in it, it must inevitably lead to a contradictory and hypocritical life. This question also implies, doesn't it, the complete denial of ideology? If you are really inquiring you cannot start with a conclusion, and all ideologies are a conclusion. So we must begin by finding out what you mean by living.

Questioner: Please, sir, let's go step by step.

KRISHNAMURTI: I am very glad that we can go into this step by step, patiently, with an inquiring mind and heart. Now what do you mean by living?

Questioner: I've never tried to put it into words. I'm be-

wildered, I don't know what to do, how to live. I've lost faith in everything – religions, philosophies and political utopias. There is a war between individuals and between nations. In this permissive society everything is allowed – killing, riots, the cynical oppression of one country by another, and nobody does anything about it because interference might mean world war. I am faced with all this and I don't know what to do; I don't know how to live at all. I don't want to live in the midst of such confusion.

KRISHNAMURTI: What is it you are asking for – a different life, or for a new life which comes about with the understanding of the old life? If you want to live a different life without understanding what has brought about this confusion, you will always be in contradiction, in conflict, in confusion. And that of course is not a new life at all. So are you asking for a new life or for a modified continuity of the old one, or to understand the old one?

Questioner: I'm not at all sure what I want, but I am beginning to see what I don't want.

KRISHNAMURTI: Is what you don't want based on your free understanding or on your pleasure and pain? Are you judging out of your revolt, or do you see the causation of this conflict and misery, and, because you see it, reject it?

Questioner: You're asking me too many things. All I know is that I want to live a different kind of life. I don't know what it means; I don't know why I'm seeking it; and, as I said, I'm utterly bewildered by it all.

KRISHNAMURTI: Your basic question is, isn't it, how are you to live in this world? Before you find out let us first see what this world is. The world is not only all that surrounds us, it is also our relationship to all these things and people, to ourselves, to ideas. That is, our relationship to property, to people, to concepts – in fact our relationship to the stream of events which we call life. This is the world. We see division into nationalities, into religious, economic, political, social and ethnical groups; the whole world is broken up and is as fragmented outwardly as its human beings are inwardly. In fact, this outer fragmentation is the manifestation of the human being's inner division.

Questioner: Yes, I see this fragmentation very clearly, and I am also beginning to see that the human being is responsible.

KRISHNAMURTI: *You* are the human being!

Questioner: Then can I live differently from what I am myself? I'm suddenly realizing that if I am to live in a totally different way there must be a new birth in me, a new mind and heart, new eyes. And I realize also that this hasn't happened. I live the way I am, and the way I am has made life as it is. But where does one go from there?

KRISHNAMURTI: You don't go anywhere from there! There is no going anywhere. The going, or the searching for the ideal, for what we think is better, gives us a feeling that we are progressing, that we are moving towards a better world. But this movement is no movement at all because the end has been projected out of our misery, confusion, greed and envy. So this end, which is supposed to be the opposite of what is, is really the same as what is, it is engendered by what is. Therefore it creates the conflict between what is and what should be. This is where our basic confusion and conflict arises. The end is not over there, not on the other side of the wall; the beginning and the end are here.

Questioner: Wait a minute, sir, please; I don't understand this at all. Are you telling me that the ideal of what should be is the result of not understanding what is? Are you telling me that what should be is what is, and that this movement from what is to what should be isn't really a movement at all?

KRISHNAMURTI: It is an idea; it is fiction. If you understand what is, what need is there for what should be?

Questioner: Is that so? I understand what is. I understand the bestiality of war, the horror of killing, and because I understand it I have this ideal of not killing. The ideal is born out of my understanding of what is, therefore it is not an escape.

KRISHNAMURTI: If you understand that killing is terrible do you have to have an ideal in order not to kill? Perhaps we are not clear about the word understanding. When we say we understand something, in that is implied, isn't it, that we have learnt all it has to say? We have explored it and discovered the truth or the falseness of it. This implies also, doesn't it, that this understanding is not an intellectual affair, but that one has felt it deeply in one's heart? There is understanding only when the mind and the heart are in perfect harmony. Then one says 'I have understood this, and finished with it', and it no longer has the vitality to breed further conflict. Do we both give the same meaning to that word understand?

Questioner: I hadn't before, but now I see that what you are saying is true. Yet I honestly don't understand, in that way, the total disorder of the world, which, as you so rightly pointed out, is my own disorder. How can I understand it? How can I completely learn about the disorder, the entire disorder and confusion of the world, and of myself?

KRISHNAMURTI: Do not use the word how, please.

Questioner: Why not?

KRISHNAMURTI: The how implies that somebody is going to give you a method, a recipe, which, if you practise it, will

183

bring about understanding. Can understanding ever come about through a method? Understanding means love and the sanity of the mind. And love cannot be practised or taught. The sanity of the mind can only come about when there is clear perception, seeing things as they are unemotionally, not sentimentally. Neither of these two things can be taught by another, nor by a system invented by yourself or by another.

Questioner: You are too persuasive, sir, or is it perhaps that you are too logical? Are you trying to influence me to see things as you see them?

KRISHNAMURTI: God forbid! Influence in any form is destructive of love. Propaganda to make the mind sensitive, alert, will only make it dull and insensitive. So we are in no way trying to influence you or persuade you, or make you depend. We are only pointing out, exploring together. And to explore together you must be free, both of me and of your own prejudices and fears. Otherwise you go round and round in circles. So we must go back to our original question: how am I to live in this world? To live in this world we must deny the world. By that we mean: deny the ideal, the war, the fragmentation, the competition, the envy and so on. We don't mean deny the world as a schoolboy revolts against his parents. We mean deny it because we understand it. This understanding is negation.

Questioner: I am out of my depth.

KRISHNAMURTI: You said you do not want to live in the confusion, the dishonesty and ugliness of this world. So you deny it. But from what background do you deny it, why do you deny it? Do you deny it because you want to live a peaceful life, a life of complete security and enclosure, or do you deny it because you see what it actually is?

Questioner: I think I deny it because I see around me what is taking place. Of course my prejudices and fear are also involved. So it is a mixture of what is actually taking place and my own anxiety.

KRISHNAMURTI: Which predominates, your own anxiety or the actual seeing of what is around you? If fear predominates, then you can't see what is actually going on around you, because fear is darkness, and in darkness you can see absolutely nothing. If you realize that, then you can see the world actually as it is, then you can see yourself actually as you are. Because you are the world, and the world is you; they are not two separate entities.

Questioner: Would you please explain more fully what you mean by the world is me and I am the world?

KRISHNAMURTI: Does this really need explaining? Do you want me to describe in detail what you are and show you that it is the same as what the world is? Will this description convince you that you are the world? Will you be convinced by a logical, sequential explanation showing you the cause and the effect? If you are convinced by careful description, will that give you understanding? Will it make you feel that you are the world, make you feel responsible for the world? It seems so clear that our human greed, envy, aggression and violence have brought about the society in which we live, a legalized acceptance of what we are. I think this is really sufficiently clear and let's not spend any more time on this issue. You see, we don't feel this, we don't love, therefore there is this division between me and the world.

Questioner: May I come back again tomorrow?

*

He came back the next day eagerly, and there was the bright light of inquiry in his eyes.

Questioner: I want, if you are willing, to go further into this

*question of how I am to live in this world. I do now under-
stand, with my heart and my mind, as you explained yesterday, the utter unimportance of ideals. I had quite a long
struggle with it and have come to see the triviality of ideals.
You are saying, aren't you, that when there are no ideals or
escapes there is only the past, the thousand yesterdays which
make up the 'me'? So when I ask: 'How am I to live in this
world?' I have not only put a wrong question, but I have also
made a contradictory statement, for I have placed the world
and the 'me' in opposition to each other. And this contradiction is what I call living. So when I ask the question,
'How am I to live in this world?' I am really trying to improve this contradiction, to justify it, to modify it, because
that's all I know; I don't know anything else.*

KRISHNAMURTI: This then is the question we have now:
must living always be in the past, must all activity spring
from the past, is all relationship the outcome of the past, is
living the complex memory of the past? That is all we know –
the past modifying the present. And the future is the outcome of this past acting through the present. So the past, the
present and the future are all the past. And this past is what
we call living. The mind is the past, the brain is the past, the
feelings are the past, and action coming from these is the
positive activity of the known. This whole process is your life
and all the relationship and activity that you know. So when
you ask how you are to live in this world you are asking for a
change of prisons.

*Questioner: I don't mean that. What I mean is: I see very
clearly that my process of thinking and doing is the past
working through the present to the future. This is all I know
and that's a fact. And I realize that unless there is a change
in this structure I am caught in it, I am of it. From this the
question inevitably arises: how am I to change?*

KRISHNAMURTI: To live in this world sanely there must be
a radical change of the mind and of the heart.

Questioner: Yes, but what do you mean by change? How am I to change if whatever I do is the movement of the past? I can only change myself, nobody else can change me. And I don't see what it means – to change.

KRISHNAMURTI: So the question 'How am I to live in this world?' has now become 'How am I to change?' – bearing in mind that the how doesn't mean a method, but is an inquiry to understand. What is change? Is there any change at all? Or can you ask whether there is any change at all only *after* there has been a total change and revolution? Let's begin again to find out what this word means. Change implies a movement from what is to something different. Is this something different merely an opposite, or does it belong to a different order altogether? If it is merely an opposite then it is not different at all, because all opposites are mutually dependent, like hot and cold, high and low. The opposite is contained within, and determined by, its opposite; it exists only in comparison, and things that are comparative have different measures of the same quality, and therefore they are similar. So change to an opposite is no change at all. Even if this going towards what seems different gives you the feeling that you are really doing something, it is an illusion.

Questioner: Let me absorb this for a moment.

KRISHNAMURTI: So what are we concerned with now? Is it possible to bring about in ourselves the birth of a new order altogether that is not related to the past? The past is irrelevant to this inquiry, and trivial, because it is irrelevant to the new order.

Questioner: How can you say it is trivial and irrelevant? We've been saying all along that the past is the issue, and now you say it is irrelevant.

KRISHNAMURTI: The past seems to be the only issue be-

187

cause it is the only thing that holds our minds and hearts. It alone is important to us. But why do we give importance to it? Why is this little space all-important? If you are totally immersed in it, utterly committed to it, then you will never listen to change. The man who is *not* wholly committed is the only one capable of listening, inquiring and asking. Only then will he be able to see the triviality of this little space. So, are you completely immersed, or is your head above the water? If your head is above the water then you can see that this little thing is trivial. Then you have room to look around. How deeply are you immersed? Nobody can answer this for you except yourself. In the very asking of this question there is already freedom and, therefore, one is not afraid. Then your vision is extensive. When this pattern of the past holds you completely by the throat, then you acquiesce, accept, obey, follow, believe. It is only when you are aware that this is not freedom that you are starting to climb out of it. So we are again asking: what is change, what is revolution? Change is not a movement from the known to the known, and all political revolutions are that. This kind of change is not what we are talking about. To progress from being a sinner to being a saint is to progress from one illusion to another. So now we are free of change as a movement from this to that.

Questioner: Have I really understood this? What am I to do with anger, violence and fear when they arise in me? Am I to give them free reign? How am I to deal with them? There must be change there, otherwise I am what I was before.

KRISHNAMURTI: Is it clear to you that these things cannot be overcome by their opposites? If so, you have only the violence, the envy, the anger, the greed. The feeling arises as the result of a challenge, and then it is named. This naming of the feeling re-establishes it in the old pattern. If you do not name it, which means you do not identify yourself with it, then the feeling is now and it will go away by itself. The naming of it strengthens it and gives it a continuity which is the whole process of thought.

Questioner: I am being driven into a corner where I see myself actually as I am, and I see how trivial I am. From there what comes next?

KRISHNAMURTI: Any movement from what I am strengthens what I am. So change *is no movement at all*. Change is the denial of change, and now only can I put this question: is there a change at all? This question can be put only when all movement of thought has come to an end, for thought must be denied for the beauty of non-change. In the total negation of all movement of thought away from what is, is the ending of what is.

RELATIONSHIP

Questioner: I have come a long way to see you. Although I am married and have children I have been away from them wandering, meditating, as a mendicant. I have puzzled greatly over this very complicated problem of relationship. When I go into a village and they give me food, I am related to the giver, as I am related to my wife and children. In another village when somebody gives me clothes I am related to the whole factory that produced them. I am related to the earth on which I walk, to the tree under which I take shelter, to everything. And yet I am alone, isolated. When I am with my wife, I am separate even during sex – it is an act of separation. When I go into a temple it is still the worshipper being related to the thing he worships: separation again. So in all relationships, as I see it, there is this separation, duality, and behind or through it, or around it, there is a peculiar sense of unity. When I see the beggar it hurts me for I am like him and I feel as he feels – lonely, desperate, sick, hungry. I feel for him, and with him, for his meaningless existence. Some rich man comes along in his big motor-car and gives me a lift, but I feel uncomfortable in his company, yet at the same time I feel for him and am related to him. So I have meditated upon this strange phenomenon of relationship. Can we on this lovely morning, overlooking this deep valley, talk over together this question?

KRISHNAMURTI: Is all relationship out of this isolation? Can there be relationship as long as there is any separateness, division? Can there be relationship if there is no contact, not only physical but at every level of our being with another? One may hold the hand of another and yet be miles away, wrapped in one's own thoughts and problems. One may be in a group and yet be painfully alone. So one

190

asks: can there be any kind of relationship with the tree, the flower, the human being, or with the skies and the lovely sunset, when the mind in its activities is isolating itself? And can there be any contact ever, with anything at all, even when the mind is *not* isolating itself?

Questioner: Everything and everybody has its own existence. Everything and everybody is shrouded in its own existence. I can never penetrate this enclosure of another's being. However much I love someone, his existence is separate from mine. I can perhaps touch him from the outside, mentally or physically, but his existence is his own, and mine is for ever on the outside of it. Similarly he cannot reach me. Must we always remain two separate entities, each in his own world, with his own limitations, within the prison of his own consciousness?

KRISHNAMURTI: Each lives within his own tissue, you in yours, he in his. And is there any possibility, ever, of breaking through this tissue? Is this tissue – this shroud, this envelope – the word? Is it made up of your concern with yourself and his with himself, your desires opposed to his? Is this capsule the past? It is all of this, isn't it? It isn't one particular thing but a whole bundle which the mind carries about. You have your burden, another has his. Can these burdens ever be dropped so that the mind meets the mind, the heart meets the heart? That is really the question, isn't it?

Questioner: Even if all these burdens are dropped, if that were possible, even then he remains in his skin with his thoughts, and I in mine with my thoughts. Sometimes the gap is narrow, sometimes it is wide, but we are always two separate islands. The gap seems to be widest when we care most about it and try to bridge it.

KRISHNAMURTI: You can identify yourself with that villager or with that flaming bougainvilia – which is a mental trick to pretend unity. Identification with something is one of the most hypocritical states – to identify oneself with a nation, with a belief and yet remain alone is a favourite trick to cheat loneliness. Or you identify yourself so completely with your belief that you are that belief, and this is a neurotic state. Now let's put away this urge to be identified with a person or an idea or a thing. That way there is no harmony, unity or love. So our next question is: can you tear through the envelope so that there is no more envelope? Then only would there be a possibility of total contact. How is one to tear through the envelope? The 'how' doesn't mean a method, but rather an inquiry which might open the door.

Questioner: Yes, no other contact can be called relationship at all, though we say it is.

KRISHNAMURTI: Do we tear the envelope bit by bit or cut through it immediately? If we tear it bit by bit, which is what analysts sometimes claim to do, the job is never done. It is not through time that you can break down this separation.

Questioner: Can I enter into the envelope of another? And isn't his envelope his very existence, his heartbeats and his blood, his feelings and his memories?

KRISHNAMURTI: Are *you* not the very envelope itself?

Questioner: Yes.

KRISHNAMURTI: The very movement to tear through the other envelope, or extend outside of your own, is the very affirmation and the action of your own envelope: you are the envelope. So you are the observer of the envelope, and you are also the envelope itself. In this case you are the observer and the observed: so is he, and that's how we remain. And you try to reach him and he tries to reach you. Is this possible? You are the island surrounded by seas, and he is also the island surrounded by seas. You see that you are both the island and the sea; there is no division between them; you are the entire earth with the sea. Therefore there is no division as the island and the sea. The other person doesn't see this. He is the island surrounded by sea; he tries to reach you, or, if you are foolish enough, you may try to reach him. Is that possible? How can there be a contact between a man who is free and another who is bound? Since you are the observer and the observed, you are the whole movement of the earth and the sea. But the other, who doesn't understand this, is still the island surrounded by water. He tries to reach you, and is everlastingly failing because he maintains his insularity. It is only when he leaves it and is, like you, open to the movement of the skies, the earth, and the sea, that there can be contact. The one who sees that the barrier is himself can no longer have a barrier. Therefore, he, in himself, is not separate at all. The other has not seen that the barrier is himself and so maintains the belief in his separateness. How can this man reach the other? It is not possible.

*

Questioner: If we may I should like to continue from where we left off yesterday. You were saying that the mind is the maker of the envelope around itself, and that this envelope is the mind. I really don't understand this. Intellectually I can agree, but the nature of perception eludes me. I should like very much to understand it – not verbally but actually feel it – so that there is no conflict in my life.

KRISHNAMURTI: There is the space between what the mind calls the envelope which it has made, and itself. There is the space between the ideal and the action. In these different fragmentations of space between the observer and the observed, or between different things it observes, is all conflict and struggle, and all the problems of life. There is the separation between this envelope around me and the envelope around another. In that space is all our existence, all our relationship and battle.

Questioner: When you talk of the division between the observer and the observed do you mean these fragmentations of space in our thinking and in our daily actions?

KRISHNAMURTI: What is this space? There is space between you and your envelope, the space between him and his envelope, and there is the space between the two envelopes. These spaces all appear to the observer. What are these spaces made of? How do they come into being? What is the quality and the nature of these divided spaces? If we could remove these fragmentary spaces what would happen?

Questioner: There would then be true contact on all levels of one's being.

KRISHNAMURTI: Is that all?

Questioner: There would be no more conflict, for all conflict is relationship across these spaces.

KRISHNAMURTI: Is that all? When this space actually disappears – not verbally or intellectually – but actually disappears – there is complete harmony, unity, between you and him, between you and another. In this harmony you and he cease and there is only this vast space which can never be broken up. The small structure of the mind comes to an end, for the mind is fragmentation.

Questioner: I really can't understand this at all, though I have a deep feeling within me that it is so. I can see that when there is love this actually takes place, but I don't know that love. It's not with me all the time. It is not in my heart. I see it only as if through a misty glass. I can't honestly grasp it with all my being. Could we, as you suggested, consider what these spaces are made of, how they come into being?

KRISHNAMURTI: Let's be quite sure that we both understand the same thing when we use the word space. There is the physical space between people and things, and there is the psychological space between people and things. Then there is also the space between the idea and the actual. So all this, the physical and psychological, is space, more or less limited and defined. We are *not* now talking of the physical space. We are talking of the psychological space between people and the psychological space in the human being himself, in his thoughts and activities. How does this space come about? It is fictitious, illusory, or is it real? Feel it, be aware of it, make sure you haven't just got a mental image of it, bear in mind that the description is never the thing. Be quite sure that you know what we are talking about. Be quite aware that this limited space, this division, exists in you: don't move from there if you don't understand. Now how does this space come about?

Questioner: We see the physical space between things . . .

KRISHNAMURTI: Don't explain anything; just feel your way into it. We are asking how this space has come into being. Don't give an explanation or a cause, but remain with this space and feel it. Then the cause and the description will have very little meaning and no value. This space has come into being because of thought, which is the 'me', the word – which is the whole division. Thought itself is this distance, this division. Thought is always breaking itself up into fragments and creating division. Thought always cuts up what it observes into fragments within space – as you and me, yours and mine, me and my thoughts, and so on. This space, which thought has created between what it observes, has become real; and it is this space that divides. Then thought tries to build a bridge over this division, thus playing a trick upon itself all the time, deceiving itself and hoping for unity.

Questioner: That reminds me of the old statement about

thought: it is a thief disguising himself as a policemen in order to catch the thief.

KRISHNAMURTI: Don't bother to quote, sir, however, ancient it is. We are considering what actually is going on. In seeing the truth of the nature of thought and its activities, thought becomes quiet. Thought being quiet, not made quiet, is there space?

Questioner: It is thought itself which now rushes in to answer this question.

KRISHNAMURTI: Exactly! Therefore we do not even ask the question. The mind now is completely harmonious, without fragmentation; the little space has ceased and there is only space. When the mind is completely quiet there is the vastness of space and silence.

Questioner: So I begin to see that my relationship to another is between thought and thought; whatever I answer is the noise of thought, and realizing it, I am silent.

KRISHNAMURTI: This silence is the benediction.

CONFLICT

Questioner: I find myself in a great deal of conflict with everything about me; and also everything within me is in conflict. People have spoken of divine order; nature is harmonious; it seems that man is the only animal who violates this order, making so much misery for others and for himself. When I wake up in the morning I see from my window little birds fighting with each other, but they soon separate and fly away, whereas I carry this war with myself and with others inside me all the time; there is no escaping it. I wonder if I can ever be at peace with myself. I must say I should like to find myself in complete harmony with everything about me and with myself. As one sees from this window the quiet sea and the light on the water, one has a feeling deep within oneself that there must be a way of living without these endless quarrels with oneself and with the world. Is there any harmony at all, anywhere? Or is there only everlasting disorder? If there is harmony, at what level can it exist? Or does it only exist on the top of some mountain which the burning valleys can never know?

KRISHNAMURTI: Can one go from one to the other? Can one change that which is to that which is not? Can disharmony be transformed into harmony?

Questioner: Is conflict necessary then? It may perhaps, after all, be the natural order of things.

KRISHNAMURTI: If one accepted that, one would have to accept everything society stands for: wars, ambitious competition, an aggressive way of life – all the brutal violence of men, inside and outside of his so-called holy places. Is this natural? Will this bring about any unity? Wouldn't it be better for us to consider these two facts – the fact of conflict with all its complicated struggles, and the fact of the mind demanding order, harmony, peace, beauty, love?

Questioner: I know nothing about harmony. I see it in the heavens, in the seasons, in the mathematical order of the universe. But that doesn't give me order in my own heart and mind; the absolute order of mathematics is not my order. I have no order, I am in deep disorder. I know there are different theories of gradual evolution towards the so-called perfection of political utopias and religious heavens, but this leaves me where I actually am. The world may perhaps be perfect in ten thousand years from now, but in the meantime I'm having hell.

KRISHNAMURTI: We see the disorder in ourselves and in society. Both are very complex. There are really no answers. One can examine all this very carefully, analyse it closely, look for causes of disorder in oneself and in society, expose them to the light and perhaps believe that one will free the mind from them. This analytical process is what most people are doing, intelligently or unintelligently, and it doesn't get anybody very far. Man has analysed himself for thousands of years, and produced no result but literature! The many saints have paralysed themselves in concepts and ideological prisons; they too are in conflict. The cause of our conflict is this everlasting duality of desire: the endless corridor of the opposites creating envy, greed, ambition, aggression, fear, and all the rest of it. Now I wonder if there isn't an altogether different approach to this problem? The acceptance of this struggle and all our efforts to get out of it have become traditional. The whole approach is traditional. In this traditional approach the mind operates but, as we see, the traditional approach of the mind creates more disorder. So the problem is not how to end disorder, but rather whether the mind can look at it freed from tradition. And then perhaps there may be no problem at all.

Questioner: I don't follow you at all.

KRISHNAMURTI: There is this fact of disorder. There is no doubt about it: it is an actual fact. The traditional approach to this fact is to analyse it, to try to discover the cause of it and overcome the cause, or else to invent its opposite and battle towards that. This is the traditional approach with its disciplines, drills, controls, suppressions, sublimations. Man has done this for thousands upon thousands of years; it has led nowhere. Can we abandon this approach completely and look at the problem entirely differently – that is, not try to go beyond it, or to resolve it, or to overcome it, or to escape from it? Can the mind do this?

Questioner: Perhaps ...

KRISHNAMURTI: Don't answer so quickly! This is a tremendous thing I am asking you. From the beginning of time man has tried to deal with all his problems, either by going beyond them, resolving them, overcoming them or escaping from them. Please do not think you can push all that aside so lightly, simply with a verbal agreement. It makes up the very structure of everybody's mind. Can the mind now, understanding all this non-verbally, actually free itself from the tradition? This traditional way of dealing with the conflict never solves it, but only adds more conflict: being violent, which is conflict, I add the additional conflict of trying to become non-violent. All social morality and all religious prescriptions are that. Are we together?

Questioner: Yes.

KRISHNAMURTI: Then do you see how far we have come? Having, through understanding, repudiated all these traditional approaches, what is the actual state of the mind now? Because the state of the mind is far more important than the conflict itself.

Questioner: I really don't know.

KRISHNAMURTI: Why don't you know? Why aren't you aware, if you have really abandoned the traditional approach, of the state of your mind? Why don't you know? Either you have abandoned it or you haven't. If you have, you would know it. If you have, then your mind is made innocent to look at the problem. You can look at the problem as though for the first time. And if you do this, *is* there a problem of conflict at all? Because you look at the problem with the old eyes it is not only strengthened but also moves in its well-worn path. So what is important is how you look at the problem – whether you look at it with new eyes or old eyes. The new eyes are freed from the conditioned responses to the problem. Even to name the problem through recognition is to approach it in the traditional way. Justification, condemnation, or translation of the problem in terms of pleasure and pain, are all involved in this habitual traditional approach of doing something about it. This is generally called positive action with regard to the problem. But when the mind brushes all that aside as being ineffectual, unintelligent, then it has become highly sensitive, highly ordered, and free.

Questioner: You're asking too much of me, I can't do it. I'm incapable of it. You're asking me to be super-human!

KRISHNAMURTI: You're making difficulties for yourself, blocking yourself, when you say you must become super-human. It's nothing of the kind. You keep on looking at things with eyes that want to interfere, that want to do something about what they see. Stop doing anything about it, for whatever you do belongs to the traditional approach. That's all. Be simple. This is the miracle of perception – to perceive with a heart and mind that are completely cleansed of the past. Negation is the most positive action.

THE RELIGIOUS LIFE

Questioner: I should like to know what a religious life is. I have stayed in monasteries for several months, meditated, led a disciplined life, read a great deal. I've been to various temples, churches and mosques. I've tried to lead a very simple, harmless life, trying not to hurt people or animals. This surely isn't all there is to a religious life? I've practised yoga, studied Zen and followed many religious disciplines. I am, and have always been, a vegetarian. As you see, I'm getting old now, and I've lived with some of the saints in different parts of the world, but somehow I feel that all this is only the outskirts of the real thing. So I wonder if we can discuss today what to you is a religious life.

KRISHNAMURTI: A sannyasi came to see me one day and he was sad. He said he had taken a vow of celibacy and left the world to become a mendicant, wandering from village to village, but his sexual desires were so imperious that one morning he decided to have his sexual organs surgically removed. For many months he was in constant pain, but somehow it healed, and after many years he fully realized what he had done. And so he came to see me and in that little room he asked me what he could do now, having mutilated himself, to become normal again – not physically, of course, but inwardly. He had done this thing because sexual activity was considered contrary to a religious life. It was considered mundane, belonging to the world of pleasure, which a real sannyasi must at all costs avoid. He said, 'Here I am, feeling completely lost, deprived of my manhood. I struggled so hard against my sexual desires, trying to control them, and ultimately this terrible thing took place. Now what am I to do? I know that what I did was wrong. My energy has almost gone and I seem to be ending my life in darkness.' He held my hand, and we sat silently for some time.

Is this a religious life? Is the denial of pleasure or beauty a way that leads to a religious life? To deny the beauty of the skies and the hills and the human form, will that lead to a religious life? But that is what most saints and monks believe. They torture themselves in that belief. Can a tortured, twisted, distorted mind ever find what is a religious life? Yet all religions assert that the only way to reality or to God, or whatever they call it, is through this torture, this distortion. They all make the distinction between what they call a spiritual or religious life and what they call a worldly life.

A man who lives only for pleasure, with occasional flashes of sorrow and piety, whose whole life is given to amusement and entertainment is, of course, a worldly man, although he may also be very clever, very scholarly, and fill his life with other people's thoughts or his own. And a man who has a gift and exercises it for the benefit of society, or for his own pleasure, and who achieves fame in the fulfilment of that gift, such a man, surely, is also worldly. But it is also worldly to go to church, or to the temple or the mosque, to pray, steeped in prejudice, bigotry, utterly unaware of the brutality that this implies. It is worldly to be patriotic, nationalistic, idealistic. The man who shuts himself up in a monastery – getting up at regular hours with a book in hand, reading and praying – is surely also worldly. And the man who goes out to do good works, whether he is a social reformer or a missionary, is just like the politician in his concern with the world. The division between the religious life and the world is the very essence of worldliness. The minds of all these people – monks, saints, reformers – are not very different from the minds of those who are only concerned with the things that give pleasure.

So it is important not to divide life into the worldly and the non-worldly. It is important not to make the distinction between the worldly and the so-called religious. Without the world of matter, the material world, we wouldn't be here.

Without the beauty of the sky and the single tree on the hill, without that woman going by and that man riding the horse, life wouldn't be possible. We are concerned with the totality of life not a particular part of it which is considered religious in opposition to the rest. So one begins to see that a religious life is concerned with the whole and not with the particular.

Questioner: I understand what you say. We have to deal with the totality of living; we can't separate the world from the so-called spirit. So the question is: in what way can we act religiously with regard to all the things in life?

KRISHNAMURTI: What do we mean by acting religiously? Don't you mean a way of life in which there is no division – division between the worldly and the religious, between what should be and what shouldn't be, between me and you, between like and dislike? This division is conflict. A life of conflict is not a religious life. A religious life is only possible when we deeply understand conflict. This understanding is intelligence. It is this intelligence that acts rightly. What most people call intelligence is merely deftness in some technical activity, or cunning in business or political chicanery.

Questioner: So my question really means how is one to live without conflict, and bring about that feeling of true sanctity which is not simply emotional piety conditioned by some religious cage – no matter how old and venerated that cage is?

KRISHNAMURTI: A man living without too much conflict in a village, or dreaming in a cave on a 'sacred' hillside, is surely not living the religious life that we are talking about. To end conflict is one of the most complex things. It needs self-observation and the sensitivity of awareness of the outer as well as of the inner. Conflict can only end where there is the understanding of the contradiction in oneself. This contradiction will always exist if there is no freedom from the known, which is the past. Freedom from the past means living in the now which is not of time, in which there is only this movement of freedom, untouched by the past, by the known.

Questioner: What do you mean by freedom from the past?

KRISHNAMURTI: The past is all our accumulated memories. These memories act in the present and create our hopes and fears of the future. These hopes and fears *are* the psychological future: without them there is no future. So the present is the action of the past, and the mind is this movement of the past. The past acting in the present creates what we call the future. This response of the past is involuntary, it is not summoned or invited, it is upon us before we know it.

Questioner: In that case, how are we going to be free of it?

KRISHNAMURTI: To be aware of this movement without choice – because choice again is more of this same movement of the past – is to observe the past in action: such observation is *not* a movement of the past. To observe without the image of thought is action in which the past has ended. To observe the tree without thought is action without the past. To observe the action of the past is again action without the past. The state of seeing is more important than what is seen. To be aware of the past in that choiceless observation is not only to act differently, but to be different. In this awareness memory acts without impediment, and efficiently. To be religious is to be so choicelessly aware that there is freedom from the known even whilst the known acts wherever it has to.

Questioner: But the known, the past, still sometimes acts even when it should not; it still acts to cause conflict.

KRISHNAMURTI: To be aware of this is also to be in a state

204

of inaction with regard to the past which is acting. So freedom from the known is truly the religious life. That doesn't mean to wipe out the known but to enter a different dimension altogether from which the known is observed. This action of seeing choicelessly is the action of love. The religious life is this action, and all living is this action, and the religious mind is this action. So religion, and the mind, and life, and love, are one.

SEEING THE WHOLE

Questioner: When I listen to you I seem to understand what you are talking about, not only verbally, but at a much deeper level. I am part of it; I fully grasp with my whole being the truth of what you say. My hearing is sharpened, and the very seeing of the flowers, the trees, and those mountains with snow, makes me feel I am part of them. In this awareness I have no conflict, no contradiction. It is as though I could do anything, and that whatever I did would be true, would not bring either conflict or pain. But unfortunately that state doesn't last. Perhaps it lasts for an hour or two while I'm listening to you. When I leave the talks it all seems to evaporate and I'm back where I was. I try to be aware of myself; I keep remembering the state I was in when I listened to your talks, keep trying to reach it, hold on to it, and this becomes a struggle. You have said, 'Be aware of your conflict, listen to your conflict, see the causes of your conflict, your conflict is yourself.' I am aware of my conflict, my pain, my sorrow, my confusion, but this awareness in no way resolves these things. On the contrary, being aware of them seems to give them vitality and duration. You talk of choiceless awareness, which again breeds another battle in me, for I am full of choice, decisions and opinions. I have applied this awareness to a particular habit I have, and it has not gone. When you are aware of some conflict or strain, this same awareness keeps looking to see if it has already gone. And this seems to remind you of it, and you never shake it off.

KRISHNAMURTI: Awareness is not a commitment to something. Awareness is an observation, both outer and inner, in which direction has stopped. You are aware, but the thing of which you are aware is not being encouraged or nourished.

Awareness is not concentration on something. It is not an action of the will choosing what it will be aware of, and analysing it to bring about a certain result. When awareness is deliberately focused on a particular object, as a conflict, that is the action of will which is concentration. When you concentrate – that is, put all your energy and thought within your chosen frontiers, whether reading a book or watching your anger – then, in this exclusion, the thing you are concentrating upon is strengthened, nourished. So here we have to understand the nature of awareness: we have to understand what we are talking about when we use the word awareness. Now, you can either be aware of a particular thing, or be aware of that particular as part of the total. The particular by itself has very little meaning, but when you see the total, then that particular has a relationship to the whole. Only in this relationship does the particular have its right meaning; it doesn't become all-important, it is not exaggerated. So the real question is: does one see the total process of life or is one concentrated on the particular, thus missing the whole field of life? To be aware of the whole field is to see also the particular, but, at the same time, to understand its relationship to the whole. If you are angry and are concerned with ending that anger, then you focus your attention on the anger and the whole escapes you and the anger is strengthened. But anger is inter-related to the whole. So when we separate the particular from the whole, the particular breeds its own problems.

Questioner: What do you mean by seeing the whole? What is this totality you talk about, this extensive awareness in which the particular is a detail? Is it some mysterious, mystical experience? If so then we are lost completely. Or is this perhaps what you are saying, that there is a whole field of existence, of which anger is a part, and that to be concerned with the part is to block out the extensive perception? But what is this extensive perception? I can only see the whole through all its particulars. And what whole do you mean?

Are you talking about the whole of the mind, or the whole of existence, or the whole of myself, or the whole of life? What whole do you mean, and how can I see it?

KRISHNAMURTI: The whole field of life: the mind, love, everything which is in life.

Questioner: How can I possibly see all that! I can understand that everything I see is partial, and that all my awareness is awareness of the particular, and that this strengthens the particular.

KRISHNAMURTI: Let's put it this way: do you perceive with your mind and your heart separately, or do you see, hear, feel, think, all together, not fragmentarily?

Questioner: I don't know what you mean.

KRISHNAMURTI: You hear a word, your mind tells you it is an insult, your feelings tell you you don't like it, your mind again intervenes to control or justify, and so on. Once again feeling takes over where the mind has concluded. In this way an event unleashes a chain-reaction of different parts of your being. What you hear had been broken up, made fragmentary, and if you concentrate on one of those fragments, you miss the total process of that hearing. Hearing can be fragmentary or it can be done with all your being, totally. So, by perception of the whole we mean perception with your eyes, your ears, your heart, your mind; not perception with each separately. It is giving your complete attention. In that attention, the particular, such as anger, has a different meaning since it is inter-related to many other issues.

Questioner: So when you say seeing the whole, you mean seeing with the whole of your being; it is a question of quality not quantity. Is that correct?

KRISHNAMURTI: Yes, precisely. But *do* you see totally in this way or are you merely verbalizing it? Do you see anger with your heart, mind, ears and eyes? Or do you see anger as something unrelated to the rest of you, and therefore of great importance? When you give importance to the whole you do not forget the particular.

Questioner: But what happens to the particular, to anger?

KRISHNAMURTI: You are aware of anger with your whole being. If you are, is there anger? Inattention is anger, not attention. So attention with your entire being is seeing the whole, and inattention is seeing the particular. To be aware of the whole, and of the particular, and of the relationship between the two, is the whole problem. We divide the particular from the rest and try to solve it. And so conflict increases and there is no way out.

Questioner: When you speak then of seeing only the particular, as anger, do you mean looking at it with only one part of your being?

KRISHNAMURTI: When you look at the particular with a fragment of your being, the division between that particular and the fragment which is looking at it grows, and so conflict increases. When there is no division there is no conflict.

Questioner: Are you saying that there is no division between this anger and me when I look at it with all my being?

KRISHNAMURTI: Exactly. Is this what you actually are doing, or are you merely following the words? What is actually taking place? This is far more important than your question.

Questioner: You ask me what is taking place. I am simply trying to understand you.

KRISHNAMURTI: Are you trying to understand me or are you seeing the truth of what we are talking about, which is independent of me? If you actually see the truth of what we are talking about, then you are your own guru and your own disciple, which is to understand yourself. This understanding cannot be learnt from another.

MORALITY

Questioner: What is it to be virtuous? What makes one act righteously? What is the foundation of morality? How do I know virtue without struggling for it? Is it an end in itself?

KRISHNAMURTI: Can we discard the morality of society which is really quite immoral? Its morality has become respectable, approved by religious sanctions; and the morality of counter-revolution also soon becomes as immoral and respectable as that of well-established society. This morality is to go to war, to kill, to be aggressive, to seek power, to give hate its place; it is all the cruelty and injustice of established authority. This is not moral. But can one actually say that it is not moral? Because we are part of this society, whether we are conscious of it or not. Social morality is our morality, and can we easily put it aside? The ease with which we put it aside is the sign of our morality – not the effort it costs us to put it aside, not the reward, not the punishment for this effort but the consummate ease with which we discard it. If our behaviour is directed by the environment in which we live, controlled and shaped by it, then it is mechanical and heavily conditioned. And if our behaviour is the outcome of our own conditioned response, is it moral? If your action is based on fear and reward, is it righteous? If you behave rightly according to some ideological concept or principle, can that action be regarded as virtuous? So we must begin to find out how deeply we have discarded the morality of authority, imitation, conformity and obedience. Isn't fear the basis of our morality? Unless these questions are fundamentally answered for oneself, one cannot know what it is to be truly virtuous. As we said, with what ease you come out of this hypocrisy is of the greatest importance. If you merely disregard it, it doesn't indicate that you are moral: you might be merely psychopathic. If you live a life of routine and contentment that is not morality either. The morality of the saint who conforms and follows the well-established tradition of sainthood is obviously not morality. So one can see that any conformity to a pattern, whether or not it is sanctioned by tradition, is not righteous behaviour. Only out of freedom can come virtue.

Can one free oneself with great skill from this network of what is considered moral? Skill in action comes with freedom, and so virtue.

Questioner: Can I free myself from social morality without fear, with the intelligence which is skill? I'm frightened at the very idea of being considered immoral by society. The young can do it, but I am middle-aged, and I have a family, and in my very blood there is respectability, the essence of the bourgeois. It is there, and I am frightened.

KRISHNAMURTI: Either you accept social morality or reject it. You can't have it both ways. You can't have one foot in hell and the other in heaven.

Questioner: So what am I to do? I see now what morality is, and yet I'm being immoral all the time. The older I grow the more hypocritical I become. I despise the social morality, and yet I want its benefits, its comfort, its security, psychological and material, and the elegance of a good address. That is my actual, deplorable state. What am I to do?

KRISHNAMURTI: You can't do anything but carry on as you are. It is much better to stop trying to be moral, stop trying to be concerned with virtue.

Questioner: But I can't, I want the other! I see the beauty and the vigour of it, the cleanliness of it. What I am holding on to is dirty and ugly, but I can't let it go.

KRISHNAMURTI: Then there is no issue. You can't have virtue and respectability. Virtue is freedom. Freedom is not an idea, a concept. When there is freedom there is attention, and only in this attention can goodness flower.

SUICIDE

Questioner: I would like to talk about suicide – not because of any crisis in my own life, nor because I have any reason for suicide, but because the subject is bound to come up when one sees the tragedy of old age – the tragedy of physical disintegration, the breaking up of the body, and the loss of real life in people when this happens. Is there any reason to prolong life when one reaches that state, to go on with the remnants of it? Would it not perhaps be an act of intelligence to recognize when the usefulness of life is over?

KRISHNAMURTI: If it was intelligence that prompted you to end life, that very intelligence would have forbidden your body to deteriorate prematurely.

Questioner: But is there not a moment when even the intelligence of the mind cannot prevent this deterioration? Eventually the body wears out – how does one recognize that time when it comes?

KRISHNAMURTI: We ought to go into this rather deeply. There are several things involved in it, aren't there? The deterioration of the body, of the organism, the senility of the mind, and the utter incapacity that breeds resistance. We abuse the body endlessly through custom, taste and negligence. Taste dictates – and the pleasure of it controls and shapes the activity of the organism. When this takes place, the natural intelligence of the body is destroyed. In magazines one sees an extraordinary variety of food, beautifully coloured, appealing to your pleasures of taste, not to what is beneficial for the body. So from youth onwards you gradually deaden and destroy the instrument which should be highly sensitive, active, functioning like a perfect machine. That is part of it, and then there is the mind which for twenty, thirty or eighty years has lived in constant battle and resistance. It knows only contradiction and conflict – emotional or intellectual. Every form of conflict is not only a distortion but brings with it destruction. These then are some of the basic inner and outer factors of deterioration – the perpetually self-centred activity with its isolating processes.

Naturally there is the physical wearing out of the body as well as the unnatural wearing out. The body loses its capacities and memories, and senility gradually takes over. You ask, should not such a person commit suicide, take a pill that will put him out? Who is asking the question – the senile, or those who are watching the senility with sorrow, with despair and fear of their own deterioration?

Questioner: Well, obviously the question from my point of view is motivated by distress at seeing senility in other people, for it has not presumably set in in myself yet. But isn't there also some action of intelligence which sees ahead into a possible breakdown of the body and asks the question whether it is not simply a waste to go on once the organism is no longer capable of intelligent life?

KRISHNAMURTI: Will the doctors allow euthanasia, will the doctors or the government permit the patient to commit suicide?

Questioner: That surely is a legal, sociological or in some people's minds, a moral question, but that isn't what we are discussing here, is it? Aren't we asking whether the individual has the right to end his own life, not whether society will permit it?

KRISHNAMURTI: You are asking whether one has the right to take one's own life – not only when one is senile or has become aware of the approach of senility, but whether it is morally right to commit suicide at any time?

214

Questioner: I hesitate to bring morality into it because that is a conditioned thing. I was attempting to ask the question on a straight issue of intelligence. Fortunately at the moment the issue does not confront me personally so I am able to look at it, I think, fairly dispassionately; but as an exercise in human intelligence, what is the answer?

KRISHNAMURTI: You are saying, can an intelligent man commit suicide? Is that it?

Questioner: Or, can suicide be the action of an intelligent man, given certain circumstances?

KRISHNAMURTI: It is the same thing. Suicide comes, after all, either from complete despair, brought about through deep frustration, or from insoluble fear, or from the awareness of the meaninglessness of a certain way of living.

Questioner: May I interrupt to say that this is generally so, but I am trying to ask the question outside any motivation. When one arrives at the point of despair then there is a tremendous motive involved and it is hard to separate the emotion from the intelligence; I am trying to stay within the realm of pure intelligence, without emotion.

KRISHNAMURTI: You are saying, does intelligence allow any form of suicide? Obviously not.

Questioner: Why not?

KRISHNAMURTI: Really one has to understand this word intelligence. Is it intelligence to allow the body to deteriorate through custom, through indulgence, through the cultivation of taste, pleasure and so on? Is that intelligence, is that the action of intelligence?

Questioner: No; but if one has arrived at a point in life where there may have been a certain amount of unintelligent use of the body which has not yet had any effect on it, one can't go back and re-live one's life.

KRISHNAMURTI: Therefore, become aware of the destructive nature of the way we live and put an end to it immediately, not at some future date. The act of immediacy in front of danger is an act of sanity, of intelligence; and the postponement as well as the pursuit of pleasure indicate lack of intelligence.

Questioner: I see that.

KRISHNAMURTI: But don't you also see something quite factual and true, that this isolating process of thought with its self-centred activity is a form of suicide? Isolation is suicide, whether it is the isolation of a nation or of a religious organization, of a family or of a community. You are already caught in that trap which will ultimately lead to suicide.

Questioner: Do you mean the individual or the group?

KRISHNAMURTI: The individual as well as the group. You are already caught in the pattern.

Questioner: Which will ultimately lead to suicide? But everybody doesn't commit suicide!

KRISHNAMURTI: Quite right, but the element of the desire to escape is already there – to escape from facing facts, from facing 'what is', and this escape is a form of suicide.

Questioner: This, I think, is the crux of what I am trying to ask, because it would seem from what you have just said that suicide is an escape. Obviously it is, ninety-nine times out of a hundred, but can there not also be – and this is my question – can there not also be a suicide that is not an escape, that is not an avoidance of what you call the 'what is', but is on the contrary a response of intelligence to 'what is'? One can say that many kinds of neurosis are forms of suicide; what I am trying to ask is whether suicide can ever be other than a neurotic response? Cannot it also be the response of facing a fact, of human intelligence acting on an untenable human condition?

KRISHNAMURTI: When you use the words 'intelligence' and 'untenable condition' it is a contradiction. The two are in contradiction.

Questioner: You have said that if one is facing a precipice, or a deadly snake about to strike, intelligence dictates a certain action, which is an action of avoidance.

KRISHNAMURTI: Is it an action of avoidance or an act of intelligence?

Questioner: Can they not be the same sometimes? If a car comes at me on the highway and I avoid it ...

KRISHNAMURTI: That is an act of intelligence.

Questioner: But it is also an act of avoiding the car.

KRISHNAMURTI: But that is the act of intelligence.

Questioner: Exactly. Therefore, is there not a corollary in living when the thing confronting you is insoluble and deadly?

KRISHNAMURTI: Then you leave it, as you leave the precipice: step away from it.

Questioner: In that case the stepping away implies suicide.

KRISHNAMURTI: No, the suicide is an act of unintelligence.

Questioner: Why?

KRISHNAMURTI: I am showing it to you.

Questioner: Are you saying that an act of suicide is categorically, inevitably, a neurotic response to life?

KRISHNAMURTI: Obviously. It is an act of unintelligence; it is an act which obviously means you have come to a point where you are so completely isolated that you don't see any way out.

Questioner: But I am trying for the purpose of this discussion to assume that there is no way out of the predicament, that one is not acting out of the motive of avoidance of suffering, that it is not stepping aside from reality.

KRISHNAMURTI: Is there in life an occurrence, a relationship, an incident from which you cannot step aside?

Questioner: Of course, there are many.

KRISHNAMURTI: Many? But why do you insist that suicide is the only way out?

Questioner: If one has a deadly disease there is no escaping it.

KRISHNAMURTI: Be careful now, be careful of what we are saying. If I have cancer, and it is going to finish me, and the doctor says, 'Well, my friend, you have got to live with it' what am I to do – commit suicide?

Questioner: Possibly.

KRISHNAMURTI: We are discussing this theoretically. If I personally had terminal cancer, then I would decide, I would consider what to do. It wouldn't be a theoretical question. I would then find out what was the most intelligent thing to do.

Questioner: Are you saying that I may not ask this question theoretically, but only if I am actually in that position?

KRISHNAMURTI: That is right. Then you will act according to your conditioning, according to your intelligence, according to your way of life. If your way of life has been avoidance

218

and escape, a neurotic business, then obviously you take a neurotic attitude and action. But if you have led a life of real intelligence, in the total meaning of that word, then that intelligence will operate when there is terminal cancer. Then I may put up with it; then I may say that I will live the few more months or years left to me.

Questioner: Or you may not say that.

KRISHNAMURTI: Or I may not say that; but don't let us say that suicide is inevitable.

Questioner: I never said that; I asked if under certain stringent circumstances, such as terminal cancer, suicide could possibly be an intelligent response to the situation.

KRISHNAMURTI: You see, there is something extraordinary in this; life has brought you great happiness, life has brought you extraordinary beauty, life has brought you great benefits, and you went with it all. Equally, when you were unhappy you went with it, which is part of intelligence: now you come to terminal cancer and you say, 'I cannot bear it any longer, I must put an end to life.' Why don't you move with it, live with it, find out about it as you go along?

Questioner: In other words, there is no reply to this question until you are in the situation.

KRISHNAMURTI: Obviously. But you see that is why it is very important, I feel, that we should face the fact, face 'what is', from moment to moment, not theorize about it. If someone is ill, desperately ill with cancer, or has become completely senile – what is the most intelligent thing to do, not for a mere observer like me, but for the doctor, the wife or the daughter?

Questioner: One cannot really answer that, because it is a problem for another human being.

KRISHNAMURTI: That's just it, that is just what I am saying.

Questioner: And one hasn't the right, it would seem to me, to decide about the life or death of another human being.

KRISHNAMURTI: But we do. All the tyrannies do. And tradition does; tradition says you must live this way, you mustn't live that way.

Questioner: And it is also becoming a tradition to keep people alive beyond the point where nature would have given in. Through medical skill people are kept alive – well, it's hard to define what is a natural condition – but it seems most unnatural to survive for as long as many people do today. But that is a different question.

KRISHNAMURTI: Yes, an entirely different question. The real question is, will intelligence allow suicide – even though doctors have said one has an incurable disease? One cannot possibly tell another what to do in this matter. It is for the human being who has the incurable disease to act according to his intelligence. If he is at all intelligent – which means that he has lived a life in which there has been love, care sensitivity and gentleness – then such a person, at the moment when it arises, will act according to the intelligence which has operated in the past.

Questioner: Then this whole conversation is in a way meaningless because that is what would have happened anyway – because people would inevitably act according to what had happened in the past. They will either blow their brains out or sit and suffer until they die, or something in between.

KRISHNAMURTI: No, it hasn't been meaningless. Listen to this; we have discovered several things – primarily that to live with intelligence is the most important thing. To live a way of life which is supremely intelligent demands an extraordinary alertness of mind and body, and we've destroyed the alertness of the body by unnatural ways of living. We are also destroying the mind, the brain, through conflict through constant repression, constant explosion and viol ence. So if one lives a way of life that is a negation of all this, then that life, that intelligence, when confronted with incurable disease will act in the moment rightly.

Questioner: I see that I have asked you a question about suicide and have been given an answer on how to live rightly.

KRISHNAMURTI: It is the only way. A man jumping over the bridge doesn't ask, 'Shall I commit suicide?' He is doing it; it is finished. Whereas we, sitting in a safe house or in a laboratory, asking whether a man should or should not commit suicide, has no meaning.

Questioner: So it is a question one cannot ask.

KRISHNAMURTI: No, it must be asked – whether one should or should not commit suicide. It must be asked, but find out what is behind the question, what is prompting the questioner, what is making him want to commit suicide. We know a man who has never committed suicide, although he is always threatening to do so, because he is completely lazy. He doesn't want to do a thing, he wants everybody to support him; such a man has already committed suicide. The man who is obstinate, suspicious, greedy for power and position, has also inwardly committed suicide. He lives behind a wall of images. So any man who lives with an image of himself, of his environment, his ecology, his political power or religion, is already finished.

Questioner: It would seem to me that what you are saying is that any life that is not lived directly . . .

KRISHNAMURTI: Directly and intelligently.

Questioner: Outside the shadows of images, of conditioning, of thinking . . . Unless one lives that way, one's life is a kind of low-key existence.

KRISHNAMURTI: Of course it is. Look at most people; they

are living behind a wall – the wall of their knowledge, their desires, their ambitious drives. They are already in a state of neurosis and that neurosis gives them a certain security which is the security of suicide.

Questioner: The security of suicide!

KRISHNAMURTI: Like a singer, for example; to him the voice is the greatest security, and when that fails he is ready to commit suicide. What is really exciting and true is to find out for oneself a way of life that is highly sensitive and supremely intelligent; and this is not possible if there is fear, anxiety, greed, envy, the building of images or the living in religious isolation. That isolation is what all religions have supplied: the believer is definitely on the threshold of suicide. Because he has put all his faith in a belief, when that belief is questioned he is afraid and is ready to take on another belief, another image, commit another religious suicide. So, can a man live without any image, without any pattern, without any time-sense? I don't mean living in such a way as not to care what happens tomorrow or what happened yesterday. That is not living. There are those who say 'Take the present and make the best of it'; that is also an act of despair. Really one should not ask whether or not it is right to commit suicide; one should ask what brings about the state of mind that has no hope – though hope is the wrong word because hope implies a future; one should ask, rather, how does a life come about that is without time? To live without time is really to have this sense of great love, because love is not of time, love is not something that was or will be; to explore this and live with it is the real question. Whether to commit suicide or not is the question of a man who is already partially dead. Hope is the most dreadful thing. Wasn't it Dante who said, 'Leave hope behind when you enter the Inferno'? To him, paradise was hope, that horrible.

Questioner: Yes, hope is its own inferno.

DISCIPLINE

Questioner: I've been brought up in a very restricted environment, in strict discipline, not only as to outward behaviour but also I was taught to discipline myself, to control my thoughts and appetites and to do certain things regularly. The result is that I find myself so hedged about that I can't do anything easily, freely and happily. When I see what is going on around me in this permissive society – the sloppiness, the dirt, the casual behaviour, the indifference to manners – I'm shocked, although at the same time I secretly desire to do some of these things myself. Discipline imposed certain values though; it brought with it frustrations and distortions, but surely some discipline is necessary – for instance, to sit decently, to eat properly, to speak with care? Without discipline one can't perceive the beauties of music or literature or painting. Good manners and training reveal a great many nuances in daily social commerce. When I observe the modern generation they have the beauty of youth, but without discipline it will soon fade away and they will become rather tiresome old men and women. There is a tragedy in all this. You see a young man, supple, eager, beautiful with clear eyes and a lovely smile, and a few years later you see him again and he is almost unrecognizable – sloppy, callous, indifferent, full of platitudes, highly respectable, hard, ugly, closed and sentimental. Surely discipline would have saved him. I, who have been disciplined almost out of existence, often wonder where the middle way is between this permissive society and the culture in which I was brought up. Isn't there a way to live without the distortion and suppression of discipline, yet to be highly disciplined within oneself?

KRISHNAMURTI: Discipline means to learn, not to conform,

not to suppress, not to imitate the pattern of what accepted authority considers noble. This is a very complex question for in it are involved several things: to learn, to be austere, to be free, to be sensitive, and to see the beauty of love.

In learning there is no accumulation. Knowledge is different from learning. Knowledge is accumulation, conclusions, formulas, but learning is a constant movement, a movement without a centre, without a beginning or an end. To learn about oneself there must be no accumulation in one's learning: if there is, it is not learning about oneself but merely adding to one's accumulated knowledge of oneself. Learning is the freedom of perception, of seeing. And you cannot learn if you are not free. So this very learning is its own discipline – you don't have to discipline yourself and then learn. Therefore discipline is freedom. This denies all conformity and control, for control is the imitation of a pattern. A pattern is suppression, suppression of 'what is', and the learning about 'what is' is denied when there is a formula of what is good and what is bad. The learning about 'what is' is the freedom from 'what is'. So learning is the highest form of discipline. Learning demands intelligence and sensitivity.

The austerity of the priest and the monk is harsh. They deny certain of their appetites but not others which custom has condoned. The saint is the triumph of harsh violence. Austerity is generally identified with self-denial through the brutality of discipline, drill and conformity. The saint is trying to break a record like the athlete. To see the falseness of this brings about its own austerity. The saint is stupid and shoddy. To see this is intelligence. Such intelligence will not go off the deep end to the opposite extreme. Intelligence is the sensitivity which understands, and therefore avoids, the extremes. But it is not the prudent mediocrity of remaining half-way between the two. To perceive all this clearly is to learn about it. To learn about it there must be freedom from all conclusions and bias. Such conclusions and bias are observation from a centre, the self, which wills and directs.

Questioner: Aren't you simply saying that to look properly you must be objective?

KRISHNAMURTI: Yes, but the word objective is not enough. What we are talking about is not the harsh objectiveness of the microscope, but a state in which there is compassion, sensitivity and depth. Discipline, as we said, is learning, and learning about austerity does not bring about violence to oneself or to another. Discipline, as it is generally understood, is the act of will, which is violence.

People throughout the world seem to think that freedom is the fruit of prolonged discipline. To see clearly is its own discipline. To see clearly there must be freedom, not a controlled vision. So freedom is not at the end of discipline, but the understanding of freedom is its own discipline. The two go together inseparably: when you separate them there is conflict. To overcome that conflict, the action of will comes into being and breeds more conflict. This is an endless chain. So freedom is at the beginning and not at the end: the beginning is the end. To learn about all this is its own discipline. Learning itself demands sensitivity. If you are not sensitive to yourself – to your environment, to your relationships – if you are not sensitive to what is happening around you, in the kitchen or in the world, then however much you discipline yourself you only become more and more insensitive, more and more self-centred – and this breeds innumerable problems. To learn is to be sensitive to yourself and to the world outside you, for the world outside is you. If you are sensitive to yourself you are bound to be sensitive to the world. This sensitivity is the highest form of intelligence. It is not the sensitivity of a specialist – the doctor, the scientist or the artist. Such fragmentation does not bring sensitivity.

How can one love if there is no sensitivity? Sentimentality and emotionalism deny sensitivity because they are terribly cruel; they are responsible for wars. So discipline is not the drill of the sergeant – whether in the parade-ground or in yourself – which is the will. Learning all day long, and during sleep, has its own extraordinary discipline which is as gentle as the new spring leaf and as swift as the light. In this there is love. Love has its own discipline, and the beauty of it escapes a mind that is drilled, shaped, controlled, tortured. Without such a discipline the mind cannot go very far.

WHAT IS

Questioner: I have read a great deal of philosophy, psychology, religion and politics, all of which to a greater or lesser degree are concerned with human relationships. I have also read your books which all deal with thought and ideas, and somehow I'm fed up with it all. I have swum in an ocean of words, and wherever I go there are more words – and actions derived from those words are offered to me: advice, exhortations, promises, theories, analyses, remedies. Of course one sets all these aside – you yourself have really done so; but for most of those who have read you, or heard you, what you say is just words. There may be people for whom all this is more than words, for whom it is utterly real, but I'm talking about the rest of us. I'd like to go beyond the word, beyond the idea, and live in total relationship to all things. For after all, that is life. You have said that one has to be a teacher and a pupil to oneself. Can I live in the greatest simplicity, without principles, beliefs, and ideals? Can I live freely, knowing that I am enslaved by the world? Crises don't knock on the door before they appear: challenges of everyday life are there before you are aware of them. Knowing all this, having been involved in many of these things, chasing various phantoms, I ask myself how I can live rightly and with love, clarity and effortless joy. I'm not asking how to live, but to live: the how denies the actual living itself. The nobility of life is not practising nobility.

KRISHNAMURTI: After stating all this, where are you? Do you really want to live with benediction, with love? If you do, then where is the problem?

Questioner: I do want to, but that doesn't get me anywhere. I've wanted to live that way for years, but I can't.

KRISHNAMURTI: So though you deny the ideal, the belief, the directive, you are very subtly and deviously asking the same thing which everybody asks: this is the conflict between the 'what is' and the 'what should be'.

Questioner: Even without the 'what should be', I see that the 'what is' is hideous. To deceive myself into not seeing it would be much worse still.

KRISHNAMURTI: If you see 'what is' then you see the universe, and denying 'what is' is the origin of conflict. The beauty of the universe is in the 'what is'; and to live with 'what is' without effort is virtue.

Questioner: The 'what is' also includes confusion, violence, every form of human aberration. To live with that is what you call virtue. But isn't it callousness and insanity? Perfection doesn't consist simply in dropping all ideals! Life itself demands that I live it beautifully, like the eagle in the sky: to live the miracle of life with anything less than total beauty is unacceptable.

KRISHNAMURTI: Then live it!

Questioner: I can't, and I don't.

KRISHNAMURTI: If you can't, then live in confusion; don't battle with it. Knowing the whole misery of it, live with it: that is 'what is'. And to live with it without conflict frees us from it.

Questioner: Are you saying that our only fault is to be self-critical?

KRISHNAMURTI: Not at all. You are not sufficiently critical. You go only so far in your self-criticism. The very entity that criticizes must be criticized, must be examined. If the examination is comparative, examination by yardstick, then that yardstick is the ideal. If there is no yardstick at all – in other words, if there is no mind that is always comparing and measuring – you can observe the 'what is', and then the 'what is' is no longer the same.

Questioner: I observe myself without a yardstick, and I'm still ugly.

KRISHNAMURTI: All examination means there is a yardstick. But is it possible to observe so that there is only observation, seeing, and nothing else – so that there is only perception without a perceiver?

Questioner: What do you mean?

KRISHNAMURTI: There is looking. The assessment of the looking is interference, distortion in the looking: that is not looking; instead it is evaluation of looking – the two are as different as chalk and cheese. Is there a perception of yourself *without* distortion, only an absolute perception of yourself as you are?

Questioner: Yes.

KRISHNAMURTI: In that perception is there ugliness?

Questioner: There is no ugliness in the perception, only in what is perceived.

KRISHNAMURTI: The way you perceive is what you are. Righteousness is in purely looking, which is attention without the distortion of measure and idea. You came to inquire how to live beautifully, with love. To look without distortion is love, and the action of that perception is the action of virtue. That clarity of perception will act all the time in living. That is living like the eagle in the sky; that is living beauty and living love.

THE SEEKER

Questioner: What is it I'm seeking? I really don't know, but there is a tremendous longing in me for something much more than comfort, pleasure and the satisfaction of fulfilment. I happen to have had all these things, but this is something much more – something at an unfathomable depth that is crying to be released, trying to tell me something. I've had this feeling for many years but when I examine it I don't seem to be able to touch it. Yet it is always there, this longing to go beyond the mountains and the skies to find something. But perhaps this thing is there right in front of me, only I don't see it. Don't tell me how to look: I've read many of your writings and I know what you mean. I want to reach out of my hand and take this thing very simply, knowing very well that I cannot hold the wind in my fist. It is said that if you operate on a tumour neatly you can pluck it out in one pocket, intact. In the same way I should like to take this whole earth, the heavens and the skies and the seas in one movement, and come upon that blessedness on the instant. Is this at all possible? How am I to cross to the other shore without taking a boat and rowing across the waters? I feel that's the only way.

KRISHNAMURTI: Yes, that's the only way – to find oneself strangely and unaccountably on the other shore, and from there to live, act and do everything that one does in daily life.

Questioner: Is it only for the few? Is it for me? I really don't know what to do. I've sat silent; I've studied, examined, disciplined myself, rather intelligently I think, and of course I've long ago discarded the temples, the shrines and the priests. I refuse to go from one system to another; it is all too futile. So you see I have come here with complete simplicity.

KRISHNAMURTI: I wonder if you really are so simple as you think! From what depth are you asking this question, and with what love and beauty? Can your mind and heart receive this? Are they sensitive to the slightest whisper of something that comes unexpectedly?

Questioner: If it is as subtle as all that, how true is it, and how real? Intimations of such subtlety are usually fleeting and unimportant.

KRISHNAMURTI: Are they? Must everything be written out on the blackboard? Please, sir, let us find out whether our minds and hearts are really capable of receiving immensity, and not just the word.

Questioner: I really don't know, that's my problem. I've done almost everything fairly intelligently, putting aside all the obvious stupidities of nationality, organized religion, belief – this endless passage of nothings. I think I have compassion, and I think my mind can grasp the subtleties of life, but that surely is not enough? So what is needed? What have I to do or not to do?

KRISHNAMURTI: Doing nothing is far more important than doing something. Can the mind be completely inactive, and thereby be supremely active? Love is not the activity of thought; it is not the action of good behaviour or social righteousness. As you cannot cultivate it, you can do nothing about love.

Questioner: I understand what you mean when you say that inaction is the highest form of action – which doesn't mean to do nothing. But somehow I cannot grasp it with my heart. Is it perhaps only because my heart is empty, tired of all action, that inaction seems to have an appeal? No. I come back to my original feeling that there is this thing of love, and I know, too, that it is the only thing. But my hand is still empty after I have said that.

KRISHNAMURTI: Does this mean that you are no longer seeking, no longer saying to yourself secretly: 'I must reach, attain, there is something beyond the furthest hills?'

Questioner: You mean I must give up this feeling I have had for so long that there is something beyond all the hills?

KRISHNAMURTI: It is not a question of giving up anything, but, as we said just now, there are only these two things: love, and the mind that is empty of thought. If you really have finished, if you really have shut the door on all the stupidities which man in his search for something has put together, if you really have finished with all these, then, are these things – love and the empty mind – just two more words, no different from any other ideas?

Questioner: I have a deep feeling that they are not, but I am not sure of it. So again I ask what I am to do.

KRISHNAMURTI: Do you know what it means to commune with what we have just said about love and the mind?

Questioner: Yes, I think so.

KRISHNAMURTI: I wonder if you do. If there is communion with these two things then there is nothing more to be said. If there is communion with these two things then all action will be from there.

Questioner: The trouble is that I still think there is something to be discovered which will put everything else in its right place, in its right order.

KRISHNAMURTI: Without these two things there is no possibility of going further. And there may be no going anywhere at all!

Questioner: Can I be in communion with it all the time? I can see that when we are together I can be somewhat in communion with it. But can I maintain it?

KRISHNAMURTI: To desire to maintain it is the noise, and therefore the losing of it.

ORGANIZATION

Questioner: I have belonged to many organizations, religious, business and political . Obviously we must have some kind of organization; without it life couldn't continue, so I've been wondering, after listening to you, what relationship there is between freedom and organization. Where does freedom begin and organization end? What is the relationship between religious organizations and Moksha or liberation?

KRISHNAMURTI: As human beings living in a very complex society, organizations are needed to communicate, to travel, to bring food, clothes and shelter, for all the business of living together whether in cities or in the country. Now this must be organized efficiently and humanely, not only for the benefit of the few but for everyone, without the divisions of nationality, race or class. This earth is ours, not yours or mine. To live happily, physically, there must be sane, rational, efficient organizations. Now there is disorder because there is division. Millions go hungry while there is vast prosperity. There are wars, conflicts and every form of brutality. Then there is the organization of belief – the organization of religions, which again breeds disunity and war. The morality which man has pursued has led to this disorder and chaos. This is the actual state of the world. And when you ask what is the relationship between organization and freedom, are you not separating freedom from everyday existence? When you separate it in this way as being something entirely different from life, isn't this, in itself, conflict and disorder? So really the question is: is it possible to live in freedom and to organize life from this freedom, in this freedom?

Questioner: Then there would be no problem. But the or-

ganization of life isn't made by yourself: others make it for you – the government and others send you to war or determine your job. So you cannot simply organize for yourself out of freedom. The whole point of my question is that the organization imposed on us by the government, by society, by morality, is not freedom. And if we reject it we find ourselves in the midst of a revolution, or some sociological reformation, which is a way of starting the same old cycle all over again. Inwardly and outwardly we are born into organization, which limits freedom. We either submit or revolt. We are caught in this trap. So there seems to be no question of organizing anything out of freedom.

KRISHNAMURTI: We do not realize that we have created society, this disorder, these walls; each one of us is responsible for it all. What we are, society is. Society is not different from us. If we are in conflict, avaricious, envious, fearful, we bring about such a society.

Questioner: There is a difference between the individual and society. I am a vegetarian; society slaughters animals. I don't want to go to war; society will force me to do so. Are you telling me that this war is my doing?

KRISHNAMURTI: Yes, it's your responsibility. You have brought it about by your nationality, your greed, envy and hate. You are responsible for war as long as you have those things in your heart, as long as you belong to any nationality, creed or race. It is only those who are free of those things who can say that they have not created this society. Therefore our responsibility is to see that we change, and to help others to change, without violence and bloodshed.

Questioner: That means organized religion.

KRISHNAMURTI: Certainly not. Organized religion is based on belief and authority.

Questioner: Where does this get us in our original question regarding the relationship between freedom and organization? Organization is always imposed or inherited from the environment, and freedom is always from the inside, and these two clash.

KRISHNAMURTI: Where are you going to start? You must start from freedom. Where there is freedom there is love. This freedom and love will show you when to cooperate and when not to cooperate. This is not an act of choice, because choice is the result of confusion. Love and freedom are intelligence. So what we are concerned with is not the division between organization and freedom but whether we can live in this world without division at all. It is division which denies freedom and love, not organization. When organization divides, it leads to war. Belief in any form, ideals, however noble or effective, breed division. Organized religion is the cause of division, just like nationality and power-groups. So be concerned with those things which divide, those things which bring about division between man and man, whether they be individual or collective. The family, the church, and the State bring about such division. What is important is the movement of thought which divides. Thought itself is always divisive, so all action based on an idea or an ideology is division. Thought cultivates prejudice, opinion, judgement. Man in himself, being divided, seeks freedom out of this division. Not being able to find it he hopes to integrate the various divisions, and of course this is not possible. You cannot integrate two prejudices. To live in this world in freedom means to live with love, eschewing every form of division. When there is freedom and love, then this intelligence will act in cooperation, and will also know when not to cooperate.

LOVE AND SEX

Questioner: I'm a married man with several children. I've lived rather a dissipated life in search of pleasure, but a fairly civilized life too, and I've made a success of it financially. But now I'm middle-aged and am feeling concerned, not only about my family but also about the way the world is going. I'm not given to brutality or violent feelings, and I have always considered that forgiveness and compassion are the most important things in life. Without these man becomes sub-human. So if I may I should like to ask you what love is. Is there really such a thing? Compassion must be part of it, but I always feel that love is something much vaster, and if we could explore it together perhaps I should then make my life into something worthwhile before it is too late. I have really come to ask this one thing – what is love?

KRISHNAMURTI: Before we begin to go into this we must be very clear that the word is not the thing, the description is not the described, because any amount of explanation, however subtle and clever, will not open the heart to the immensity of love. This we must understand, and not merely stick to words: words are useful for communication, but in talking about something that is really non-verbal we must establish a communion between us, so that both of us feel and realize the same thing at the same time, with a fullness of mind and heart. Otherwise we will be playing with words. How can one approach this really very subtle thing that cannot be touched by the mind? We must go rather hesitatingly. Shall we first see what it is not, and then perhaps we may be able to see what it is? Through negation we may come upon the positive, but merely to pursue the positive leads to assumptions and conclusions which bring about division. You are asking what love is. We are saying we may come upon it when we know what it is not. Anything that brings about a division, a separation, is not love, for in that there is conflict, strife and brutality.

Questioner: What do you mean by a division, a separation that brings about strife – what do you mean by it?

KRISHNAMURTI: Thought in its very nature is divisive. It is thought that seeks pleasure and holds it. It is thought that cultivates desire.

Questioner: Will you go into desire a bit more?

KRISHNAMURTI: There is the seeing of a house, the sensation that it is lovely, then there is the desire to own it and to have pleasure from it, then there is the effort to get it. All this constitutes the centre, and this centre is the cause of division. This centre is the feeling of a 'me', which is the cause of division, because this very feeling of 'me' is the feeling of separation. People have called this the ego and all kinds of other names – the 'lower self' as opposed to some idea of a 'higher self' – but there is no need to be complicated about it; it is very simple. Where there is the centre, which is the feeling of 'me', which in its activities isolates itself, there is division and resistance. And all this is the process of thought. So when you ask what is love, it is not of this centre. Love is not pleasure and pain, nor hate nor violence in any form.

Questioner: Therefore in this love you speak of there can be no sex because there cannot be desire?

KRISHNAMURTI: Don't, please, come to any conclusion. We are investigating, exploring. Any conclusion or assumption prevents further inquiry. To answer this question we have also to look at the energy of thought. Thought, as we have said, sustains pleasure by thinking about something that has been pleasurable, cultivating the image, the picture. Thought engenders pleasure. Thinking about the sexual act becomes lust, which is entirely different from the act of sex. What most people are concerned with is the passion of lust. Craving before and after sex is lust. This craving is thought. Thought is not love.

Questioner: Can there be sex without this desire of thought?

KRISHNAMURTI: You have to find out for yourself. Sex plays an extraordinarily important part in our lives because it is perhaps the only deep, first-hand experience we have. Intellectually and emotionally we conform, imitate, follow, obey. There is pain and strife in all our relationships, except in the act of sex. This act, being so different and beautiful, we become addicted to, so it in turn becomes a bondage. The bondage is the demand for its continuation – again the action of the centre which is divisive. One is so hedged about – intellectually, in the family, in the community, through social morality, through religious sanctions – so hedged about that there is only this one relationship left in which there is freedom and intensity. Therefore we give tremendous importance to it. But if there were freedom all around then this would not be such a craving and such a problem. We make it a problem because we can't get enough of it, or because we feel guilty at having got it, or because in getting it we break the rules which society has laid down. It is the old society which calls the new society permissive because for the new society sex is a part of life. In freeing the mind from the bondage of imitation, authority, conformity and religious prescriptions, sex has its own place, but it won't be all-consuming. From this one can see that freedom is essential for love – not the freedom of revolt, not the freedom of doing what one likes nor of indulging openly or secretly one's cravings, but rather the freedom which comes in the understanding of this whole structure and nature of the centre. Then freedom is love.

Questioner: So freedom is not licence?

KRISHNAMURTI: No. Licence is bondage. Love is not hate, nor jealousy, nor ambition, nor the competitive spirit with its fear of failure. It is not the love of god nor the love of man – which again is a division. Love is not of the one or of the many. When there is love it is personal and impersonal, with and without an object. It is like the perfume of a flower; one or many can smell it: what matters is the perfume, not to whom it belongs.

Questioner: Where does forgiveness come in all this?

KRISHNAMURTI: When there is love there can be no forgiveness. Forgiveness comes only after you have accumulated rancour; forgiveness is resentment. Where there is no wound there is no need for healing. It is inattention that breeds resentment and hate, and you become aware of them and then forgive. Forgiveness encourages division. When you are conscious that you are forgiving, then you are sinning. When you are conscious that you are tolerant, then you are intolerant. When you are conscious that you are silent, then there is no silence. When you deliberately set about to love, then you are violent. As long as there is an observer who says, 'I am' or 'I am not', love cannot be.

Questioner: What place has fear in love?

KRISHNAMURTI: How can you ask such a question? Where one is, the other is not. When there is love you can do what you will.

PERCEPTION

Questioner: You use different words for perception. You sometimes say 'perception', but also 'observe', 'see', 'understand', 'be aware of'. I suppose you use all these words to mean the same thing: to see clearly, completely, wholly. Can one see anything totally? We're not talking of physical or technical things, but psychologically can you perceive or understand anything totally? Isn't there always something concealed so that you only see partially? I'd be most obliged if you could go into this matter rather extensively. I feel this is an important question because it may perhaps be a clue to a great many things in life. If I could understand myself totally then perhaps I would have all my problems solved and be a happy super-human being. When I talk about it I feel rather excited at the possibility of going beyond my little world with its problems and agonies. So what do you mean by perceiving, seeing? Can one see oneself completely?

KRISHNAMURTI: We always look at things partially. Firstly because we are inattentive and secondly because we look at things from prejudices, from verbal and psychological images about what we see. So we never see anything completely. Even to look objectively at nature is quite arduous. To look at a flower without any image, without any botanical knowledge – just to observe it – becomes quite difficult because our mind is wandering, uninterested. And even if it is interested it looks at the flower with certain appreciations and verbal descriptions which seem to give the observer a feeling that he has really looked at it. Deliberate looking is not looking. So we really never look at the flower. We look at it through the image. Perhaps it is fairly easy to look at something that doesn't deeply touch us, as when we go to the

241

cinema and see something which stirs us for the moment but which we soon forget. But to observe ourselves without the image – which is the past, our accumulated experience and knowledge – happens very rarely. We have an image about ourselves. We think we ought to be this and not that. We have built a previous idea about ourselves and through it we look at ourselves. We think we are noble or ignoble and seeing what we actually are either depresses us or frightens us. So we cannot look at ourselves; and when we do, it is partial observation, and anything that is partial or incomplete doesn't bring understanding. It is only when we can look at ourselves totally that there is a possibility of being free from what we observe. Our perception is not only with the eyes, with the senses, but also with the mind, and obviously the mind is heavily conditioned. So intellectual perception is only partial perception, yet perceiving with the intellect seems to satisfy most of us, and we think we understand. A fragmentary understanding is the most dangerous and destructive thing. And that is exactly what is happening all over the world. The politician, the priest, the businessman, the technician; even the artist – all of them see only partially. And therefore they are really very destructive people. As they play a great part in the world their partial perception becomes the accepted norm, and man is caught in this. Each of us is at the same time the priest, the politician, the businessman, the artist, and many other fragmentary entities. And each of us is also the battlefield of all these conflicting opinions and judgements.

Questioner: I see this clearly. I'm using the word see intellectually, of course.

KRISHNAMURTI: If you see this totally, not intellectually or verbally or emotionally, then you will act and live quite a different kind of life. When you see a dangerous precipice or are faced by a dangerous animal there is no partial understanding or partial action; there is complete action.

Questioner: But we are not faced with such dangerous crises every moment of our lives.

KRISHNAMURTI: We *are* faced with such dangerous crises all the time. You have become accustomed to them, or are indifferent to them, or you leave it to others to solve the problems; and these others are equally blind and lopsided.

Questioner: But how am I to be aware of these crises all the time, and why do you say there is a crisis all the time?

KRISHNAMURTI: The whole of life is in each moment. Each moment is a challenge. To meet this challenge inadequately is a crisis in living. We don't want to see that these are crises, and we shut our eyes to escape from them. So we become blinder, and the crises augment.

Questioner: But how am I to perceive totally? I'm beginning to understand that I see only partially, and also to understand the importance of looking at myself and the world with complete perception, but there is so much going on in me that it is difficult to decide what to look at. My mind is like a great cage full of restless monkeys.

KRISHNAMURTI: If you see one movement totally, in that totality every other movement is included. If you understand one problem completely, then you understand all human problems, for they are all inter-related. So the question is: can one understand, or perceive, or see, one problem so completely that in the very understanding of it one has understood the rest? This problem must be seen while it is happening, not after or before, as memory or as an example. For instance, it is no good now for us to go into anger or fear; the thing to do is to observe them as they arise. Perception is instantaneous: you understand something instantly or not at all: seeing, hearing, understanding are instantaneous. Listening and looking have duration.

Questioner: My problem goes on. It exists in a span of time. You are saying that seeing is instantaneous and therefore out of time. What gives jealousy or any other habit, or any other problem, duration?

KRISHNAMURTI: Don't they go on because you have not looked at them with sensitivity, choiceless awareness, intelligence? You have looked partially and therefore allowed them to continue. And in addition, wanting to get rid of them is another problem with duration. The incapacity to deal with something makes of it a problem with duration, and gives it life.

Questioner: But how am I to see that whole thing instantly? How am I to understand so that it never comes back?

KRISHNAMURTI: Are you laying emphasis on never or on understanding? If you lay emphasis on never it means you want to escape from it permanently, and this means the creation of a second problem. So we have only one question, which is how to see the problem so completely that one is free of it. Perception can only be out of silence, not out of a chattering mind. The chattering may be the wanting to get rid of it, reduce it, escape from it, suppress it or find a substitute for it, but it is only a quiet mind that sees.

Questioner: How am I to have a quiet mind?

KRISHNAMURTI: You don't see the truth that only a quiet mind sees. How to get a quiet mind doesn't arise. It is the truth that the mind must be quiet, and seeing the truth of this frees the mind from chattering. Perception, which is intelligence, is then operating, not the assumption that you must be silent in order to see. Assumption can also operate but that is a partial, fragmentary operation. There is no relationship between the partial and the total; the partial cannot grow into the total. Therefore seeing is of the greatest importance. Seeing is attention, and it is only inattention that gives rise to a problem.

Questioner: How can I be attentive all the time? It's impossible!

KRISHNAMURTI: That's quite right, it *is* impossible. But to be aware of your inattention is of the greatest importance, not how to be attentive all the time. It is greed that asks the question, 'How can I be attentive all the time?' One gets lost in the practice of being attentive. The practice of being attentive is inattention. You cannot practise to be beautiful, or to love. When hate ceases the other is. Hate can cease only when you give your whole attention to it, when you learn and do not accumulate knowledge about it. Begin very simply.

Questioner: What is the point of your talking if there is nothing we can practise after having heard you?

KRISHNAMURTI: The hearing is of the greatest importance, not what you practise afterwards. The hearing is the instantaneous action. The practice gives duration to problems. Practice is total inattention. Never practise: you can only practise mistakes. Learning is always new.

SUFFERING

Questioner: I seem to have suffered a great deal all my life, not physically, but through death and loneliness and the utter futility of my existence. I had a son whom I greatly loved. He died in an accident. My wife left me, and that caused a great deal of pain. I suppose I am like thousands of other middle-class people with sufficient money and a steady job. I'm not complaining of my circumstances but I want to understand what sorrow means, why it comes at all. One has been told that wisdom comes through sorrow, but I have found quite the contrary.

KRISHNAMURTI: I wonder what you have learnt from suffering? Have you learnt anything at all? What has sorrow taught you?

Questioner: It has certainly taught me never to be attached to people, and a certain bitterness, a certain aloofness, and not to allow my feelings to run away with me. It has taught me to be very careful not to get hurt again.

KRISHNAMURTI: So, as you say, it hasn't taught you wisdom; on the contrary it has made you more cunning, more insensitive. Does sorrow teach one anything at all except the obvious self-protective reactions?

Questioner: I have always accepted suffering as part of my life, but I feel now, somehow, that I'd like to be free of it, free of all the tawdry bitterness and indifference without again going through all the pain of attachment. My life is so pointless and empty, utterly self-enclosed and insignificant. It's a life of mediocrity, and perhaps that mediocrity is the greatest sorrow of all.

KRISHNAMURTI: There is the personal sorrow and the sorrow of the world. There is the sorrow of ignorance and the sorrow of time. This ignorance is the lack of knowing oneself, and the sorrow of time is the deception that time can cure, heal and change. Most people are caught in that deception and either worship sorrow or explain it away. But in either case it continues, and one never asks oneself if it can come to an end.

Questioner: But I am asking now if it can come to an end, and how? How am I to end it? I understand that it's no good running away from it, or resisting it with bitterness and cynicism. What am I to do to end the grief which I have carried for so long?

KRISHNAMURTI: Self-pity is one of the elements of sorrow. Another element is being attached to someone and encouraging or fostering his attachment to you. Sorrow is not only there when attachment fails you but its seed is in the very beginning of that attachment. In all this the trouble is the utter lack of knowing oneself. Knowing oneself is the ending of sorrow. We are afraid to know ourselves because we have divided ourselves into the good and the bad, the evil and the noble, the pure and the impure. The good is always judging the bad, and these fragments are at war with each other. This war is sorrow. To end sorrow is to see the fact and not invent its opposite, for the opposites contain each other. Walking in this corridor of opposites is sorrow. This fragmentation of life into the high and the low, the noble and the ignoble, God and the Devil, breeds conflict and pain. When there is sorrow, there is no love. Love and sorrow cannot live together.

Questioner: Ah! But love can inflict sorrow on another. I may love another and yet bring him sorrow.

KRISHNAMURTI: Do you bring it, if you love, or does he? If another is attached to you, with or without encouragement, and you turn away from him and he suffers, is it you or he who has brought about his suffering?

Questioner: You mean I am not responsible for someone else's sorrow, even if it is on my account? How does sorrow ever end then?

KRISHNAMURTI: As we have said, it is only in knowing oneself completely that sorrow ends. Do you know yourself at a glance, or hope to after a long analysis? Through analysis you cannot know yourself. You can only know yourself without accumulation, in relationship, from moment to moment. This means that one must be aware, without any choice, of what is actually taking place. It means to see oneself as one is, without the opposite, the ideal, without the knowledge of what one has been. If you look at yourself with the eyes of resentment or rancour then what you see is coloured by the past. The shedding of the past all the time when you see yourself is the freedom from the past. Sorrow ends only when there is the light of understanding, and this light is not lit by one experience or by one flash of understanding; this understanding is lighting itself all the time. Nobody can give it to you – no book, trick, teacher or saviour. The understanding of yourself is the ending of sorrow.

THE HEART AND THE MIND

Questioner: Why is it that man has divided his being into different compartments – the intellect and the emotions? Each seems to exist independently of the other. These two driving forces in life are often so contradictory that they seem to tear apart the very fabric of our being. To bring them together so that man can act as a total entity has always been one of the principal aims of life. And added to these two things within man there is a third which is his changing environment. So these two contradictory things within him are further in opposition to the third which appears to be outside himself. Here is a problem so confusing, so contradictory, so vast that the intellect invents an outside agency called God to bring them together, and this further complicates the whole business. There is only this one problem in life.

KRISHNAMURTI: You seem to be carried away by your own words. Is this really a problem to you or are you inventing it in order to have a good discussion? If it is for a discussion then it has no real content. But if it is a real problem then we can go into it deeply. Here we have a very complex situation, the inner dividing itself into compartments and further separating itself from its environment. And still further, it separates the environment, which it calls society, into classes, races and economic, national and geographic groups. This seems to be what is actually going on in the world and we call it living. Being unable to solve this problem we invent a super-entity, an agency that we hope will bring about a harmony and a binding quality in ourselves and between us. This binding quality which we call religion brings about another factor of division in its turn. So the question becomes: what will bring about a complete harmony of living in which there are no divisions but a state in which the intellect and the heart are both the expression of a total entity? That entity is not a fragment.

Questioner: I agree with you, but how is this to be brought about? This is what man has always longed for and has sought through all religions and all political and social utopias.

KRISHNAMURTI: You ask how. The 'how' is the great mistake. It is the separating factor. There is your 'how' and my 'how' and somebody else's 'how'. So if we never used that word we would be really inquiring and not seeking a method to achieve a determined result. So can you put away altogether this idea of a recipe, a result? If you can define a result you already know it and therefore it is conditioned and not free. If we put away the recipe then we are both capable of inquiring if it is at all possible to bring about a harmonious whole without inventing an outside agency, for all outside agencies, whether they are environmental or super-environmental, only increase the problem.

First of all, it is the mind that divides itself as feeling, intellect and environment; it is the mind that invents the outside agency; it is the mind that creates the problem.

Questioner: This division is not only in the mind. It is even stronger in the feelings. The Muslims and Hindus do not think themselves separate, they feel themselves separate, and it is this feeling that actually makes them separate and makes them destroy each other.

KRISHNAMURTI: Exactly: the thinking and the feeling are one; they have been one from the beginning and that is exactly what we are saying. So our problem is not the integration of the different fragments but the understanding of this mind and heart which are one. Our problem is not how to get rid of classes or how to build better utopias or breed better political leaders or new religious teachers. Our problem is the mind. To come to this point not theoretically but to see it actually is the highest form of intelligence. For then you do not belong to any class or religious group; then you are not a Muslim, a Hindu, a Jew or a Christian. So we now have only one issue: why does the mind of man divide? It not only divides its own functions into feelings and thoughts but separates itself as the 'I' from the 'you', and the 'we' from the 'they'. The mind and the heart are one. Don't let us forget it. Remember it when we use the word 'mind'. So our problem is, why does the mind divide?

Questioner: Yes.

KRISHNAMURTI: The mind is thought. All the activity of thought is separation, fragmentation. Thought is the response of memory which is the brain. The brain must respond when it sees a danger. This is intelligence, but this same brain has somehow been conditioned not to see the danger of division. Its actions are valid and necessary when they deal with facts. Equally, it will act when it sees the fact that division and fragmentation are dangerous to it. This is not an idea or an ideology or a principle or a concept – all of which are idiotic and separative: it is a fact. To see danger the brain has to be very alert and awake, all of it, not just a segment of it.

Questioner: How is it possible to keep the whole brain awake?

KRISHNAMURTI: As we said, there is no 'how' but only seeing the danger, that is the whole point. The seeing is not the result of propaganda or conditioning; the seeing is with the whole brain. When the brain is completely awake then the mind becomes quiet. When the brain is completely awake there is no fragmentation, no separation, no duality. The quality of this quietness is of the highest importance. You can make the mind quiet by drugs and all kinds of tricks but such deceptions breed various other forms of illusion and contradiction. This quietness is the highest form of intelligence which is never personal or impersonal, never yours or mine. Being anonymous, it is whole and immaculate. It defies description for it has no quality. This is awareness, this is attention, this is love, this is the highest. The brain must be completely awake, that's all. As the man in the jungle must keep terribly awake to survive, so the man in the jungle of the world must keep terribly awake to live completely.

BEAUTY AND THE ARTIST

Questioner: I wonder what an artist is? There on the banks of the Ganges, in a dark little room, a man sits weaving a most beautiful saree in silk and gold, and in Paris in his atelier another man is painting a picture which he hopes will bring him fame. Somewhere there is a writer cunningly spinning out stories stating the old, old problem of man and woman; then there is the scientist in his laboratory and the technician putting together a million parts so that a rocket may go to the moon. And in India a musician is living a life of great austerity in order to transmit faithfully the distilled beauty of his music. There is the housewife preparing a meal, and the poet walking alone in the woods. Aren't these all artists in their own way? I feel that beauty is in the hands of everybody, but they don't know it. The man who makes beautiful clothes or excellent shoes, the woman who arranged those flowers on your table, all of them seem to work with beauty. I often wonder why it is that the painter, the sculptor, the composer, the writer – the so-called creative artist – have such extraordinary importance in this world and not the shoemaker or the cook. Aren't they creative too? When you consider all the varieties of expression which people consider beautiful, then what place has a true artist in life, and who is the true artist? It is said that beauty is the very essence of all life. Is that building over there, which is considered to be so beautiful, the expression of that essence? I should greatly appreciate it if you would go into this whole question of beauty and the artist.

KRISHNAMURTI: Surely the artist is one who is skilled in action? This action is in life and not outside of life. Therefore if it is living skilfully that truly makes an artist. This skill can operate for a few hours in the day when he is play-

ing an instrument, writing poems or painting pictures, or i
can operate a bit more if he is skilled in many such fragments – like those great men of the Renaissance who worked
in several different media. But the few hours of music or
writing may contradict the rest of his living which is in dis
order and confusion. So is such a man an artist at all? The
man who plays the violin with artistry and keeps his eye or
his fame isn't interested in the violin, he is only exploiting i
to be famous, the 'me' is far more important than the music
and so it is with the writer or the painter with an eye or
fame. The musician identifies his 'me' with what he con
siders to be beautiful music, and the religious man identifies
his 'me' with what he considers to be the sublime. All these
are skilled in their particular little fields but the rest of the
vast field of life is disregarded. So we have to find out what is
skill in action, in living, not only in painting or in writing or
in technology, but how one can live the whole of life with
skill and beauty. Are skill and beauty the same? Can a
human being – whether he be an artist or not – live the
whole of his life with skill and beauty? Living is action and
when that action breeds sorrow it ceases to be skilful. So can
a man live without sorrow, without friction, without jealousy
and greed, without conflict of any kind? The issue is not who
is an artist and who is not an artist but whether a human
being, you or another, can live without torture and dis
tortion. Of course it is profane to belittle great music, great
sculpture, great poetry or dancing, or to sneer at it; that is to
be unskilled in one's own life. But the artistry and beauty
which is skill in action should operate throughout the day
not just during a few hours of the day. This is the real chal
lenge, not just playing the piano beautifully. You must play
it beautifully if you touch it at all, but that is not enough. I
is like cultivating a small corner of a huge field. We are
concerned with the whole field and that field is life. What we
always do is to neglect the whole field and concentrate or
fragments, our own or other people's. Artistry is to be com

pletely awake and therefore to be skilful in action in the whole of life, and this is beauty.

Questioner: What about the factory worker or the office employee? Is he an artist? Doesn't his work preclude skill in action and so deaden him that he has no skill in anything else either? Is he not conditioned by his work?

KRISHNAMURTI: Of course he is. But if he wakes up he will either leave his work or so transform it that it becomes artistry. What is important is not the work but the waking up to the work. What is important is not the conditioning of the work but to wake up.

Questioner: What do you mean, wake up?

KRISHNAMURTI: Are you awakened only by circumstances, by challenges, by some disaster or joy? Or is there a state of being awake without any cause? If you are awakened by an event, a cause, then you depend on it, and when you depend on something – whether it be a drug, sex, painting or music – you are allowing yourself to be put to sleep. So any dependence is the end of skill, the end of artistry.

Questioner: What is this other awakened state that has no cause? You are talking about a state in which there is neither a cause nor an effect. Can there be a state of mind that is not the result of some cause? I don't understand that because surely everything we think and everything we are is the result of a cause? There is the endless chain of cause and effect.

KRISHNAMURTI: This chain of cause and effect is endless because the effect becomes the cause and the cause begets further effects, and so on.

Questioner: Then what action is there outside this chain?

KRISHNAMURTI: All we know is action with a cause, a motive, action which is a result. All action is in relationship. If relationship is based on cause it is cunning adaptation, and therefore inevitably leads to another form of dullness. Love is the only thing that is causeless, that is free; it is beauty, it is skill, it is art. Without love there is no art. When the artist is playing beautifully there is no 'me'; there is love and beauty, and this is art. This is skill in action. Skill in action is the absence of the 'me'. Art is the absence of the 'me'. But when you neglect the whole field of life and concentrate only in a little part – however much the 'me' may then be absent, you are still living unskilfully and therefore you are not an artist of life. The absence of 'me' in living is love and beauty, which brings its own skill. This is the greatest art: living skilfully in the whole field of life.

Questioner: Oh Lord! How am I to do that? I see it and feel it in my heart but how can I maintain it?

KRISHNAMURTI: There is no way to maintain it, there is no way to nourish it, there is no practising of it; there is only the seeing of it. Seeing is the greatest of all skills.

DEPENDENCE

*Questioner: I should like to understand the nature of de-
pendence. I have found myself depending on so many things
– on women, on different kinds of amusement, on good wine,
on my wife and children, on my friends, on what people say.
Fortunately I no longer depend on religious entertainment,
but I depend on the books I read to stimulate me and on
good conversation. I see that the young are also dependent,
perhaps not so much as I am, but they have their own particular forms of dependence. I have been to the East and
have seen how there they depend on the guru and the
family. Tradition there has greater importance and is more
deeply rooted than it is here in Europe, and, of course, very
much more so than in America. But we all seem to depend
on something to sustain us, not only physically but, much
more, inwardly. So I am wondering whether it is at all possible to be really free of dependence, and should one be free
of it?*

KRISHNAMURTI: I take it you are concerned with the
psychological inward attachments. The more one is attached
the greater the dependence. The attachment is not only to
persons but to ideas and to things. One is attached to a particular environment, to a particular country and so on. And
from this springs dependence and therefore resistance.

Questioner: Why resistance?

KRISHNAMURTI: The object of my attachment is my ter-
ritorial or my sexual domain. This I protect, resisting any
form of encroachment on it from others. I also limit the
freedom of the person to whom I am attached and limit my
own freedom. So attachment is resistance. I am attached to

something or somebody. That attachment is possessiveness; possessiveness is resistance, so attachment is resistance.

Questioner: Yes, I see that.

KRISHNAMURTI: Any form of encroachment on my possessions leads to violence, legally or psychologically. So attachment is violence, resistance, imprisonment – the imprisonment of oneself and of the object of attachment. Attachment means this is mine and not yours; keep off! So this relationship is resistance against others. The whole world is divided into mine and yours: my opinion, my judgement, my advice, my God, my country – an infinity of such nonsense. Seeing all this taking place, not in abstraction but actually in our daily life, we can ask why there is this attachment to people, things and ideas. Why does one depend? All being is relationship and all relationship is in this dependence with its violence, resistance and domination. We have made the whole world into this. Where one possesses one must dominate. We meet beauty, love springs up, and immediately it turns to attachment and all this misery begins and the love has gone out of the window. Then we ask, 'What has happened to our great love?' This is actually what is happening in our daily life. And, seeing all this, we can now ask: why is man invariably attached, not only to that which is lovely, but also to every form of illusion and to so many idiotic fancies?

Freedom is not a state of non-dependence; it is a positive state in which there isn't any dependence. But it is not a result, it has no cause. This must be understood very clearly before we can go into the question of why man depends or falls into the trap of attachment with all its miseries. Being attached we try to cultivate a state of independence – which is another form of resistance.

Questioner: So what is freedom? You say it is not the negation of dependence or the ending of dependence; you say it is not freedom from something, but just freedom. So what is it? Is it an abstraction or an actuality?

KRISHNAMURTI: It is not an abstraction. It is the state of mind in which there is no form of resistance whatsoever. It is not like a river accommodating itself to boulders here and there, going round or over them. In this freedom there are no boulders at all, only the movement of the water.

Questioner: But the boulder of attachment is there, in this river of life. You can't just speak about another river in which there are no boulders.

KRISHNAMURTI: We are not avoiding the boulder or saying it doesn't exist. We must first understand freedom. It is not the same river as the one in which there are the boulders.

Questioner: I have still got my river with its boulders, and that's what I came to ask about, not about some other unknown river without boulders. That's no good to me.

KRISHNAMURTI: Quite right. But you must understand what freedom is in order to understand your boulders. But don't let us flog this simile to death. We must consider both freedom and attachment.

Questioner: What has my attachment to do with freedom or freedom with my attachment?

KRISHNAMURTI: In your attachment there is pain. You want to be rid of this pain, so you cultivate detachment which is another form of resistance. In the opposite there is no freedom. These two opposites are identical and mutually strengthen each other. What you are concerned with is how to have the pleasures of attachment without its miseries. You cannot. That is why it is important to understand that freedom does not lie in detachment. In the process of understanding attachment there is freedom, not in running away from attachment. So our question now is, why are human beings attached, dependent?

Being nothing, being a desert in oneself, one hopes through another to find water. Being empty, poor, wretched, insufficient, devoid of interest or importance, one hopes through another to be enriched. Through the love of another one hopes to forget oneself. Through the beauty of another one hopes to acquire beauty. Through the family, through the nation, through the lover, through some fantastic belief, one hopes to cover this desert with flowers. And God is the ultimate lover. So one puts hooks into all these things. In this there is pain and uncertainty, and the desert seems more arid than ever before. Of course it is neither more nor less arid; it is what it was, only one has avoided looking at it while escaping through some form of attachment with its pain, and then escaping from that pain into detachment. But one remains arid and empty as before. So instead of trying to escape, either through attachment or through detachment, can we not become aware of this fact of this deep inward poverty and inadequacy, this dull hollow isolation? That is the only thing that matters, not attachment or detachment. Can you look at it without any sense of condemnation or evaluation? When you do, are you looking at it as an observer who looks at the observed, or without the observer?

Questioner: What do you mean, the observer?

KRISHNAMURTI: Are you looking at it from a centre with all its conclusions of like and dislike, opinion, judgement, the desire to be free of this emptiness and so on – are you looking at this aridness with the eyes of conclusion – or are you looking with eyes that are completely free? When you look at it with completely free eyes there is no observer. If there is no observer, is there the thing observed as loneliness, emptiness, wretchedness?

Questioner: Do you mean to say that that tree doesn't exist if I look at it without conclusions, without a centre which is the observer?

KRISHNAMURTI: Of course the tree exists.

Questioner: Why does loneliness disappear but not the tree when I look without the observer?

KRISHNAMURTI: Because the tree is not created by the centre, by the mind of the 'me'. But the mind of the 'me' in all its self-centred activity has created this emptiness, this isolation. And when that mind, without the centre, looks, the self-centred activity ends. So the loneliness is not. Then the mind functions in freedom. Looking at the whole structure of attachment and detachment, and the movement of pain and pleasure, we see how the mind of the 'me' builds its own desert and its own escapes. When the mind of the 'me' is still, then there is no desert and there is no escape.

BELIEF

Questioner: I am one of those people who really believe in God. In India I followed one of the great modern saints who, because he believed in God, brought about great political changes there. In India the whole country throbs to the beat of God. I have heard you talk against belief so probably you don't believe in God. But you are a religious person and therefore there must be in you some kind of feeling of the Supreme. I have been all over India and through many parts of Europe, visiting monasteries, churches and mosques, and everywhere I have found this very strong, compelling belief in God whom one hopes shapes one's life. Now since you don't believe in God, although you are a religious person, what exactly is your position with regard to this question? Why don't you believe? Are you an atheist? As you know, in Hinduism you can be an atheist or a theist and yet be equally well a Hindu. Of course it's different with the Christians. If you don't believe in God you can't be a Christian. But that's beside the point. The point is that I have come to ask you to explain your position and demonstrate to me its validity. People follow you and therefore you have a responsibility, and therefore I am challenging you in this way.

KRISHNAMURTI: Let us first of all clear up this last point. There are no followers, and I have no responsibility to you or to the people who listen to my talks. Also I am not a Hindu or anything else, for I don't belong to any group, religious or otherwise. Each one must be a light to himself. Therefore there is no teacher, no disciple. This must be clearly understood from the very beginning otherwise one is influenced, one becomes a slave to propaganda and persuasion. Therefore anything that is being said now is not dogma or creed or persuasion: we either meet together in

262

understanding or we don't. Now, you said most emphatically that you believe in God and you probably want through that belief to experience what one might call the godhead. Belief involves many things. There is belief in facts that you may not have seen but can verify, like the existence of New York or the Eiffel Tower. Then you may believe that your wife is faithful though you don't actually know it. She might be unfaithful in thought yet you believe she is faithful because you don't actually see her going off with someone else; she may deceive you in daily thought, and you must certainly have done the same too. You believe in reincarnation, don't you, though there is no certainty that there is any such thing? However, that belief has no validity in your life, has it? All Christians believe that they must love but they do not love – like everyone else they go about killing, physically or psychologically. There are those who do not believe in God and yet do good. There are those who believe in God and kill for that belief; those who prepare for war because they claim they want peace, and so on. So one has to ask oneself what need there is to believe at all in anything, though this doesn't deny the extraordinary mystery of life. But belief is one thing and 'what is' is another. Belief is a word, a thought, and this is not the thing, any more than your name is actually you.

Through experience you hope to touch the truth of your belief, to prove it to yourself, but this belief conditions your experience. It isn't that the experience comes to prove the belief, but rather that the belief begets the experience. Your belief in God will give you the experience of what you call God. You will always experience what you believe and nothing else. And this invalidates your experience. The Christian will see virgins, angels and Christ, and the Hindu will see similar deities in extravagant plurality. The Muslim, the Buddhist, the Jew and the Communist are the same. Belief conditions its own supposed proof. What is important is not what you believe but only why you believe at all. Why *do* you believe? And what difference does it make to what actually *is* whether you believe one thing or another? Facts are not influenced by belief or disbelief. So one has to ask why one believes at all in anything; what is the basis of belief? Is it fear, is it the uncertainty of life – the fear of the unknown, the lack of security in this ever-changing world? Is it the insecurity of relationship, or is it that faced with the immensity of life, and not understanding it, one encloses oneself in the refuge of belief? So, if I may ask you, if you had no fear at all, would you have any belief?

Questioner: I am not at all sure that I am afraid, but I love God, and it is this love that makes me believe in Him.

KRISHNAMURTI: Do you mean to say you are devoid of fear? And therefore know what love is?

Questioner: I have replaced fear with love and so to me fear is non-existent, and therefore my belief is not based on fear.

KRISHNAMURTI: Can you substitute love for fear? Is that not an act of thought which is afraid and therefore covers up the fear with the word called love, again a belief? You have covered up that fear with a word and you cling to the word, hoping to dissipate fear.

Questioner: What you are saying disturbs me greatly. I am not at all sure I want to go on with this, because my belief and my love have sustained me and helped me to lead a decent life. This questioning of my belief brings about a sense of disorder of which, quite frankly, I am afraid.

KRISHNAMURTI : So there *is* fear, which you are beginning to discover for yourself. This disturbs you. Belief comes from fear and is the most destructive thing. One must be free of fear and of belief. Belief divides people, makes them hard, makes them hate each other and cultivate war. In a roundabout way, unwillingly, you are admitting that fear begets

264

belief. Freedom from belief is necessary to face the fact of fear. Belief like any other ideal is an escape from 'what is'. When there is no fear then the mind is in quite a different dimension. Only then can you ask the question whether there is a God or not. A mind clouded by fear or belief is incapable of any kind of understanding, any realization of what truth is. Such a mind lives in illusion and can obviously not come upon that which is Supreme. The Supreme has nothing to do with your or anybody else's belief, opinion or conclusion.

Not knowing, you believe, but to know is not to know. To know is within the tiny field of time and the mind that says, 'I know', is bound by time and so cannot possibly understand that which *is*. After all, when you say, 'I know my wife and my friend', you know only the image or the memory, and this is the past. Therefore you can never actually know anybody or anything. You cannot know a living thing, only a dead thing. When you see this you will no longer think of relationship in terms of knowing. So one can never say, 'There is no God', or 'I know God.' Both these are a blasphemy. To understand that which *is* there must be freedom, not only from the known but also from the fear of the known and from the fear of the unknown.

Questioner: You speak of understanding that which 'is' and yet you deny the validity of knowing. What is this understanding if it is not knowing?

KRISHNAMURTI: The two are quite different. Knowing is always related to the past and therefore it binds you to the past. Unlike knowing, understanding is not a conclusion, not accumulation. If you have listened you have understood. Understanding is attention. When you attend completely you understand. So the understanding of fear is the ending of fear. Your belief can therefore no longer be the predominant factor; the understanding of fear is predominant. When there is no fear there is freedom. It is only then that one can find what is true. When that which 'is' is not distorted by fear then that which 'is' is true. It is not the word. You cannot measure truth with words. Love is not a word nor a belief nor something that you can capture and say, 'It is mine.' Without love and beauty that which you call God is nothing at all.

DREAMS

Questioner: I have been told by professionals that dreaming is as vital as daytime thinking and activity, and that I would find my daily living under great stress and strain if I did not dream. They insist, and here I'm using not their jargon but my own words, that during certain periods of sleep the movement of the eyelids indicates refreshing dreams and that these bring a certain clarity to the brain. I am wondering whether the stillness of the mind which you have often spoken about might not bring greater harmony to living than the equilibrium brought about by patterns of dreams. I should also like to ask why the language of dreams is one of symbols.

KRISHNAMURTI: Language itself is a symbol, and we are used to symbols: we see the tree through the image which is the symbol of the tree, we see our neighbour through the image we have about him. Apparently it is one of the most difficult things for a human being to look at anything directly, not through images, opinions, conclusions, which are all symbols. And so in dreams symbols play a large part and in this there is great deception and danger. The meaning of a dream is not always clear to us, although we realize it is in symbols and try to decipher them. When we see something, we speak of it so spontaneously that we do not recognize that words are also symbols. All this indicates, doesn't it, that there is direct communication in technical matters but seldom in human relationships and understanding? You don't need symbols when somebody hits you. That is a direct communication. This is a very interesting point: the mind refuses to see things directly, to be aware of itself without the word and the symbol. You say the sky is blue. The listener then deciphers this according to his own reference of

blueness and transmits it to you in his own cipher. So we live
in symbols, and dreams are a part of this symbolic process.
We are incapable of direct and immediate perception without the symbols, the words, the prejudices and conclusions.
The reason for this is also quite apparent: it is part of the
self-centred activity with its defences, resistances, escapes
and fears. There is a ciphered response in the activity of the
brain, and dreams must naturally be symbolic because
during the waking hours we are incapable of direct response or perception.

*Questioner: It seems to me that this then is an inherent
function of the brain.*

KRISHNAMURTI: Inherent means something permanent,
inevitable and lasting. Surely any psychological state can be
changed. Only the deep, constant demand of the brain for
the physical security of the organism is inherent. Symbols
are a device of the brain to protect the psyche; this is the
whole process of thought. The 'me' is a symbol, not an
actuality. Having created the symbol of the 'me', thought
identifies itself with its conclusion, with the formula, and
then defends it: all misery and sorrow come from this.

Questioner: Then how do I get around it?

KRISHNAMURTI: When you ask how to get around it, you
are still holding on to the symbol of the 'me', which is
fictitious; you become something separate from what you
see, and so duality arises.

*Questioner: May I come back another day to continue
this?*

*

*Questioner: You were good enough to let me come back, and
I should like to continue where we left off. We were talking
about symbols in dreams and you pointed out that we live by*

symbols, deciphering them according to our gratification.
We do this not only in dreams but in everyday life; it is our
usual behaviour. Most of our actions are based on the in-
terpretation of the symbols or images that we have.
Strangely, after having talked with you the other day, my
dreams have taken a peculiar turn. I have had very dis-
turbing dreams and the interpretation of those dreams took
place as they were happening within the dreams. It was a
simultaneous process; the dream was being interpreted by
the dreamer. This has never happened to me before.

KRISHNAMURTI: During our waking hours, there is always
the observer, different from the observed, the actor, separate
from his action. In the same way there is the dreamer separate from his dream. He thinks it is separate from himself
and therefore in need of interpretation. But is the dream
separate from the dreamer, and is there any need to interpret it? When the observer is the observed what need is
there to interpret, to judge, to evaluate? This need would
exist only if the observer were different from the thing observed. This is very important to understand. We have separated the thing observed from the observer and from this
arises not only the problem of interpretation but also conflict,
and the many problems connected with it. This division is an
illusion. This division between groups, races, nationalities, is
fictitious. We are beings, undivided by names, by labels.
When the labels become all important, division takes place,
and then wars and all other struggles come into being.

Questioner: How then do I understand the content of the
dream? It must have significance. Is it an accident that I
dream of some particular event or person?

KRISHNAMURTI: We should really look at this quite
differently. Is there anything to understand? When the observer thinks he is different from the thing observed there is
an attempt to understand that which is outside himself. The
same process goes on within him. There is the observer wish-

ing to understand the thing he observes, which is himself. But when the observer *is* the observed, there is no question of understanding; there is only observation. You say that there is something to understand in the dream, otherwise there would be no dream, you say that the dream is a hint of something unresolved that one should understand. You use the word 'understand', and in that very word is the dualistic process. You think there is an 'I', and a thing to be understood, whereas in reality these two entities are one and the same. Therefore your search for a meaning in the dream is the action of conflict.

Questioner: Would you say the dream is an expression of something in the mind?

KRISHNAMURTI: Obviously it is.

Questioner: I do not understand how it is possible to regard a dream in the way you are describing it. If it has no significance, why does it exist?

KRISHNAMURTI: The 'I' is the dreamer, and the dreamer wants to see significance in the dream which he has invented or projected, so both are dreams, both are unreal. This unreality has become real to the dreamer, to the observer who thinks of himself as separate. The whole problem of dream interpretation arises out of this separation, this division between the actor and the action.

Questioner: I am getting more and more confused, so may we go over it again differently? I can see that a dream is the product of my mind and not separate from it, but dreams seem to come from levels of the mind which have not been explored, and so they seem to be intimations of something alive in the mind.

KRISHNAMURTI: It is not your particular mind in which there are hidden things. Your mind is the mind of man; your consciousness is the whole of man. But when you particularize it as *your* mind, you limit its activity, and because of this limitation, dreams arise. During waking hours observe without the observer, who is the expression of limitation. Any division is a limitation. Having divided itself into a 'me' and a 'not me', the 'me' the observer, the dreamer, has many problems – among them dreams and the interpretation of dreams. In any case, you will see the significance or the value of a dream only in a limited way because the observer is always limited. The dreamer perpetuates his own limitation, therefore the dream is always the expression of the incomplete, never of the whole.

Questioner: Pieces are brought back from the moon in order to understand the composition of the moon. In the same way we try to understand human thinking by bringing back pieces from our dreams, and examining what they express.

KRISHNAMURTI: The expressions of the mind are the fragments of the mind. Each fragment expresses itself in its own way and contradicts other fragments. A dream may contradict another dream, one action another action, one desire another desire. The mind lives in this confusion. A part of the mind says it must understand another part, such as a dream, an action or a desire. So each fragment has its own observer, its own activity; then a super-observer tries to bring them all into harmony. The super-observer is also a fragment of the mind. It is these contradictions, these divisions, that breed dreams.

So the real question is not the interpretation or the understanding of a particular dream; it is the perception that these many fragments are contained in the whole. Then you see yourself as a whole and not as a fragment of a whole.

Questioner: Are you saying, sir, that one should be aware during the day of the whole movement of life, not just one's family life, or business life, or any other individual aspect of life?

KRISHNAMURTI: Consciousness is the whole of man and does not belong to a particular man. When there is the consciousness of one particular man there is the complex problem of fragmentation, contradiction and war. When there is awareness of the total movement of life in a human being during the waking hours, what need is there for dreams at all? This total awareness, this attention, puts an end to fragmentation and to division. When there is no conflict whatsoever the mind has no need for dreams.

Questioner: This certainly opens a door through which I see many things.

TRADITION

Questioner: Can one really be free of tradition? Can one be free of anything at all? Or is it a matter of side-stepping it and not being concerned with any of it? You talk a great deal about the past and its conditioning – but can I be really free of this whole background of my life? Or can I merely modify the background according to the various outward demands and the challenges, adjust myself to it rather than become free of it? It seems to me that this is one of the most important things, and I'd like to understand it because I always feel that I am carrying a burden, the weight of the past. I would like to put it down and walk away from it, never come back to it. Is that possible?

KRISHNAMURTI: Doesn't tradition mean carrying the past over to the present? The past is not only one's particular set of inheritances but also the weight of all the collective thought of a particular group of people who have lived in a particular culture and tradition. One carries the accumulated knowledge and experience of the race and the family. All this is the past – the carrying over from the known to the present – which shapes the future. Is not the teaching of all history a form of tradition? You are asking if one can be free of all this. First of all, why does one want to be free? Why does one want to put down this burden? Why?

Questioner: I think it's fairly simple. I don't want to be the past – I want to be myself; I want to be cleansed of this whole tradition so that I can be a new human being. I think in most of us there is this feeling of wanting to be born anew.

KRISHNAMURTI: You cannot possibly be the new just by wishing for it. Or by struggling to be new. You have not only to understand the past but also you have to find out who you are. Are you not the past? Are you not the continuation of what has been, modified by the present?

Questioner: My actions and my thoughts are, but my existence isn't.

KRISHNAMURTI: Can you separate the two, action and thought, from existence? Are not thought, action, existence, living and relationship all one? This fragmentation into 'me' and 'not-me' is part of this tradition.

Questioner: Do you mean that when I am not thinking, when the past is not operating, I am obliterated, that I have ceased to exist?

KRISHNAMURTI: Don't let us ask too many questions, but consider what we began with. Can one be free of the past – not only the recent but the immemorial, the collective, the racial, the human, the animal? You are all that, you are not separate from that. And you are asking whether you can put all that aside and be born anew. The 'you' *is* that, and when you wish to be reborn as a new entity, the new entity you imagine is a projection of the old, covered over with the word 'new'. But underneath, you are the past. So the question is, can the past be put aside or does a modified form of tradition continue for ever, changing, accumulating, discarding, but always the past in different combinations? The past is the cause and the present is the effect, and today, which is the effect of yesterday, becomes the cause of tomorrow. This chain is the way of thought, for thought is the past. You are asking whether one can stop this movement of yesterday into today. Can one look at the past to examine it, or is that not possible at all? To look at it the observer must be outside it – and he isn't. So here arises another issue. If the observer himself is the past then how can the past be isolated for observation?

Questioner: I can look at something objectively . . .

KRISHNAMURTI: But you, who are the observer, are the past trying to look at itself. You can objectify yourself only as an image which you have put together through the years in every form of relationship, and so the 'you' which you objectify is memory and imagination, the past. You are trying to look at yourself as though you were a different entity from the one who is looking, but you *are* the past, with its old judgements, evaluations and so on. The action of the past is looking at the memory of the past. Therefore there is never relief from the past. The continuous examination of the past by the past perpetuates the past; this is the very action of the past, and this is the very essence of tradition.

Questioner: Then what action is possible? If I am the past – and I can see that I am – then whatever I do to chisel away the past is adding to it. So I am left helpless! What can I do? I can't pray because the invention of a god is again the action of the past. I can't look to another, for the other is also the creation of my despair. I can't run away from it all because at the end of it I am still there with my past. I can't identify myself with some image which is not of the past because that image is my own projection too. Seeing all this, I am really left helpless, and in despair.

KRISHNAMURTI: Why do you call it helplessness and despair? Aren't you translating what you see as the past into an emotional anxiety because you cannot achieve a certain result? In so doing you are again making the past act. Now, can you look at all this movement of the past, with all its traditions, without wanting to be free of it, change it, modify it or run away from it – simply observe it without any reaction?

Questioner: But as we have been saying all through this conversation, how can I observe the past if I am the past? I can't look at it at all!

KRISHNAMURTI: Can you look at yourself, who are the

past, without any movement of thought, which is the past? If you can look without thinking, evaluating, liking, disliking, judging, then there *is* a looking with eyes that are not touched by the past. It is to look in silence, without the noise of thought. In this silence there is neither the observer nor the thing which he is looking at as the past.

Questioner: Are you saying that when you look without evaluation or judgement the past has disappeared? But it hasn't – there are still the thousands of thoughts and actions and all the pettiness which were rampant only a moment ago. I look at them and they are still there. How can you say that the past has disappeared? It may momentarily have stopped acting ...

KRISHNAMURTI: When the mind is silent that silence is a new dimension, and when there is any rampant pettiness it is instantly dissolved, because the mind has now a different quality of energy which is not the energy engendered by the past. This is what matters: to have that energy that dispels the carrying over of the past. The carrying over of the past is a different kind of energy. The silence wipes the other out; the greater absorbs the lesser and remains untouched. It is like the sea, receiving the dirty river and remaining pure. This is what matters. It is only this energy that can wipe away the past. Either there is silence or the noise of the past In this silence the noise ceases and the new is this silence. It is not that *you* are made new. This silence is infinite and the past is limited. The conditioning of the past breaks down in the fullness of silence.

CONDITIONING

Questioner: You have talked a great deal about conditioning and have said that one must be free of this bondage, otherwise one remains imprisoned always. A statement of this kind seems so outrageous and unacceptable! Most of us are very deeply conditioned and we hear this statement and throw up our hands and run away from such extravagant expression, but I have taken you seriously – for, after all, you have more or less given your life to this kind of thing, not as a hobby but with deep seriousness – and therefore I should like to discuss it with you to see how far the human being can uncondition himself. Is it really possible, and if so, what does it mean? Is it possible for me, having lived in a world of habits, traditions and the acceptance of orthodox notions in so many matters – is it possible for me really to throw off this deep-rooted conditioning? What exactly do you mean by conditioning, and what do you mean by freedom from conditioning?

KRISHNAMURTI: Let us take the first question first. We are conditioned – physically, nervously, mentally – by the climate we live in and the food we eat, by the culture in which we live, by the whole of our social, religious and economic environment, by our experience, by education and by family pressures and influences. All these are the factors which condition us. Our conscious and unconscious responses to all the challenges of our environment – intellectual, emotional, outward and inward – all these are the action of conditioning. Language is conditioning; all thought is the action, the response of conditioning.

Knowing that we are conditioned we invent a divine agency which we piously hope will get us out of this mechanical state. We either postulate its existence outside or inside ourselves – as the atman, the soul, the Kingdom of Heaven which is within, and who knows what else! To these beliefs we cling desperately, not seeing that they themselves are part of the conditioning factor which they are supposed to destroy or redeem. So not being able to uncondition ourselves in this world, and not even seeing that conditioning is the problem, we think that freedom is in Heaven, in Moksha, in Nirvana. In the Christian myth of original sin and in the whole eastern doctrine of Samsara, one sees that the factor of conditioning has been felt, though rather obscurely. If it had been clearly seen, naturally these doctrines and myths would not have arisen. Nowadays the psychologists also try to get to grips with this problem, and in doing so condition us still further. Thus the religious specialists have conditioned us, the social order has conditioned us, the family which is part of it has conditioned us. All this is the past which makes up the open as well as the hidden layers of the mind. *En passant* it is interesting to note that the so-called individual doesn't exist at all, for his mind draws on the common reservoir of conditioning which he shares with everybody else, so the division between the community and the individual is false: there is only conditioning. This conditioning is action in all relationships – to things, people and ideas.

Questioner: Then what am I to do to free myself from it all? To live in this mechanical state is not living at all, and yet all action, all will, all judgements are conditioned – so there is apparently nothing I can do about conditioning which isn't conditioned! I am tied hand and foot.

KRISHNAMURTI: The very factor of conditioning in the past, in the present and in the future, is the 'me' which thinks in terms of time, the 'me' which exerts itself; and now it exerts itself in the demand to be free; so the root of all conditioning is the thought which is the 'me'. The 'me' is the very essence of the past, the 'me' is time, the 'me' is sorrow –

the 'me' endeavours to free itself from itself, the 'me' makes efforts, struggles to achieve, to deny, to become. This struggle to become is time in which there is confusion and the greed for the more and the better. The 'me' seeks security and not finding it transfers the search to heaven; the very 'me' that identifies itself with something greater in which it hopes to lose itself – whether that be the nation, the ideal or some god – is the factor of conditioning.

Questioner: You have taken everything away from me, What am I without this 'me'?

KRISHNAMURTI: If there is no 'me' you are unconditioned, which means you are nothing.

Questioner: Can the 'me' end without the effort of the 'me'?

KRISHNAMURTI: The effort to become something is the response, the action, of conditioning.

Questioner: How can the action of the 'me' stop?

KRISHNAMURTI: It can stop only if you see this whole thing, the whole business of it. If you see it in action, which is in relationship, the seeing is the ending of the 'me'. Not only is this seeing an action which is not conditioned but also it acts upon conditioning.

Questioner: Do you mean to say that the brain – which is the result of vast evolution with its infinite conditioning – can free itself?

KRISHNAMURTI: The brain is the result of time; it is conditioned to protect itself physically, but when it tries to protect itself psychologically then the 'me' begins, and all our misery starts. It is this effort to protect itself psychologically that is the affirmation of the 'me'. The brain can learn, can acquire knowledge technologically, but when it acquires knowledge psychologically then that knowledge asserts itself in relationship as the 'me' with its experiences, its will and its violence. This is what brings division, conflict and sorrow to relationship.

Questioner: Can this brain be still and only operate when it has to work technologically – only operate when knowledge is demanded in action, as for example in learning a language, driving a car or building a house?

KRISHNAMURTI: The danger in this is the dividing of the brain into the psychological and the technological. This again becomes a contradiction, a conditioning, a theory. The real question is whether the brain, the whole of it, can be still, quiet, and respond efficiently only when it has to in technology or in living. So we are not concerned with the psychological or the technological; we ask only, can this whole mind be completely still and function only when it has to? We say it can and this is the understanding of what meditation is.

*

Questioner: If I may I should like to continue where we left off yesterday. You may remember that I asked two questions: I asked what is conditioning and what is freedom from conditioning, and you said let us take the first question first. We hadn't time to go into the second question, so I should like to ask today, what is the state of the mind that is free from all its conditioning? After talking with you yesterday it became very clear to me how deeply and strongly I am conditioned, and I saw – at least I think I saw – an opening, a crack in this structure of conditioning. I talked the matter over with a friend and in taking certain factual instances of conditioning I saw very clearly how deeply and venomously one's actions are affected by it. As you said at the end, meditation is the emptying of the mind of all conditioning so that there is no distortion or illusion. How is one to be free of all distortion, all illusion? What is illusion?

KRISHNAMURTI: It is so easy to deceive oneself, so easy to convince oneself of anything at all. The feeling that one must *be* something is the beginning of deception, and, of course, this idealistic attitude leads to various forms of hypocrisy. What makes illusion? Well, one of the factors is this constant comparison between what is and what should be, or what might be, this measurement between the good and the bad – thought trying to improve itself, the memory of pleasure, trying to get more pleasure, and so on. It is this desire for more, this dissatisfaction, which makes one accept or have faith in something, and this must inevitably lead to every form of deception and illusion. It is desire and fear, hope and despair, that project the goal, the conclusion to be experienced. Therefore this experience has no reality. All so-called religious experiences follow this pattern. The very desire for enlightenment must also breed the acceptance of authority, and this is the opposite of enlightenment. Desire, dissatisfaction, fear, pleasure, wanting more, wanting to change, all of which is measurement – this is the way of illusion.

Questioner: Do you really have no illusion at all about anything?

KRISHNAMURTI: I am not all the time measuring myself or others. This freedom from measurement comes about when you are really living with what is – neither wishing to change it nor judging it in terms of good and bad. Living with something is not the acceptance of it: it is there whether you accept it or not. Living with something is not identifying yourself with it either.

Questioner: Can we go back to the question of what this freedom is that one really wants? This desire for freedom expresses itself in everybody, sometimes in the stupidest ways, but I think one can say that in the human heart there is always this deep longing for freedom which is never re-

alized; there is this incessant struggle to be free. I know I am not free; I am caught in so many wants. How am I to be free, and what does it mean to be really honestly free?

KRISHNAMURTI: Perhaps this may help us to understand it: total negation is that freedom. To negate everything we consider to be positive, to negate the total social morality, to negate all inward acceptance of authority, to negate everything one has said or concluded about reality, to negate all tradition, all teaching, all knowledge except technological knowledge, to negate all experience, to negate all the drives which stem from remembered or forgotten pleasures, to negate all fulfilment, to negate all commitments to act in a particular way, to negate all ideas, all principles, all theories. Such negation is the most positive action, therefore it is freedom.

Questioner: If I chisel away at this, bit by bit, I shall go on for ever and that itself will be my bondage. Can it all wither away in a flash, can I negate the whole human deception, all the values and aspiration and standards, immediately? Is it really possible? Doesn't it require enormous capacity, which I lack, enormous understanding, to see all this in a flash and leave it exposed to the light, to that intelligence you have talked about? I wonder, sir, if you know what this entails. To ask me, an ordinary man with an ordinary education, to plunge into something which seems like an incredible nothingness ... Can I do it? I don't even know what it means to jump into it! It's like asking me to become all of a sudden the most beautiful, innocent, lovely human being. You see I am really frightened now, not the way I was frightened before, I am faced now with something which I know is true, and yet my utter incapacity to do it binds me. I see the beauty of this thing, to be really completely nothing, but. ...

KRISHNAMURTI: You know, it is only when there is emptiness in oneself, not the emptiness of a shallow mind but the emptiness that comes with the total negation of everything one has been and should be and will be – it is only in this emptiness that there is creation; it is only in this emptiness that something new can take place. Fear is the thought of the unknown, so you are really frightened of leaving the known, the attachments, the satisfactions, the pleasurable memories, the continuity and security which give comfort. Thought is comparing this with what it thinks is emptiness. This imagination of emptiness is fear, so fear is thought. To come back to your question – can the mind negate everything it has known, the total content of its own conscious and unconscious self, which is the very essence of yourself? Can you negate yourself completely? If not, there is no freedom. Freedom is not freedom from something – that is only a reaction; freedom comes in total denial.

Questioner: But what is the good of having such freedom? You are asking me to die, aren't you?

KRISHNAMURTI: Of course! I wonder how you are using the word 'good' when you say what is the good of this freedom? Good in terms of what? The known? Freedom is the absolute good and its action is the beauty of everyday life. In this freedom alone there is living, and without it how can there be love? Everything exists and has its being in this freedom. It is everywhere and nowhere. It has no frontiers. Can you die now to everything you know and not wait for tomorrow to die? This freedom is eternity and ecstasy and love.

HAPPINESS

Questioner: What is happiness? I have always tried to find it but somehow it hasn't come my way. I see people enjoying themselves in so many different ways and many of the things they do seem so immature and childish. I suppose they are happy in their own way, but I want a different kind of happiness. I have had rare intimations that it might be possible to get it, but somehow it has always eluded me. I wonder what I can do to feel really completely happy?

KRISHNAMURTI: Do you think happiness is an end in itself? Or does it come as a secondary thing in living intelligently?

Questioner: I think it is an end in itself because if there is happiness then whatever you do will be harmonious; then you will do things effortlessly, easily, without any friction. I am sure that whatever you do out of this happiness will be right.

KRISHNAMURTI: But is this so? Is happiness an end in itself? Virtue is not an end in itself. If it is, then it becomes a very small affair. Can you seek happiness? If you do then probably you will find an imitation of it in all sorts of distractions and indulgences. This is pleasure. What is the relationship between pleasure and happiness?

Questioner: I have never asked myself.

KRISHNAMURTI: Pleasure which we pursue is mistakenly called happiness, but can you pursue happiness, as you pursue pleasure? Surely we must be very clear as to whether pleasure is happiness. Pleasure is gratification, satisfaction, indulgence, entertainment, stimulation. Most of us think

284

pleasure is happiness, and the greatest pleasure we consider to be the greatest happiness. And is happiness the opposite of unhappiness? Are you trying to be happy because you are unhappy and dissatisfied? Has happiness got an opposite at all? Has love got an opposite? Is your question about happiness the result of being unhappy?'

Questioner: I am unhappy like the rest of the world and naturally I don't want to be, and that is what is driving me to seek happiness.

KRISHNAMURTI: So happiness to you is the opposite of unhappiness. If you were happy you wouldn't seek it. So what is important is not happiness but whether unhappiness can end. That is the real problem, isn't it? You are asking about happiness because you are unhappy and you ask this question without finding out whether happiness is the opposite of unhappiness.

Questioner: If you put it that way, I accept it. So my concern is how to be free from the misery I am in.

KRISHNAMURTI: Which is more important – to understand unhappiness or to pursue happiness? If you pursue happiness it becomes an escape from unhappiness and therefore it will always remain, covered over perhaps, hidden, but always there, festering inside. So what is your question now?

Questioner: My question now is why am I miserable? You have very neatly pointed out to me my real state, rather than given me the answer I want, so now I am faced with this question, how am I to get rid of the misery I am in?

KRISHNAMURTI: Can an outside agency help you to get rid of your own misery, whether that outside agency be God, a master, a drug or a saviour? Or can one have the intelligence to understand the nature of unhappiness and deal with it immediately?

Questioner: I have come to you because I thought you might help me, so you could call yourself an outside agency. I want help and I don't care who gives it to me.

KRISHNAMURTI: In accepting or giving help several things are involved. If you accept it blindly you will be caught in the trap of one authority or another, which brings with it various other problems, such as obedience and fear. So if you start off wanting help, not only do you not get help – because nobody can help you anyway – but in addition you get a whole series of new problems; you are deeper in the mire than ever before.

Questioner: I think I understand and accept that. I have never thought it out clearly before. How then can I develop the intelligence to deal with unhappiness on my own, and immediately? If I had this intelligence surely I wouldn't be here now, I wouldn't be asking you to help me. So my question now is, can I get this intelligence in order to solve the problem of unhappiness and thereby attain happiness?

KRISHNAMURTI: You are saying that this intelligence is separate from its action. The action of this intelligence is the seeing and the understanding of the problem itself. The two are not separate and successive; you don't first get intelligence and then use it on the problem like a tool. It is one of the sicknesses of thinking to say that one should have the capacity first and then use it, the idea or the principle first and then apply it. This itself is the very absence of intelligence and the origin of problems. This is fragmentation. We live this way and so we speak of happiness and unhappiness, hate and love, and so on.

Questioner: Perhaps this is inherent in the structure of language.

KRISHNAMURTI: Perhaps it is but let's not make too much fuss about it here and wander away from the issue. We are saying that intelligence, and the action of that intelligence – which is seeing the problem of unhappiness – are one indivisibly. Also that this is not separate from ending unhappiness or getting happiness.

Questioner: How am I to get that intelligence?

KRISHNAMURTI: Have you understood what we have been saying?

Questioner: Yes.

KRISHNAMURTI: But if you have understood you have seen that this seeing *is* intelligence. The only thing you can do is to see; you cannot cultivate intelligence in order to see. Seeing is not the cultivation of intelligence. Seeing is more important than intelligence, or happiness, or unhappiness. There is only seeing or not seeing. All the rest – happiness, unhappiness and intelligence – are just words.

Questioner: What is it, then, to see?

KRISHNAMURTI: To see means to understand how thought creates the opposites. What thought creates is not real. To see means to understand the nature of thought, memory, conflict, ideas; to see all this as a total process is to understand. This is intelligence; seeing totally is intelligence; seeing fragmentarily is the lack of intelligence.

Questioner: I am a bit bewildered. I think I understand, but it is rather tenuous; I must go slowly. What you are saying is, see and listen completely. You say this attention is intelligence and you say that it must be immediate. One can only see now. I wonder if I really see now, or am I going home to think over what you have said, hoping to see later?

KRISHNAMURTI: Then you will never see; in thinking about it you will never see it because thinking prevents seeing. Both of us have understood what it means to see.

This seeing is not an essence or an abstraction or an idea. You cannot see if there is nothing to see. Now you have a problem of unhappiness. See it completely, including your wanting to be happy and how thought creates the opposite. See the search for happiness and the seeking help in order to get happiness. See disappointment, hope, fear. All of this must be seen completely, as a whole, not separately. See all this now, give your whole attention to it.

Questioner: I am still bewildered. I don't know whether I have got the essence of it, the whole point. I want to close my eyes and go into myself to see if I have really understood this thing. If I have then I have solved my problem.

LEARNING

Questioner: You have often talked about learning. I don't quite know what you mean by it. We are taught to learn at school and at the University, and life also teaches us many things – to adjust ourselves to environment and to our neighbours, to our wife or husband, to our children. We seem to learn from almost everything, but I am sure that when you speak about learning this isn't quite what you mean because you also seem to deny experience as a teacher. But when you deny experience aren't you denying all learning? After all, through experience, both in technology and in human everyday living, we learn everything we know. So could we go into this question?

KRISHNAMURTI: Learning through experience is one thing – it is the accumulation of conditioning – and learning all the time, not only about objective things but also about oneself, is something quite different. There is the accumulation which brings about conditioning – this we know – and there is the learning which we speak about. This learning is observation – to observe without accumulation, to observe in freedom. This observation is not directed from the past. Let us keep those two things clear.

What do we learn from experience? We learn things like languages, agriculture, manners, going to the moon, medicine, mathematics. But have we learnt about war through making war? We have learnt to make war more deadly, more efficient, but we haven't learnt *not* to make war. Our experience in warfare endangers the survival of the human race. Is this learning? You may build a better house, but has experience taught you how to live more nobly inside it? We have learnt through experience that fire burns and that has become our conditioning but we have also learnt through our conditioning that nationalism is good. Yet experience should also teach us that nationalism is deadly. All the evidence is there. The religious experience, as based on our conditioning, has separated man from man. Experience has taught us to have better food, clothes and shelter, but it has not taught us that social injustice prevents the right relationship between man and man. So experience conditions and strengthens our prejudices, our peculiar tendencies and our particular dogmas and beliefs. We do not learn what stupid nonsense all this is; we do not learn to live in the right relationship with other men. This right relationship is love. Experience teaches me to strengthen the family as a unit opposed to society and to other families. This brings about strife and division, which makes it ever more important to strengthen the family protectively, and so the vicious circle continues. We accumulate, and call this 'learning through experience', but more and more this learning brings about fragmentation, narrowness and specialization.

Questioner: Are you making out a case against technological learning and experience, against science and all accumulated knowledge? If we turn our backs on that we shall go back to savagery.

KRISHNAMURTI: No, I am not making out such a case at all. I think we are misunderstanding each other. We said that there are two kinds of learning: accumulation through experience, and acting from that accumulation, which is the past, and which is absolutely necessary wherever the action of knowledge is necessary. We are not against this; that would be too absurd!

Questioner: Gandhi tried to keep the machine out of life and started all that business which they call 'home industries' or 'Cottage industries' in India. Yet he used modern mechanized transport. This shows the inconsistency and hypocrisy of his position.

KRISHNAMURTI: Let's leave other people out of this. We arc saying that there are two kinds of learning – one, acting through the accumulation of knowledge and experience, and the other, learning without accumulation, but learning all the time in the very act of living. The former is absolutely necessary in all technical matters, but relationship, behaviour, are not technical matters, they are living things and you have to learn about them all the time. If you act from what you have learnt about behaviour, then it becomes mechanical and therefore relationship becomes routine.

Then there is another very important point: in all the learning which is accumulation and experience, profit is the criterion that determines the efficiency of the learning. And when the motive of profit operates in human relationships then it destroys those relationships because it brings about isolation and division. When the learning of experience and accumulation enters the domain of human behaviour, the psychological domain, then it must inevitably destroy. Enlightened self-interest on the one hand is advancement, but on the other hand it is the very seat of mischief, misery and confusion. Relationship cannot flower where there is self-interest of any kind, and that is why relationship cannot flower where it is guided by experience or memory.

Questioner: I see this, but isn't religious experience something different? I am talking about the experience gathered and passed on in religious matters – the experiences of the saints and gurus, the experience of the philosophers. Isn't this kind of experience beneficial to us in our ignorance?

KRISHNAMURTI: Not at all! The saint must be recognized by society and always conforms to society's notions of sainthood – otherwise he wouldn't be called a saint. Equally the guru must be recognized as such by his followers who are conditioned by tradition. So both the guru and the disciple are part of the cultural and religious conditioning of the particular society in which they live. When they assert that they have come into contact with reality, that they know, then you may be quite sure that what they know is not reality. What they know is their own projection from the past. So the man who says he knows, does not know. In all these so-called religious experiences a cognitive process of recognition is inherent. You can only recognize something you have known before, therefore it is of the past, therefore it is time-binding and not timeless. So-called religious experience does not bring benefit but merely conditions you according to your particular tradition, inclination, tendency and desire, and therefore encourages every form of illusion and isolation.

Questioner: Do you mean to say that you cannot experience reality?

KRISHNAMURTI: To experience implies that there must be an experiencer and the experience is the essence of all conditioning. What he experiences is the already-known.

Questioner: What do you mean when you talk about the experiencer? If there is no experiencer do you mean you disappear?

KRISHNAMURTI: Of course. The 'you' is the past and as long as the 'you' remains or the 'me' remains, that which is immense cannot be. The 'me' with his shallow little mind, experience and knowledge, with his heart burdened with jealousies and anxieties – how can such an entity understand that which has no beginning and no ending, that which is ecstasy? So the beginning of wisdom is to understand yourself. Begin understanding yourself.

Questioner: Is the experiencer different from that which he experiences, is the challenge different from the reaction to the challenge?

KRISHNAMURTI: The experiencer *is* the experienced, otherwise he could not recognize the experience and would not call it an experience; the experience is already in him before he recognizes it. So the past is always operating and recognizing itself; the new becomes swallowed up by the old. Similarly it is the reaction which determines the challenge; the challenge is the reaction, the two are not separate; without a reaction there would be no challenge. So the experience of an experiencer, or the reaction to a challenge which comes from the experiencer, are old, for they are determined by the experiencer. If you come to think of it, the word 'experience' means to go through something and finish with it and not store it up, but when we talk about experience we actually mean the opposite. Every time you speak of experience you speak of something stored from which action takes place, you speak of something which you have enjoyed and demand to have again, or have disliked and fear to have repeated.

So really to live is to learn without the cumulative process.

SELF-EXPRESSION

Questioner: Expression seems to me so important. I must express myself as an artist otherwise I feel stifled and deeply frustrated. Expression is part of one's existence. As an artist it is as natural that I should give myself to it as that a man should express his love for a woman in words and gestures. But through all this expression there is a sort of pain which I don't quite understand. I think most artists would agree with me that there is deep conflict in expressing one's deepest feelings on canvas, or in any other medium. I wonder if one can ever be free of this pain, or does expression always bring pain?

KRISHNAMURTI: What is the need of expression, and where does the suffering come into all this? Isn't one always trying to express more and more deeply, extravagantly, fully, and is one ever satisfied with what one has expressed? The deep feeling and the expression of it are not the same thing; there is a vast difference between the two, and there is always frustration when the expression doesn't correspond to the strong feeling. Probably this is one of the causes of pain, this discontent with the inadequacy of the utterance which the artist gives to his feeling. In this there is conflict and the conflict is a waste of energy. An artist has a strong feeling which is fairly authentic; he expresses it on canvas. This expression pleases some people and they buy his work; he gets money and reputation. His expression has been noticed and becomes fashionable. He refines it, pursues it, develops it, and is all the time imitating himself. This expression becomes habitual and stylized; the expression becomes more and more important and finally more important than the feeling; the feeling eventually evaporates. The artist is left with the social consequences of being a successful painter: the market place of the salon and the gallery, the connoisseur, the critics; he is enslaved by the society for which he paints. The feeling has long since disappeared, the expression is an empty shell remaining. Consequently even this expression eventually loses its attraction because it had nothing to express; it is a gesture, a word without a meaning. This is part of the destructive process of society. This is the destruction of the good.

Questioner: Can't the feeling remain, without getting lost in expression?

KRISHNAMURTI: When expression becomes all-important because it is pleasurable, satisfying or profitable, then there is a cleavage between expression and feeling. When the feeling *is* the expression then the conflict doesn't arise, and in this there is no contradiction and hence no conflict. But when profit and thought intervene, then this feeling is lost through greed. The passion of feeling is entirely different from the passion of expression, and most people are caught in the passion of expression. So there is always this division between the good and the pleasurable.

Questioner: Can I live without being caught in this current of greed?

KRISHNAMURTI: If it is the feeling which is important you will never ask about expression. Either you have got the feeling or you haven't. If you ask about the expression, you are not asking about artistry but about profit. Artistry is that which is never taken into account: it is the living.

Questioner: So what is it, to live? What is it to be, and to have that feeling which is complete in itself? I have now understood that expression is beside the point.

KRISHNAMURTI: It is living without conflict.

PASSION

Questioner: What is passion? You've talked about it and apparently you give it a special meaning. I don't think I know that meaning. Like every man I have sexual passion and passions for superficial things like fast driving or cultivating a beautiful garden. Most of us indulge in some form of passionate activity. Talk about his special passion and you see a man's eyes sparkle. We know the word passion comes from the Greek word for suffering, but the feeling I get when you use this word is not one of suffering but rather of some driving quality like that of the wind which comes roaring out of the west, chasing the clouds and the rubbish before it. I'd like to possess that passion. How does one come by it? What is it passionate about? What is the passion you mean?

KRISHNAMURTI: I think we should be clear that lust and passion are two different things. Lust is sustained by thought, driven by thought, it grows and gathers substance in thought until it explodes sexually, or, if it is the lust for power, in its own violent forms of fulfilment. Passion is something entirely different; it is not the product of thought nor the remembrance of a past event; it is not driven by any motive of fulfilment; it is not sorrow either.

Questioner: Is all sexual passion lust? Sexual response is not always the result of thought; it may be contact as when you suddenly meet somebody whose loveliness overpowers you.

KRISHNAMURTI: Wherever thought builds up the image of pleasure it must inevitably be lust and not the freedom of passion. If pleasure is the main drive then it is lust. When sexual feeling is born out of pleasure it is lust. If it is born out of love it is not lust, even though great delight may then be present. Here we must be clear and find out for ourselves whether love excludes pleasure and enjoyment. When you see a cloud and delight in its vastness and the light on it, there is of course pleasure, but there is a great deal more than pleasure. We are not condemning this at all. If you keep returning to the cloud in thought, or in fact, for a stimulation, then you are indulging in an imaginative flight of fancy, and obviously here pleasure and thought are the incentives operating. When you first looked at that cloud and saw its beauty there was no such incentive of pleasure operating. The beauty in sex is the absence of the 'me', the ego, but the thought of sex is the affirmation of this ego, and that is pleasure. This ego is all the time either seeking pleasure or avoiding pain, wanting fulfilment and thereby inviting frustration. In all this the feeling of passion is sustained and pursued by thought, and therefore it is no longer passion but pleasure. The hope, the pursuit, of remembered passion is pleasure.

Questioner: What is passion itself, then?

KRISHNAMURTI: It has to do with joy and ecstasy, which is not pleasure. In pleasure there is always a subtle form of effort – a seeking, striving, demanding, struggling to keep it, to get it. In passion there is no demand and therefore no struggle. In passion there is not the slightest shadow of fulfilment, therefore there can be neither frustration nor pain. Passion is the freedom from the 'me', which is the centre of all fulfilment and pain. Passion does not demand because it *is*, and I am not speaking of something static. Passion is the austerity of self-abnegation in which the 'you' and the 'me' is not; therefore passion is the essence of life. It is this that moves and lives. But when thought brings in all the problems of having and holding, then passion ceases. Without passion creation is not possible.

Questioner: What do you mean by creation?

KRISHNAMURTI: Freedom.

Questioner: What freedom?

KRISHNAMURTI: Freedom from the 'me' which depends on environment and is the product of environment – the me which is put together by society and thought. This freedom is clarity, the light that is not lit from the past. Passion is only the present.

Questioner: This has fired me with a strange new feeling.

KRISHNAMURTI: That is the passion of learning.

Questioner: What particular action in my daily living will ensure that this passion is burning and operating?

KRISHNAMURTI: Nothing will ensure it except the attention of learning, which is action, which is now. In this there is the beauty of passion, which is the total abandonment of the 'me' and its time.

ORDER

Questioner: In your teaching there are a thousand details. In my living I must be able to resolve them all into one action, now, which permeates all I do, because in my living I have only the one moment right before me in which to act. What is that one action in daily living which will bring all the details of your teaching to one point, like a pyramid inverted on its point?

KRISHNAMURTI: ... dangerously!

Questioner: Or, to put it differently, what is the one action which will bring the total intelligence of living into focus in one instant in the present?

KRISHNAMURTI: I think the question to ask is how to live a really intelligent, balanced, active life, in harmonious relationship with other human beings, without confusion, adjustment and misery. What is the one act that will summon this intelligence to operate in whatever you are doing? There is so much misery, poverty and sorrow in the world. What are you, as a human being, to do facing all these human problems? If you use the opportunity to help others for your own fulfilment, then it is exploitation and mischief. So we can put that aside from the beginning. The question really is, how are we to live a highly intelligent, orderly life without any kind of effort? It seems that we always approach this problem from the outside, asking ourselves, 'What am I to do, confronted with all the many problems of mankind – economic, social, human?' We want to work this out in terms of the outer.

Questioner: No, I am not asking you how I can tackle or solve the problems of the world, economic, social or political.

That would be too absurd! All I want to know is how to live righteously in this world exactly as it is, because it is as it is now, right here before me, and I can't will it into any other shape. I must live now in this world as it is, and in these circumstances solve all the problems of living. I am asking how to make this living a life of Dharma, which is that virtue that is not imposed from without, that does not conform to any precept, is not cultivated by any thought.

KRISHNAMURTI: Do you mean you want to find yourself immediately, suddenly, in a state of grace which is great intelligence, innocency, love – to find yourself in this state without having a past or a future, and to act from this state?

Questioner: Yes! That is it exactly.

KRISHNAMURTI: This has nothing to do with achievement, success or failure. There must surely be only one way to live: what is it?

Questioner: That is my question.

KRISHNAMURTI: To have inside you that light that has no beginning and no ending, that is not lit by your desire, that is not yours or someone else's. When there is this inward light, whatever you do will always be right and true.

Questioner: How do you get that light, now, without all the struggle, the search, the longing, the questioning?

KRISHNAMURTI: It is only possible when you really die to the past completely, and this can be done only when there is complete order in the brain. The brain cannot stand disorder. If there is disorder all its activities will be contradictory, confused, miserable and it will bring about mischief in itself and around itself. This order is not the design of thought, the design of obedience to a principle, to authority, or to some form of imagined goodness. It is disorder in the

300

brain that brings about conflict; then all the various resistances cultivated by thought to escape from this disorder arise – religious and otherwise.

Questioner: How can this order be brought about to a brain that is disorderly, contradictory, in itself?

KRISHNAMURTI: It can be done by watchfulness throughout the day, and then, before sleeping, by putting everything that has been done during the day in order. In that way the brain does not go to sleep in disorder. This does not mean that the brain hypnotizes itself into a state of order when there is really disorder in and about it. There must be order during the day, and the summing up of this order before sleeping is the harmonious ending of the day. It is like a man who keeps accounts and balances them properly every evening so that he starts afresh the next day, so that when he goes to sleep his mind is quiet, empty, not worried, confused, anxious or fearful. When he wakes up there is this light which is not the product of thought or of pleasure. This light is intelligence and love. It is the negation of the disorder of the morality in which we have been brought up.

Questioner: Can I have this light immediately? That is the question I asked right at the beginning, only I put it differently.

KRISHNAMURTI: You can have it immediately when the 'me' is not. The 'me' comes to an end when it sees for itself that it must end; the seeing is the light of understanding.

THE INDIVIDUAL AND THE COMMUNITY

Questioner: I don't quite know how to ask this question but I have a strong feeling that relationship between the individual and the community, these two opposing entities, has been a long history of mischief. The history of the world, of thought, of civilization, is, after all, the history of the relationship between these two opposing entities. In all societies the individual is more or less suppressed; he must conform and fit into the pattern which the theorists have determined. The individual is always trying to break out of these patterns, and continuous battle between the two is the result. Religions talk about the individual soul as something separate from the collective soul. They emphasize the individual. In modern society – which has become so mechanical, standardized and collectively active – the individual is trying to identify himself, inquiring what he is, asserting himself. All struggle leads nowhere. My question is, what is wrong with all this?

KRISHNAMURTI: The only thing that really matters is that there be an action of goodness, love and intelligence in living. Is goodness individual or collective, is love personal or impersonal, is intelligence yours, mine or somebody else's? If it is yours or mine then it is not intelligence, or love, or goodness. If goodness is an affair of the individual or of the collective, according to one's particular preference or decision, then it is no longer goodness. Goodness is not in the backyard of the individual nor in the open field of the collective; goodness flowers only in freedom from both. When there is this goodness, love and intelligence, then action is not in terms of the individual or the collective. Lacking goodness, we divide the world into the individual and the collective, and further divide the collective into innumerable groups according to religion, nationality and class. Having created these divisions we try to bridge them by forming new groups which are again divided from other groups. We see that every great religion supposedly exists to bring about the brotherhood of man and, in actual fact, prevents it. We always try to reform that which is already corrupt. We don't eradicate corruption fundamentally but simply re-arrange it.

Questioner: Are you saying that we need not waste time in these endless bargainings between the individual and the collective, or try to prove that they are different or that they are similar? Are you saying that only goodness, love and intelligence are the issue, and that these lie beyond the individual or the collective?

KRISHNAMURTI: Yes.

Questioner: So the real question seems to be how love, goodness and intelligence can act in daily living.

KRISHNAMURTI: If these act, then the question of the individual and the collective is academic.

Questioner: How are they to act?

KRISHNAMURTI: They can act only in relationship: all existence is in relationship. So the first thing is to become aware of one's relationship to everything and everybody, and to see how in this relationship the 'me' is born and acts. This 'me' that is both the collective and the individual; it is the 'me' that separates; it is the 'me' that acts collectively or individually, the 'me' that creates heaven and hell. To be aware of this is to understand it. And the understanding of it is the ending of it. The ending of it is goodness, love and intelligence.

MEDITATION AND ENERGY

Questioner: This morning I should like to go into the deeper meaning, or deeper sense, of meditation. I have practised many forms of it, including a little Zen. There are various schools which teach awareness but they all seem rather superficial, so can we leave all that aside and go into it more deeply?

KRISHNAMURTI: We must also set aside the whole meaning of authority, because in meditation any form of authority, either one's own or the authority of another, becomes an impediment and prevents freedom – prevents a freshness, a newness. So authority, conformity and imitation must be set aside completely. Otherwise you merely imitate, follow what has been said, and that makes the mind very dull and stupid. In that there is no freedom. Your past experience may guide, direct or establish a new path, and so even that must go. Then only can one go into this very deep and extraordinarily important thing called meditation. Meditation is the essence of energy.

Questioner: For many years I have tried to see that I do not become a slave to the authority of someone else or to a pattern. Of course there is a danger of deceiving myself but as we go along I shall probably find out. But when you say that meditation is the essence of energy, what do you mean by the words energy and meditation?

KRISHNAMURTI: Every movement of thought, every action demands energy. Whatever you do or think needs energy, and this energy can be dissipated through conflict, through various forms of unnecessary thought, emotional pursuits and sentimental activities. Energy is wasted in conflict which arises in duality, in the 'me' and the 'not-me', in the division between the observer and the observed, the thinker and the thought. When this wastage is no longer taking place there is a quality of energy which can be called an awareness – an awareness in which there is no evaluation, judgement, condemnation or comparison but merely an attentive observation, a seeing of things exactly as they are, both inwardly and outwardly, without the interference of thought, which is the past.

Questioner: This I find very difficult to understand. If there were no thought at all, would it be possible to recognize a tree, or my wife or neighbour? Recognition is necessary, isn't it, when you look at a tree or the woman next door?

KRISHNAMURTI: When you observe a tree is recognition necessary? When you look at that tree, do you say it is a tree or do you just look? If you begin to recognize it as an elm, an oak or a mango tree then the past interferes with direct observation. In the same way, when you look at your wife, if you look with memories of annoyances or pleasures you are not really looking at her but at the image which you have in your mind about her. That prevents direct perception: direct perception does not need recognition. Outward recognition of your wife, your children, your house or your neighbour is, of course, necessary, but why should there be an interference of the past in the eyes, the mind and the heart? Doesn't it prevent you from seeing clearly? When you condemn or have an opinion about something, that opinion or prejudice distorts observation.

Questioner: Yes, I see that. That subtle form of recognition does distort, I see that. You say all these interferences of thought are a waste of energy. You say observe without any form of recognition, condemnation, judgement; observe without naming, for that naming, recognition, condemnation are a waste of energy. That can be logically and actually understood. Then there is the next point which is

*the division, the separateness, or, rather, as you have often
put it in your talks, the space that exists between the observer and the observed which creates duality; you say that
this also is a waste of energy and brings about conflict. I find
everything you say logical but I find it extraordinarily
difficult to remove that space, to bring about harmony between the observer and the observed. How is this to be
done?*

KRISHNAMURTI: There is no how. The how means a system,
a method, a practice which becomes mechanical. Again we
have to be rid of the significance of the word 'how'.

*Questioner: Is it possible? I know the word possible implies a
future, an effort, a striving to bring about harmony, but one
must use certain words. I hope we can go beyond those
words, so is it possible to bring about a union between the
observer and the observed?*

KRISHNAMURTI: The observer is always casting its shadow
on the thing it observes. So one must understand the structure and the nature of the observer, not how to bring about a
union between the two. One must understand the movement
of the observer and in that understanding perhaps the observer comes to an end. We must examine what the observer
is: it is the past with all its memories, conscious and unconscious, its racial inheritance, its accumulated experience
which is called knowledge, its reactions. The observer is
really the conditioned entity. He is the one who asserts that
he is, and *I am*. In protecting himself, he resists, dominates,
seeking comfort and security. The observer then sets himself
apart as something different from that which he observes,
inwardly or outwardly. This brings about a duality and from
this duality there is conflict, which is the wastage of energy.
To be aware of the observer, his movement, his self-centred
activity, his assertions, his prejudices, one must be aware of
all these unconscious movements which build the separatist
feeling that he is different. It must be observed without any

form of evaluation, without like and dislike; just observe it in daily life, in its relationships. When this observation is clear, isn't there then a freedom from the observer?

Questioner: You are saying, sir, that the observer is really the ego; you are saying that as long as the ego exists, he must resist, divide, separate, for in this separation, this division, he feels alive. It gives him vitality to resist, to fight, and he has become accustomed to that battle; it is his way of living. Are you not saying that this ego, this 'I', must dissolve through an observation in which there is no sense of like or dislike, no opinion or judgement, but only the observing of this 'I' in action? But can such a thing really take place? Can I look at myself so completely, so truly, without distortion? You say that when I do look at myself so clearly then the 'I' has no movement at all. And you say this is part of meditation?

KRISHNAMURTI: Of course. This *is* meditation.

Questioner: This observation surely demands extraordinary self-discipline.

KRISHNAMURTI: What do you mean by self-discipline? Do you mean disciplining the self by putting him in a strait-jacket, or do you mean learning about the self, the self that asserts, that dominates, that is ambitious, violent and so on – learning about it? The learning is, in itself, discipline. The word discipline means to learn and when there is learning, not accumulating, when there is actual learning, which needs attention, that learning brings about its own responsibility, its own activity, its own dimensions: so there is no discipline as something imposed upon it. Where there is learning there is no imitation, no conformity, no authority. If this is what you mean by the word discipline, then surely there is freedom to learn?

Questioner: You are taking me too far and perhaps too

deeply, and I can't quite go with you where this learning is concerned. I see very clearly that the self as the observer must come to an end. It is logically so, and there must be no conflict: that is very clear. But you are saying that this very observation is learning and in learning there is always accumulation; this accumulation becomes the past. Learning is an additive process, but you are apparently giving it a different meaning altogether. From what I have understood you are saying that learning is a constant movement without accumulation. Is that so? Can learning be without accumulation?

KRISHNAMURTI: Learning is its own action. What generally happens is that having learnt – we act upon what we have learnt. So there is division between the past and action, and hence there is a conflict between what should be and what is, or what has been and what is. We are saying that there can be action in the very movement of learning: that is, learning is doing; it is not a question of having learnt and then acting. This is very important to understand because having learnt, and acting from that accumulation, is the very nature of the 'me', the 'I', the ego or whatever name one likes to give it. The 'I' is the very essence of the past and the past impinges on the present and so on into the future. In this there is constant division. Where there is learning there is a constant movement; there is no accumulation which can become the 'I'.

Questioner: But in the technological field there must be accumulated knowledge. One can't fly the Atlantic or run a car, or even do most of the ordinary daily things without knowledge.

KRISHNAMURTI: Of course not, sir; such knowledge is absolutely necessary. But we are talking about the psychological field in which the 'I' operates. The 'I' can use technological knowledge in order to achieve something, a position or prestige; the 'I' can use that knowledge to function, but if in functioning the 'I' interferes, things begin to go wrong, for the 'I', through technical means, seeks status. So the 'I' is not concerned merely with knowledge in scientific fields; it is using it to achieve something else. It is like a musician who uses the piano to become famous. What he is concerned with is fame and not the beauty of the music in itself or for itself. We are not saying that we must get rid of technological knowledge; on the contrary, the more technological knowledge there is the better living conditions will be. But the moment the 'I' uses it, things begin to go wrong.

Questioner: I think I begin to understand what you are saying. You are giving quite a different meaning and dimension to the word learning, which is marvellous. I am beginning to grasp it. You are saying that meditation is movement of learning and in that there is freedom to learn about everything, not only about meditation, but about the way one lives, drives, eats, talks, everything.

KRISHNAMURTI: As we said, the essence of energy is meditation. To put it differently – so long as there is a meditator there is no meditation. If he attempts to achieve a state described by others, or some flash of experience ...

Questioner: If I may interrupt you, sir, are you saying that learning must be constant, a flow, a line without any break, so that learning and action are one, or a constant movement? I don't know what word to use, but I am sure you understand what I mean. The moment there is a break between learning, action and meditation, that break is a disharmony, that break is conflict. In that break there is the observer and the observed and hence the whole wastage of energy; is that what you are saying?

KRISHNAMURTI: Yes, that is what we mean. Meditation is not a state; it is a movement, as action is a movement. And as we said just now, when we separate action from learning, then the observer comes between the learning and the action; then he becomes important; then he uses action and learning for ulterior motives. When this is very clearly understood as one harmonious movement of acting, of learning, of meditation, there is no wastage of energy and this is the beauty of meditation. There is only one movement. Learning is far more important than meditation or action. To learn there must be complete freedom, not only consciously but deeply, inwardly – a total freedom. And in freedom there is this movement of learning, acting, meditating as a harmonious whole. The word whole not only means health but holy. So learning is holy, acting is holy, meditation is holy. This is really a sacred thing and the beauty is in itself and not beyond it.

ENDING THOUGHT

Questioner: I wonder what you really mean by ending thought. I talked to a friend about it and he said it is some kind of oriental nonsense. To him thought is the highest form of intelligence and action, the very salt of life, indispensable. It has created civilization, and all relationship is based on it. All of us accept this, from the greatest thinker to the humblest labourer. When we don't think we sleep, vegetate or day-dream; we are vacant, dull and unproductive, whereas when we are awake we are thinking, doing, living, quarrelling: these are the only two states we know. You say, be beyond both – beyond thought and vacant inactivity. What do you mean by this?

KRISHNAMURTI: Very simply put, thought is the response of memory, the past. The past is an infinity or a second ago. When thought acts it is this past which is acting as memory, as experience, as knowledge, as opportunity. All will is desire based on this past and directed towards pleasure or the avoidance of pain. When thought is functioning it is the past, therefore there is no new living at all; it is the past living in the present, modifying itself and the present. So there is nothing new in life that way, and when something new is to be found there must be the absence of the past, the mind must not be cluttered up with thought, fear, pleasure, and everything else. Only when the mind is uncluttered can the new come into being, and for this reason we say that thought must be still, operating only when it has to – objectively, efficiently. All continuity is thought; when there is continuity there is nothing new. Do you see how important this is? It's really a question of life itself. Either you live in the past, or you live totally differently: that is the whole point.

311

Questioner: I think I do see what you mean, but how in the world is one to end this thought? When I listen to the bird there is thought telling me instantly it is the blackbird; when I walk down the street thought tells me I am walking down the street and tells me all I recognize and see; when I play with the notion of not thinking it is again thought that plays this game. All meaning and understanding and communication are thought. Even when I am not communicating with someone else I am doing so with myself. When I am awake, I think, when I am asleep I think. The whole structure of my being is thought. Its roots lie far deeper than I know. All I think and do and all I am is thought, thought creating pleasure and pain, appetites, longings, resolutions, conclusions, hopes, fears and questions. Thought commits murder and thought forgives. So how can one go beyond it? Isn't it thought again which seeks to go beyond it?

KRISHNAMURTI: We both said, when thought is still, something new can be. We both saw that point clearly and to understand it clearly is the ending of thought.

Questioner: But that understanding is also thought.

KRISHNAMURTI: Is it? You assume that it is thought, but is it, actually?

Questioner: It is a mental movement with meaning, a communication to oneself.

KRISHNAMURTI: If it is a communication to oneself it is thought. But is understanding a mental movement with meaning?

Questioner: Yes it is.

KRISHNAMURTI: The meaning of the word and the understanding of that meaning is thought. That is necessary in life. There thought must function efficiently. It is a technological matter. But you are not asking that. You are asking how thought, which is the very movement of life as you know it, can come to an end. Can it only end when you die? That is really your question, isn't it?

Questioner: Yes.

KRISHNAMURTI That is the right question. Die! Die to the past, to tradition.

Questioner: But how?

KRISHNAMURTI: The brain is the source of thought. The brain is matter and thought is matter. Can the brain – with all its reactions and its immediate responses to every challenge and demand – can that brain be very still? It is not a question of ending thought, but of whether the brain can be completely still. Can it act with full capacity when necessary and otherwise be still? This stillness is not physical death.

See what happens when the brain is completely still. See what happens.

Questioner: In that space there was a blackbird, the green tree, the blue sky, the man hammering next door, the sound of the wind in the trees and my own heartbeat, the total quietness of the body. That is all.

KRISHNAMURTI: If there was recognition of the blackbird singing, then the brain was active, was interpreting. It was not still. This really demands tremendous alertness and discipline, the watching that brings its own discipline, not imposed or brought about by your unconscious desire to achieve a result or a pleasurable new experience. Therefore during the day thought must operate effectively, sanely, and also watch itself.

Questioner: That is easy, but what about going beyond it?

KRISHNAMURTI: Who is asking this question? Is it the

desire to experience something new or is it the inquiry? If it is the inquiry, then you must inquire and investigate the whole business of thinking and be completely familiar with it, know all its tricks and subtleties. If you have done this you will know that the question of going beyond thought is an empty one. Going beyond thought is knowing what thought is.

THE NEW HUMAN BEING

Questioner: I am a reformer, a social worker. Seeing the extraordinary injustice there is in the world, my whole life has been dedicated to reform. I used to be a Communist but I can't go along with Communism any more, it has ended in tyranny. Nevertheless, I am still dedicated to reforming society so that man can live in dignity, beauty and freedom, and realize the potential which nature seems to have given him, and which he himself seems always to have stolen from his fellow man. In America there is a certain kind of freedom, and yet standardization and propaganda are very strong there – all the mass media exert a tremendous pressure on the mind. It seems that the power of television, this mechanical thing that man has invented, has developed its own personality, its own will, its own momentum; and though probably nobody – perhaps not even any one group – is deliberately using it to influence society, its trend shapes the very souls of our children. And this is the same in varying degrees in all democracies. In China there seems to be no hope at all for the dignity or freedom of man, while in India the government is weak, corrupt and inefficient. It seems to me that all the social injustice in the world absolutely must be changed. I want passionately to do something about it, yet I don't know where to begin to tackle it.

KRISHNAMURTI: Reform needs further reform, and this is an endless process.

So let us look at it differently. Let us put aside the whole thought of reform; let us wipe it out of our blood. Let us completely forget this idea of wanting to reform the world. Then let us see actually what is happening, right throughout the world. Political parties always have a limited programme which, even if fulfilled, invariably brings about mischief,

315

which then has to be corrected once again. We are always talking about political action as being a most important action, but political action is not the way. Let us put it out of our minds. All social and economic reforms come under this category. Then there is the religious formula of action based on belief, idealism, dogmatism, conformity to some so-called divine recipe. In this is involved authority and acceptance, obedience and the utter denial of freedom. Though religions talk of peace on earth they contribute to the disorder because they are a factor of division. Also the churches have always taken some political stand in times of crisis, so they are really political bodies, and we have seen that all political action is divisive. The churches have never really denied war: on the contrary they have waged war. So when one puts aside the religious recipes, as one puts aside the political formulas – what is left, and what is one to do? Naturally civic order must be maintained: you have to have water in the taps. If you destroy civic order you have to start again from the beginning. So, what is one to do?

Questioner: That is what I am actually asking you.

KRISHNAMURTI: Be concerned with radical change, with total revolution. The only revolution is the revolution between man and man, between human beings. That is our only concern. In this revolution there are no blueprints, no ideologies, no conceptual utopias. We must take the fact of the actual relationship between men and change that radically. That is the real thing. And this revolution must be immediate, it must not take time. It is not achieved through evolution, which is time.

Questioner: What do you mean? All historical changes have taken place in time; none of them has been immediate. You are proposing something quite inconceivable.

KRISHNAMURTI: If you take time to change, do you suppose that life is in suspension during the time it takes to change

It isn't in suspension. Everything you are trying to change is being modified and perpetuated by the environment, by life itself. So there is no end to it. It is like trying to clean the water in a tank which is constantly being refilled with dirty water. So time is out.

Now, what is to bring about this change? It cannot be will, or determination, or choice, or desire, because all these are part of the entity that has to be changed. So we must ask what actually is possible, with the action of will and assertiveness which is always the action of conflict.

Questioner: Is there any action which is not the action of will and assertiveness?

KRISHNAMURTI: Instead of asking this question let us go much deeper. Let us see that actually it is *only* the action of will and assertiveness that needs to be changed at all, because the only mischief in relationship is conflict, between individuals or within individuals, and conflict *is* will and assertiveness. Living without such action does not mean that we live like vegetables. Conflict is our main concern. All the social maladies you mentioned are the projection of this conflict in the heart of each human being. The only possible change is a radical transformation of yourself in all your relationships, not in some vague future, but now.

Questioner: But how can I completely eradicate this conflict in myself, this contradiction, this resistance, this conditioning? I understand what you mean intellectually, but I can only change when I feel it passionately, and I don't feel it passionately. It is merely an idea to me; I don't see it with my heart. If I try to act on this intellectual understanding I am in conflict with another, deeper, part of myself.

KRISHNAMURTI: If you really see this contradiction passionately, then that very perception is the revolution. If you see in yourself this division between the mind and the heart, actually see it, not conceive of it theoretically, but see it, then the problem comes to an end. A man who is passionate about the world and the necessity for change, must be free from political activity, religious conformity and tradition – which means, free from the weight of time, free from the burden of the past, free from all the action of will: this is the new human being. This only is the social, psychological, and even the political revolution.

MORE ABOUT PENGUINS
AND PELICANS

For further information about books available from
Penguins please write to Dept EP, Penguin Books Ltd,
Harmondsworth, Middlesex UB7 0DA.

In the U.S.A.: For a complete list of books available
from Penguins in the United States write to Dept CS,
Penguin Books, 625 Madison Avenue, New York, New
York 10022.

In Canada: For a complete list of books available from
Penguins in Canada write to Penguin Books Canada
Ltd, 2801 John Street, Markham, Ontario L3R 1B4.

In Australia: For a complete list of books available from
Penguins in Australia write to the Marketing
Department, Penguin Books Australia Ltd, P.O. Box
257, Ringwood, Victoria 3134.

In New Zealand: For a complete list of books available
from Penguins in New Zealand write to the Marketing
Department, Penguin Books (N.Z.) Ltd, P.O. Box 4019,
Auckland 10.

THE PENGUIN
KRISHNAMURTI READER

Edited by Mary Lutyens

Extracts from his influential books – *The First and Last Freedom*, *Life Ahead* and *This Matter of Culture*

This Penguin reader introduces to a wide public the most extraordinary Eastern teacher now living, a man who was educated by Annie Besant to be the World Teacher and the salvation of the nations; who rejected this Messianic role, announcing that he did not seek disciples; but whose gentle, simple and human example inspired Aldous Huxley and continues to influence seekers after truth in our own day.

Krishnamurti does not have a 'Philosophy'. He hopes to liberate us from all systems – from the bonds of ideology and received opinion as well as from organized religion, from the tyranny of the mind as well as the tyranny of the body. His message, addressed directly to every individual in his audience, is one of unity and wholeness, of total understanding and total love. As the *Observer* said of one of his books, 'for those who wish to listen, it will have a value beyond words'.